Events That Changed
America in the
Nineteenth Century

Also Available in
The Greenwood Press "Events That Changed America" Series

Events That Changed America in the Twentieth Century
John E. Findling and Frank W. Thackeray, editors

Events That Changed America in the Nineteenth Century

edited by
John E. Findling
&
Frank W. Thackeray

THE GREENWOOD PRESS
"EVENTS THAT CHANGED AMERICA" SERIES

GREENWOOD PRESS
Westport, Connecticut • London

Library of Congress Cataloging-in-Publication Data

Events that changed America in the nineteenth century / edited by John
E. Findling & Frank W. Thackeray.
    p.   cm.—(Greenwood Press "Events that changed America"
series)
    Includes bibliographical references and index.
    ISBN 0–313–29081–4 (alk. paper)
    1. United States—History—1783–1865.   2. United States—
History—1865–1898.   I. Findling, John E.   II. Thackeray, Frank W.
III. Series.
E337.5.E9   1997
973—dc20   96–25007

British Library Cataloguing in Publication Data is available.

Library of Congress Catalog Card Number: 96–25007
ISBN: 0–313–29081–4

First published in 1997

Greenwood Press, 88 Post Road West, Westport, CT 06881
An imprint of Greenwood Publishing Group, Inc.

Printed in the United States of America

∞™

The paper used in this book complies with the
Permanent Paper Standard issued by the National
Information Standards Organization (Z39.48–1984).

10 9 8 7 6 5 4 3 2 1

Contents

Illustrations

Preface

This book, which describes and evaluates the significance of ten of the most important events in the United States during the nineteenth century, is the second in a multivolume series intended to acquaint readers with the seminal events of American history. An earlier volume, published in 1996, highlighted events in the twentieth century, and future volumes will cover the most important events of earlier centuries. There is also an ongoing series of volumes addressing the global experience.

Our collective classroom experience provided the inspiration for this project. Having encountered thousands of entry-level college students whose knowledge of the history of their country is sadly deficient, we determined to prepare a series of books that would concentrate on the most important events affecting those students (and others as well) in the hope that they would better understand their country and how it came to be. We hope these books will stimulate readers to delve further into the events covered and to take a greater interest in history in general.

Each chapter begins with an introduction that presents factual material about the event in a clear, concise, chronological order. It is followed by a longer interpretive essay by a specialist exploring the ramifications of the event under consideration. Each essay concludes with an annotated bibliography of the most important works about the event. The ten chapters are followed by three appendixes that provide additional useful information. Appendix A is a glossary of names, events, organizations, and terms mentioned but not fully explained in the introductions and essays. Appendix B is a timeline of key nineteenth-century events, and Appendix C is a listing of presidents, vice presidents, and secretaries of state in the nineteenth century.

The events covered in this book were selected on the basis of our combined teaching and research activities. Colleagues and contributors made suggestions as well, and for this we thank them. Of course, another pair of editors might have arrived at a somewhat different list than we did, but we believe that we have assembled a group of events that truly changed America in the nineteenth century.

Numerous people behind the scenes deserve much of the credit for the final product. Barbara Rader, our editor at Greenwood Publishing Group, has encouraged us from the very beginning. The staff of the Photographic Division of the Library of Congress provided genial assistance to us as we selected the photographs that appear in this book. Our student research assistant, Bob Marshall, was helpful at many stages of the project. We are especially grateful to Brigette Colligan, who was always ready to type or retype whatever we asked her to. Various staff members of the Indiana University Southeast computer center cheerfully unscrambled disks and turned mysterious word processing programs into something we could work with. We benefited from funds that IUS provided to hire student research assistants and pay for other costs associated with the project. Special thanks to Roger and Amy Baylor and Kate O'Connell for making their establishment available to us, enabling us to confer about this project and discuss its many facets with our colleagues and former students in a congenial atmosphere. Among those who helped us make this a better book are John Newman, Sam Sloss, Shelia Anderson, Kim Pelle, Rick Kennedy, Jo Ann Waterbury, Brook Dutko, Andrew Trout, and Kathy Nichols. We also thank Robert A. Divine and Lewis L. Gould of the University of Texas for their assistance in locating authors for some of the essays. Most important, we thank our authors, whose essays were well conceived and thoughtful and whose patience when the project seemed to lag was much appreciated.

Finally, we express our appreciation to our spouses, Carol Findling and Kathy Thackeray, and to our children, Jamey Findling and Alex and

Max Thackeray, whose interest in our work and forbearance during its long gestation made it all worthwhile.

John E. Findling
Frank W. Thackeray

On December 20, 1803, the U.S. flag was raised over the Place d'Armée in New Orleans, marking the formal transfer of the Louisiana territory. (Reproduced from the Collections of the Library of Congress)

1

The Louisiana Purchase, 1803

INTRODUCTION

When Thomas Jefferson was elected president in 1800, the change to Republican control meant a change in foreign policy from Alexander Hamilton's tough realism and commercial orientation to Jefferson's nationalistic assertiveness. Jefferson and his secretary of state, James Madison, took seriously any slights to U.S. national dignity and had confidence in the nation's ability to defend itself. In power, Jefferson and Madison sought to implement an ideal, based on a moralistic approach of American concepts of what was right and wrong, with the assumption that these American concepts were universally valid. It was a distinctive approach to foreign affairs—a blend of high purpose and selfish national interest.

The first test of Jefferson's foreign policy came in 1802, when the president decided to confront the Barbary pirates, who stopped ships in the vicinity of their ports on Africa's Mediterranean coast and demanded a payment called a tribute. Although this practice had been going on since at least the 1780s, Jefferson considered it an affront to American honor and sent U.S. naval vessels to the area to protect U.S. commercial shipping. A naval battle at Tripoli, one of the pirate ports, resulted in the destruction of several enemy ships, but when an American ship ran aground pursuing a pirate ship, its crew was captured, creating an early hostage crisis. After further sea and land battles and a final payment of $60,000, the crew was released, and the sultan of Tripoli pledged not to interfere further with U.S. shipping.

Jefferson's greatest achievement in office, though it strained his constitutional principles, was the Louisiana Purchase. This territory is a funnel-shaped area that included many of the present-day plains states west of the Mississippi River and stretched down to the port city of New Orleans. Spain had acquired this territory in 1763 as a result of the French and Indian War. But in 1800, Napoleon Bonaparte, now the unquestioned ruler of France, reacquired Louisiana from Spain in exchange for some territory elsewhere. Napoleon wanted to develop Louisiana into a source of food for his possessions in the French West Indies and end their dependence on the United States. But in 1800, his hands were tied in Europe with all the military activity there; neither men nor money was available to occupy and develop Louisiana.

Another problem cropped up when Napoleon tried to establish a naval base at Santo Domingo (Haiti) for protection against the British navy. A slave insurrection, led by the Haitian hero Toussaint L'Ouverture, broke out in 1801. Napoleon sent a military force to the island, and most Americans presumed that it would easily put down the trouble in Santo Domingo and then move on to occupy New Orleans and perhaps West and East Florida as well. Should this happen, it would threaten U.S. security and might lead to the eventual absorption of adjacent U.S. territory into the French empire. To prevent this, Jefferson was prepared to make an alliance with Great Britain.

As it turned out, French forces proved nearly helpless against both the Haitian rebels and an outbreak of yellow fever. In the end, Napoleon lost some 70,000 men, and Haiti became independent. This catastrophe caused the French emperor to reassess his plans about an American empire. He decided that perhaps it was not such a good idea after all; conquering Europe might be a better choice.

Meanwhile, with its problems in Haiti, France made no move to occupy Louisiana, and nothing really was different from the time Spain had controlled the territory. Indeed, the Spanish still exercised nominal authority in Louisiana, including control over the use of the port of New Orleans, which Americans had been guaranteed under the provisions of Pinckney's Treaty (1795). But in October 1802, Spain suddenly withdrew permission for Americans to use New Orleans, in violation of the treaty. This left the city open for French occupation and caused a good deal of political turmoil in Washington, where Jefferson's Federalist opponents urged him to send troops to seize New Orleans and the Floridas.

At this point, in January 1803, Jefferson appointed James Monroe as a special envoy to go to Paris to buy the territory around New Orleans, as well as the territory of Florida, which the president suspected might also have gone from Spain to France. Monroe was to work with Robert Livingston, the U.S. minister to France, and the two diplomats were instructed to go to England with suggestions for an alliance if Napoleon was unwilling to sell.

At about the time Monroe arrived in Paris in April 1803, however, Napoleon received even more bad news from Santo Domingo and made the offer to sell not just the New Orleans area but the whole of the Louisiana Territory. Monroe and Livingston knew a good deal when they saw one and concluded the sale on April 30, 1803. No one specified exactly what had been bought—simply the territory that had been in the hands of Spain—but the price was $15 million. At the time of the sale, Monroe and Livingston were not quite certain what had been purchased; later, it was found that the sale did not include the Floridas but did encompass some 828,000 square miles of territory, bought for the princely sum of three cents an acre.

There were certain irregularities about the sale that threatened to cause problems. France had never officially taken over the land from Spain, and French constitutional law decreed a vote of its legislature to approve the sale of territory. Moreover, nothing in the U.S. Constitution said anything about the authority of the president to buy territory, and Jefferson considered a constitutional amendment to authorize the purchase. But there was reason to believe that Napoleon might withdraw the offer if there was any kind of delay, so Jefferson put principles aside and sent the treaty to Congress. Some Federalists thought the purchase expensive and unnecessary, and others worried about the incorporation of 50,000 new French-Creole citizens, but the Senate ratified the treaty by a 24–7 vote and the House of Representatives appropriated the money by a wide margin. The formal transfer of sovereignty took place in New Orleans on December 20, 1803. Although the Floridas were not included in the sale, Jefferson said, "If we push them strongly with one hand, holding out a price in the other, we shall certainly obtain the Floridas, and all in good time."

After the Louisiana Purchase, Jefferson hoped to continue his expansionist drive and acquire both Florida and Texas from Spain. He tried unsuccessfully to get Napoleon's help in this, and then he had to deal with his former vice president, Aaron Burr, now a hated political rival, who led an expedition down the Mississippi River that Jefferson (and many others) believed was aimed at creating a secessionist republic in Louisiana under Burr's rule. Burr was arrested, but the onset of maritime troubles with Great Britain prevented Jefferson from making any further progress in acquiring Florida or Texas.

Jefferson remained confident that the acquisition of Florida would be the second step in the century-long process of U.S. expansion. In 1818, long after Jefferson had left the presidency, the Spanish still owned Florida. Near the town of Apalachicola in what is now the Florida panhandle, a group of Seminole Indians and their chief, Billy Bowlegs, were causing trouble for the United States by crossing the border into Alabama and scalping unsuspecting settlers. Complicating the situation was the fact that the Indians were apparently being advised and encouraged by two resident British subjects, an elderly Scottish trader named Alexander Arbuthnot and a young English adventurer named Robert C. Ambrister.

President James Monroe responded to the Indian depredations by ordering Andrew Jackson, then a frontier military officer, to raise a force and subdue the Seminoles, even if it meant chasing them into Florida. Jackson, whose regard for Indians was scant indeed, chased the Seminoles to the Gulf Coast at the town of St. Mark's, where a gunboat flying the Union Jack was anchored in the harbor. Two Seminole chiefs, associates of Billy Bowlegs, rowed out, intending to seek sanctuary among the friendly British. To their surprise, they met Jackson, who had been flying the British flag on an American gunboat as a trick. The next day, Jackson entered St. Mark's over the protests of the Spanish governor, hauled down the Spanish flag, hanged the two Indians without a trial, and arrested Arbuthnot, who kept a trading ship there. Next, Jackson set out after Billy Bowlegs, who, with his contingent of Indians, had escaped from St. Mark's. Jackson learned how they managed to escape when Ambrister and a few accomplices stumbled into his camp by mistake, and on one of the men was found a secret note from Arbuthnot warning the Indians of Jackson's pursuit and offering ten kegs of gunpowder. Jackson was upset.

In a quickly assembled court-martial, Arbuthnot was tried for espionage and inciting the Indians against the United States, while Ambrister was tried for actively leading the Indians into war against the United States. Arbuthnot put up a defense, but Ambrister pleaded guilty and threw himself on the mercy of the court. It mattered little. Both were found guilty and sentenced to death, and Jackson threw aside considerations of mercy for the two, terming them "unprincipled villains" and "wretches who by false promises delude and excite an Indian tribe to all the horrid deeds of savage war." Ambrister went to his death before a firing squad, while Arbuthnot was hanged from the topsail yardarm of his own trading ship.

Although Great Britain and Spain protested Jackson's arbitrary actions, no diplomatic crises ensued. Britain acted with restraint, disclaiming the actions of its subjects in the light of more serious considerations, such as profitable trade relations with the United States. Spain's protests were dismissed by Secretary of State John Quincy Adams, who said that Spain got what it deserved for failing to keep order on its borders. In the negotiations that followed, Spain agreed to cede all of Florida to the United States in exchange for U.S. payment of $5 million owed to Americans who had lost goods to Spanish ships during the recent Napoleonic wars. Additionally, the United States gave up some dubious claims to Texas in return for Spanish claims to the Oregon Territory and a clarification of the boundary between the United States and Spanish America. This began at the Sabine River (which separates Louisiana and Texas today) and then moved northwestward in a series of steps to the Rocky Mountains, to a point where the Oregon Territory began. The assumption of Spanish claims to that territory gave the United States equal standing with Great Britain in what is now the Pacific Northwest and satisfied Adams's desire to have a claim to the Columbia River basin. In 1819, the deal was concluded in the Adams-Onís Treaty, or, as it sometimes called, the Transcontinental Treaty. Two years later, the Senate ratified the treaty.

The Louisiana Purchase and the acquisition of Florida were the first two steps toward the completion of American expansion across the North American continent. Jefferson died in 1826, but he would have approved the continuation of U.S. territorial acquisition across the Rocky Mountains to the Pacific Ocean and deep into Mexico. His expansionist policy, based on an assumption of U.S. moral superiority and the pursuit of practical national interests, was one of his most important legacies.

INTERPRETIVE ESSAY
Steven E. Siry

Thomas Jefferson never journeyed more than a hundred miles west of Monticello, yet since at least the Revolutionary War, he had dreamed of an American "empire of liberty." Believing that freedom was threatened by the consolidation of power in the hands of a few people, the Virginian wanted to maintain an open and roughly equal society. In particular, Jefferson emphasized territorial expansion in conjunction with access to foreign markets as the best way to keep America dominated by independent landowning farmers to prevent the problems associated with urban centers and preserve social equality and civic responsibility. Furthermore, westward expansion would secure America's borders and thus help reduce the threat from foreign powers.

The Jefferson administration's acquisition of the Louisiana Territory from France in 1803 expanded America's "empire of liberty" by more than doubling the size of the nation. Eventually all or part of 15 states would be carved out of the territory. There existed, however, great uncertainty about the territory's extent since the treaty of 1803 did not delineate clear boundaries. In response to American inquiries concerning the territory's exact boundaries, the French foreign minister asserted: "You have made a noble bargain for yourselves, and I suppose you will make the most of it."

If America's vast new domain were to serve the needs of the agrarian republic, it would have to be explored and made ready for settlement. Thus in the summer of 1803, President Jefferson sent an expedition to the trans-Mississippi West. Led by Jefferson's personal secretary, Meriwether Lewis, and a young army officer, William Clark, the expedition wanted to find a useful transcontinental route to the Pacific Ocean, study the terrain and animals, and develop a fur trade with the Indians. The "Corps of Discovery" left St. Louis in May 1804 and went up the Missouri River. With a Shoshone woman, Sacajawea, acting as their interpreter, the group of explorers followed the Snake and Columbia Rivers to the Pacific Ocean. Using the same route, the expedition returned to St. Louis in September 1806. The expedition's report greatly increased American interest in the fur trade of the trans-Mississippi West and suggested, incorrectly, that the route to the Pacific could easily lead to increased trade with China.

In addition, in 1805–1806, Lieutenant Zebulon Pike explored the sources of the Mississippi River into northern Minnesota. Later he ventured into New Mexico and Colorado, where he sighted the peak that now bears his name. Pike subsequently reported that the Great Plains was a treeless waste on which settlers could never survive. Major Stephen H. Long, leader of an expedition in 1819–1820, supported Pike's report and misleadingly referred to the region as the Great American Desert.

During the time of Pike's explorations, Aaron Burr and 60 followers went down the Mississippi River on flatboats, either to capture Texas from the Spanish or to set up an independent nation in the Mississippi Valley. Whatever the purpose of Burr's adventure, President Jefferson had his former vice president arrested, and peace was maintained with Spain. A grand jury indicted Burr for treason on charges that he was attempting to cause the secession of lands in the Louisiana Territory and to become the head of a new republic in the trans-Mississippi area. Chief Justice John Marshall, a political opponent of Jefferson, presided at the trial and interpreted the Constitution's treason clause as tightly as possible by barring evidence of conspiracy until it had been proved that Burr had raised a military force. The jury consequently found Burr not guilty.

The Louisiana Purchase, which had secured access to the Gulf of Mexico, was supposed to promote the Jeffersonian vision of an expanding agrarian republic based on unimpeded access to foreign markets. But the renewal of the Anglo-French conflict in 1803 had limited American access to these markets. As a result, Jefferson and his handpicked successor, James Madison, imposed economic sanctions against Great Britain and France between 1806 and 1812 to liberate American commerce from foreign restrictions. These sanctions, however, fueled the growth of manufacturing in the United States and thus ironically began to undermine the Jeffersonian vision of an agrarian-dominated nation. Eventually British violations of American neutrality, which placed restrictions on access to foreign markets and created political divisions within the Democratic-Republican party, led to President Madison's June 1812 decision to request a declaration of war against Great Britain.

After the War of 1812, there developed a renewed interest in western expansion. Over the next decade, the government established military posts on the Minnesota, Mississippi, Missouri, and Arkansas Rivers. The posts helped to expand America's agrarian republic by securing the frontier, promoting the fur trade, and supporting white settlement. In addition, the Anglo-American Convention of 1818 adjusted the poorly defined northern boundary of the Louisiana Territory by asserting that the Canadian-American border would start at the Lake of the Woods and then run westward along the forty-ninth parallel to the "Stony [Rocky] Mountains."

Following the Louisiana Purchase, American diplomats had tried to obtain part of Florida by arguing that it had always been included in the Louisiana Territory, but the Spanish refused to accept this view. Then as Spain's power declined, the United States took West Florida between 1810 and 1813. Finally in 1819, as a result of the Adams-Onís Treaty (also known as the Transcontinental Treaty), the United States acquired East Florida, and Spain recognized that previously occupied West Florida was part of the Louisiana Purchase. Furthermore, the treaty established a new boundary line that started at the mouth of the Sabine River, moved in a northwestward direction to the forty-second parallel, and then went straight west to the Pacific Ocean. The United States thus surrendered its vague claims for Texas arising from the Louisiana Purchase. President James Monroe and his cabinet did not know that the Spanish government would have retreated even on the Sabine boundary; therefore the Monroe administration, which considered Florida to be more important than Texas, did not pursue the issue. Despite the failure to acquire Texas, the Adams-Onís Treaty embraced the grand Jeffersonian vision of an expanding empire of liberty.

By 1819 the United States had 11 slave and 11 free states, with the Ohio River and the southern and western boundary of Pennsylvania defining the line between them. The dividing line had not been extended across the Mississippi River, although slavery had existed there since the French and Spanish had controlled the area.

In 1818 the Missouri legislature petitioned Congress for admission to the Union as a slave state, an action that heightened northern fears over the extension of slavery. Thus, in early 1819, a New York Congressman, James Tallmadge, Jr., offered an amendment to the Missouri statehood bill that would bar further importation of slaves into Missouri and free, at age 25, all those born there. By the narrowest of margins, the amendment was defeated in Congress, and the northern majority fell short of its objective of keeping slavery out of the rest of the Louisiana Territory. Ultimately Congress decided to admit Missouri as a slave state and Maine as a free state. In addition, Congress prohibited slavery in the rest of the Louisiana Territory north of the southern boundary of Missouri (the 36°30' parallel). Northern and southern nationalists praised the Missouri Compromise, but sectional conflict had only been postponed.

White settlers had also started moving into the area south of Missouri. Bordering the state of Louisiana (1812) on the north was the Arkansas

Territory, which had been created in 1819. The settlement of Arkansas continued slowly, partly due to the swamps and mountains that covered significant areas in the territory. However, as more eastern states became crowded, the overflow of population moved into Arkansas. In 1836, with a population of fewer than 100,000, Arkansas was admitted to the Union to offset the admission of Michigan, whose citizens were "free-soil," or antislavery.

During the period between 1820 and 1835, Americans engaged in fur trading in the Rocky Mountains region. Traders from St. Louis, known as the Gateway to the West, met in the wilderness each summer with mountain men and Indians to barter for beaver pelts. By the mid-1830s, the beavers had almost been exterminated. Trade until after 1860 then shifted to bison robes.

Among the earliest people to settle west of the Mississippi River were Native American tribes from the South and the Old Northwest that the federal government forcibly relocated in present-day Kansas and Oklahoma. Then in the 1840s, white Americans, especially those moving along the overland trails to the Far West, made extensive contacts with the approximately 250,000 Native Americans who lived on the Great Plains. The Pawnee, Omaha, Oto, Ponca, and Kansa lived nearest the Missouri and Iowa frontier. Unlike other Plains Indians, these border tribes lived in villages and raised crops while supplementing their diets with buffalo meat in the summer. The Central Plains Indians included the Brule and Oglala Sioux, the Cheyenne, the Shoshone, and the Arapaho. These were aggressive nomadic tribes who used horses to attack the border Indians and to track the buffalo for as much as five hundred miles.

Although their cultures varied, all the Indians of the Great Plains shared a neolithic culture using stone and bone tools. The warriors carried bows and arrows, stone-tipped lances, and shields made of buffalo hide so tough they could deflect bullets. The warriors also used a secret system of signals to execute intricate cavalry maneuvers.

The migration of whites along the overland trails across the Plains to the Pacific coast led to conflict with the Indians. Whites fed their oxen and horses on the grass that both the Indians' horses and the buffalo needed. The whites also began to hunt the buffalo for profit and sport. As the great buffalo herds began to shrink, the Indian tribes increasingly fought each other for the dwindling supply of food.

The discovery of gold in California, which brought 20,000 people across the Plains in 1849 alone, led to federal action. The vast number of gold seekers turned the Platte Valley into a wasteland for the tribes. In addition, diseases carried by white immigrants killed thousands of Indians. To manage the Indians better and to uphold the Jeffersonian vision of an expanding agrarian civilization, the government decided to construct a chain of forts to protect the pioneers. Furthermore, according to the Fort Laramie Treaty (1851), the federal government would compensate the Indians for the destruction of the buffalo and other resources and annually provide various goods to the tribes. In return, the tribes had to stay within certain boundaries, and some tribal lands were sold.

When the Fort Laramie Treaty was signed, there were few white settlers in the area west of the Mississippi River, east of the Rocky Mountains, and north of the Missouri Compromise line of 36°30'. Nevertheless, in 1854 Senator Stephen A. Douglas introduced a bill to organize that area as an important prelude to building a transcontinental railroad and to promoting white settlement in the region. To win southern backing, Douglas added a clause to his bill that explicitly repealed the antislavery provision of the Missouri Compromise. In the territory north of 36°30' the status of slavery would be determined by the territorial legislature. This was known as popular sovereignty. After a bitter debate, Congress passed the Kansas-Nebraska Act. No other piece of legislation in American history has produced such immediate and far-reaching changes. The act divided the northern Democrats and led directly to the collapse of the Whig party and the formation of the Republican party, which opposed the extension of slavery into any territory.

After the passage of the Kansas-Nebraska Act, thousands of settlers moved to Kansas. As proslavery and antislavery groups competed for control in the area, violence eventually escalated until the territory became known as "Bleeding Kansas." In 1857 proslavery forces wanted to elect delegates to a convention at Lecompton, the territorial capital, to write a constitution and seek admission to the Union as a slave state. Since an overwhelming majority of the settlers in the territory held free-state views, the success of the proslavery plan depended on holding a rigged election for convention delegates. But the antislavery settlers boycotted the election. Unless a fair election was held, Congress would reject the Lecompton Constitution which protected slavery.

The proslavery forces now permitted a vote on allowing or preventing the future importation of slaves into Kansas. But the free-soilers, still unable to vote for the abolition of slavery in Kansas, again boycotted the election, and consequently the proslavery constitution that had no restrictions on importing slaves was ratified. However, the bill to admit Kansas to the Union as a slave state was defeated in the House of Representatives. The Lecompton controversy thus greatly worsened the sectional controversy. In Kansas the antislavery forces soon took control of the government and repealed Kansas's laws protecting slavery. By 1860 only two slaves remained in Kansas, and in late January 1861, after six southern states had seceded from the Union, Kansas was admitted to the Union as a free state.

In 1860 some 4.3 million Americans lived west of the Mississippi River. To increase this trans-Mississippi population and to promote agrarian expansion, Congress in 1862 passed the Homestead Act, which gave 160 acreas of land to anyone who would pay a $10 registration fee and pledge to live on the land and cultivate part of it for five years. Between 1862 and 1900 nearly 400,000 families obtained land under the act. But the Homestead Act's land allotment was not suited to the semiarid area comprising much of the Louisiana Territory. On the Great Plains, annual precipitation averages less than 20 inches and annual runoff less than 1 inch. Lacking irrigation, a 160-acre farm was too small to be self-supporting on the Great Plains. In 1873 in an attempt to adjust the Homestead Act to western conditions, Congress passed the Timber Culture Act, which allowed homesteaders to purchase an additional 160 acres if they planted trees on one-fourth of the land within four years. The act successfully encouraged forestation and increased farms to a self-supporting size.

During the Civil War, Indian revolts occurred in the trans-Mississippi West. The Indians opposed encroachments by miners, hunters, and settlers on their lands and denounced the failure of the government to provide annual supplies of the quality stated in treaties. Moreover, builders of the first transcontinental railroad, completed in 1869, wanted rights of way through tribal lands and brought thousands of white settlers to ensure profits for their operation.

As a result of the conflict, a government commission in 1867 recommended that two large Indian districts should be formed to hold all the Plains Indians. The northern and southern districts were to comprise roughly what is now South Dakota and Oklahoma. In the end only the latter was created. Over the next 20 years the slaughter of millions of buffalo on the Plains, the construction of several transcontinental railroads, and the rising tide of white settlers broke the Indians' resistance. Between 1867 and 1887 many of the tribes of the Plains and elsewhere were assigned to the Indian Territory.

But in 1875 the federal government permitted gold prospectors to move into the Black Hills of the Dakota Territory, a sacred part of the Sioux reservation. Led by Chiefs Sitting Bull, Crazy Horse, and Rain-in-the-Face, the Sioux went to war and achieved initial success, especially with their stunning victory in 1876 over the troops led by General George A. Custer at the Battle of Little Big Horn. Nevertheless, the U.S. army eventually defeated the Sioux.

In 1887 Congress passed the Dawes Severalty Act, which asserted that whenever the president believed an Indian tribe sufficiently civilized to become farmers and the reservation land fertile enough for cultivation, the tribal land should be divided among the Indians. For at least 25 years the federal government would retain full title on behalf of the Indians. During that period the Indians could not sell the land and a mortgage could not be put on it. The government would also confer U.S. citizenship on all Indians obtaining a trust title. The government would sell surplus land, and proceeds would be held in trust for the tribe.

By the late 1880s, their situation made many Indians receptive to the visionary message of Wovoka, a Paiute prophet who asserted that natural disasters would soon destroy the white race and allow the Native Americans to reclaim their lands. Dancing and meditating Indians demonstrated their faith in the prophecy and called on their ancestors to return to life. This Ghost Dance movement did not advocate Indian violence against whites, but settlers became very concerned. Some of the Sioux left their reservations and in late December 1890 at Wounded Knee Creek in South Dakota, the army killed over 200 men, women, and children of the tribe.

Between 1870 and 1900, a tremendous number of settlers, including many Canadian and European immigrants, flocked to the Great Plains. Numerous pioneers' accounts contain expressions of relief on emerging from the eastern forest wilderness to the openness of the Great Plains, which they frequently referred to as a "garden." Nevertheless, many settlers soon found the vast, treeless Plains depressing. Several "prairie realists" wrote of the settlers' many hardships and bitter disappointments. One of these writers was Hamlin Garland, who grew up on farms in Iowa and the Dakota Territory. In *Main-Travelled Roads* (1891), he described the drudgery and the misery of life on the prairie. The "Main-Travelled Road in the West," asserted Garland, "[is] long and wearyful, and has a dull little town at one end, and a home of toil at the other. Like the main-travelled road of life, it is traversed by many classes of people, but the poor and weary predominate."

Life on the Plains was not always so discouraging as Garland suggested, although settlers were forced to adapt to the new environment in many ways. For example, due to a lack of firewood, the settlers burned corncobs and twisted wheat, and the farmers used sod "bricks" to build their houses.

The dramatic increase in settlers on the Great Plains after 1870 resulted in an immense increase in food production in the United States. Intensive farming was developed from the eastern boundary of the Louisiana Territory to the rainfall line of the one hundredth meridian. In particular, on the central Plains was the "corn-hog belt," and in the Red River Valley of western Minnesota and eastern North Dakota emerged one of the world's most productive granaries. In combination with great increases being made in other countries, agricultural overproduction became a worldwide development, which caused steadily declining farm prices and produced a period of significant distress for American farmers.

But a greater-than-normal dry cycle on the Great Plains began in 1887 and continued for nearly ten years. Since many of the Plains farmers were not experienced at dry-land farming, they had one crop failure after another. Usually the prices of grain and meat rise during a period of crop failures. In the 1890s, however, prices remained extremely low because of the substantial production of crops by the farmers of the Midwest and in foreign countries. Consequently, between a third and a half of the farmers in Nebraska, South Dakota, Colorado, and western Kansas were ruined.

In the late 1880s, in response to the economic crisis, Farmers' Alliances were created on the northern Great Plains and in the South. These groups blamed their problems on a conspiracy of bankers, railroad owners, and Republican and Democratic party leaders. Beginning in 1890, Farmers' Alliances in local elections backed candidates who would work to assist farmers. Victories on the local level prompted agrarian leaders to meet at Omaha, Nebraska, in July 1892 to create the National People's party, commonly called the Populist party, and to nominate a candidate to run for the presidency. The Populists' "Omaha platform" called for the federal government to increase significantly its involvement in the economy to assist the farmers. The Populists wanted a graduated income tax, government regulation of transportation and communications systems, the direct election of U.S. senators, a new government-controlled banking system, and, especially, the unlimited coinage of silver to boost commodity prices through inflation of the money supply.

Winning only 9 percent of the popular vote in 1892, the Populist leaders in 1896 decided to back Nebraska's William Jennings Bryan, the Democratic party's nominee for president, who espoused ideas that the farming community supported. Bryan particularly opposed the gold standard and endorsed the purchase and coinage of silver at the ratio of 16 to 1 of gold. But Bryan was defeated by the Republican party's candidate, William McKinley, who campaigned in favor of the gold standard. Soon after the election, the Populist party virtually disappeared. Despite its short life, its ideas would substantially influence the reform movements of the Progressive era.

In addition to the climatic problems on the Great Plains, farmers in the 1870s and 1880s also clashed with cattlemen over the use of the land. Commercial cattle ranching on the Plains developed rapidly after the Civil War. Ranchers used cattle drives to take longhorns to newly built railroad connections for shipment to slaughtering and packing houses in cities such as Kansas City and St. Louis. By the late 1870s huge ranches had been established in western Kansas, Nebraska, eastern Colorado, the Dakotas, and elsewhere.

As this occurred, the public became fascinated with the cowboys who worked for the cattle barons. The romantic portrayal of the cowboy was promoted by "dime" novels and better-written books, such as Owen Wister's *The Virginian* (1902). Moreover, Wild West shows, featuring Calamity Jane, "Buffalo Bill" Cody, and other living legends of the West, traveled to cities in the East and Europe and contributed to the romantic mythmaking about the trans-Mississippi West and the cowboys.

Ranchers in the 1880s overstocked their herds, and hungry cattle grew weak as grass became scarce. Then in 1886 a harsh winter featuring several blizzards killed 90 percent of the cattle. The cattle ranchers subsequently began to replace the longhorns with new breeds, to fence in the cattle using the newly invented barbed wire, and to feed the herds grain during the winter. In short, ranching was rapidly becoming a modern business.

In 1904 the United States commemorated the one hundredth anniversary of the Louisiana Purchase by holding an exposition in St. Louis. Millions of visitors at the fair gazed upon a statue of Thomas Jefferson and learned of his part in the founding of the West. The Louisiana Purchase International Exposition ended with a substantial surplus, and the funds were used to build in St. Louis the first significant memorial to Jefferson. It was especially meant to honor Jefferson's acquisition of the Louisiana Territory, which was the most far reaching act of his life for the nation. As Merrill Peterson asserted in *The Jeffersonian Image in the American Mind* (1962): "The Declaration [of Independence] and the Louisiana Purchase were viewed as promise and fulfillment, the abstract idea and the thing itself, the dream of freedom and the awakening of national destiny." But ironically, by the centennial of the Louisiana Purchase it was not a "destiny" that upheld the Jeffersonian vision of a republic dominated by independent landowning farmers. During the nineteenth century, as the United States became a more industrialized and urbanized nation, the Jeffersonian vision increasingly had succumbed to the imperatives of modernity.

SELECTED BIBLIOGRAPHY

Ambrose, Stephen E. *Undaunted Courage: Meriwether Lewis, Thomas Jefferson, and the Opening of the American West.* New York: Simon & Schuster, 1996. Authoritative account of the Lewis and Clark expedition (1804–1806), which first made Americans aware of what was included in the Louisiana Purchase.

Andrist, Ralph K. *The Long Death: The Last Days of the Plains Indian.* New York: Macmillan, 1964. A well-written account of the Plains Indian wars.

Banning, Lance. *The Jeffersonian Persuasion: Evolution of a Party Ideology.* Ithaca, NY: Cornell University Press, 1978. Argues that Jeffersonian thought was an Americanization of the anti-urban British political ideology that the country gentry espoused.

Barney, William L. *The Passage of the Republic: An Interdisciplinary History of Nineteenth-Century America.* Lexington, MA: D. C. Heath and Company, 1987. A study of the transformation of the United States from its eighteenth-century roots into a market society, including an overview of the diplomatic and political issues related to the Louisiana Territory.

Billington, Ray Allen. *America's Frontier Heritage.* New York: Holt, Rinehart & Winston, 1966. Uses the literature of numerous disciplines to present a view of the frontier's important role in the development of democratic institutions in the United States.

Dangerfield, George. *The Awakening of American Nationalism, 1815–1828.* New York: Harper & Row, 1965. Provides insightful coverage of the Anglo-American Convention of 1818, the Adams-Onís Treaty, and the Missouri Compromise.

DeConde, Alexander. *This Affair of Louisiana.* New York: Scribner's, 1976. Provides an analysis of the Louisiana Purchase within the larger context of the history of manifest destiny.

Dick, Everett N. *The Sod-house Frontier, 1854–1890: A Social History of the Northern Plains from the Creation of Kansas and Nebraska to the Admission of the Dakotas.* New York: Appleton-Century, 1937. A study of the entire process of settlement, which the author claims was mostly uniform throughout Kansas, Nebraska, and the Dakotas.

Dykstra, Robert R. *The Cattle Towns: A Social History of the Kansas Cattle Trading Centers: Abilene, Ellsworth, Wichita, Dodge City, and Caldwell, 1867–1885.* New York: Alfred A. Knopf, 1976. A study of the bitter local conflicts between rival interests that led to major problems in the cattle towns.

Ellis, David M., ed. *The Frontier in American Development: Essays in Honor of Paul Wallace Gates.* Ithaca, NY: Cornell University Press, 1969. Contains several articles dealing with the agrarian development of the Great Plains and its impact on U.S. history.

Fite, Gilbert C. *The Farmer's Frontier, 1865–1900.* New York: Holt, Rinehart and Winston, 1966. A study of the economic conditions that resulted in widespread agrarian protest.

Goetzmann, William H. *Army Exploration in the American West, 1803–1863.* New Haven, CT: Yale University Press, 1959. An analysis of the role played by the U.S. Army in exploring the trans-Mississippi West, especially the actions by the topographical engineers from 1838 to 1863.

Goodwyn, Lawrence. *Democratic Promise: The Populist Movement in America.* New York: Oxford University Press, 1976. A revisionist work that downplays the Populists' radicalism and views the Populist movement as a cooperative, democratic challenge to an inegalitarian political and financial system.

Greever, William S. *The Bonanza West: The Story of the Western Mining Rushes, 1848–1900.* Norman: University of Oklahoma Press, 1963. Presents detailed information on the mining expeditions in the Dakotas.

Hicks, John D. *The Populist Revolt: A History of the Farmers' Alliance and the People's Party.* Minneapolis: University of Minnesota Press, 1931. A comprehensive work on the Populists.

Hofstadter, Richard. *The Age of Reform: From Bryan to F.D.R.* New York: Alfred A. Knopf, 1955. A Pulitzer Prize–winning book that describes the Populists as unsophisticated reformers and criticizes them for espousing myths, including a conspiracy theory of history, that obscured the real reasons for the farmers' economic problems.

Lamar, Howard R., *The Trader on the American Frontier: Myth's Victim.* College Station: Texas A&M University Press, 1977. Contends that farmers had no need of Indian trade, and this eventually caused the decline of commercial contact with the Indians and led to the demise of the Indian way of life.

————, ed. *The Reader's Encyclopedia of the American West.* New York: Crowell, 1977. A reference work with information on the Louisiana Territory and related topics.

Limerick, Patricia Nelson. *The Legacy of Conquest: The Unbroken Past of the American West.* New York: W. W. Norton, 1987. A synthesis of recent scholarship that argues that the American West was a cultural meeting ground and an area of conquest, especially due to ethnic conflicts and competition for resources.

McCoy, Drew R. *The Elusive Republic: Political Economy in Jeffersonian America.* Chapel Hill: University of North Carolina Press, 1980. Describes the European ideas behind Jefferson's dream of an agrarian empire of liberty and analyzes the relationship between the Jeffersonian view of the political economy and party politics.

Merk, Frederick. *History of the Westward Movement.* New York: Alfred A. Knopf, 1978. A wide-ranging volume that contains information about farming and the cattle industry on the Great Plains.

Milner, Clyde A., II, Carol A. O'Connor, and Martha A. Sandweiss, eds. *The Oxford History of the American West.* New York: Oxford University Press, 1994. A valuable reference work that contains entries on the Louisiana Territory and related topics.

Moore, Glover. *The Missouri Controversy, 1819–1821.* Lexington: University of Kentucky Press, 1953. The fullest account of the Missouri crisis.

Nash, Roderick. *Wilderness and the American Mind.* Rev. ed. New Haven, CT: Yale University Press, 1973. Provides useful insights on pioneers' first impressions of the Great Plains.

Paterson, Thomas G., J. Garry Clifford, and Kenneth J. Hagan. *American Foreign Policy: A History to 1914.* 3d ed. Lexington, MA: D. C. Heath and Company, 1988. A general history that includes coverage of American diplomacy dealing with the Louisiana Territory.

Peterson, Merrill D. *The Jefferson Image in the American Mind.* New York: Oxford University Press, 1962. A detailed study that shows the changing views over a century and a half of Jefferson's ideas and actions, including the purchase of the Louisiana Territory.

Prucha, Francis Paul. *The Great Father: The United States Government and the American Indians.* Vol. 1. Lincoln: University of Nebraska Press, 1984. A survey of the policies of the national government toward the Indians in the nineteenth century.

Rawley, James A. *Race and Politics: "Bleeding Kansas" and the Coming of the Civil War.* Philadelphia: Lippincott, 1969. Covers the consequences of the Kansas-Nebraska Act.

Smith, Henry Nash. *Virgin Land: The American West as Symbol and Myth.* Cambridge, MA: Harvard University Press, 1950. An important interdisciplinary work that includes an analysis of "dime" novels' mythical portrayal of western heroes.

Turner, Frederick Jackson. *The Frontier in American History.* New York: Holt, Rinehart, and Winston, 1920. A collection of essays that includes Turner's seminal paper written in 1893, which asserts that the American nation was unique in its character and development because it had been shaped less by transatlantic ties than by the conquest of a series of frontiers across the North American continent.

Utley, Robert M. *Frontier Regulars: The United States Army and the Indian, 1866–1891.* New York: Macmillan, 1973. A survey of the U.S. army's victory over the Plains Indians.

Webb, Walter Prescott. *The Great Plains.* Boston: Ginn and Company, 1931. Offering an environmental interpretation, this work, which affected many subsequent studies of the Great Plains, argues that the essential characteristics of the region are its level surface, treelessness, and semiaridity, which have also been the principal factors in shaping a way of life on the Plains different from that fashioned in the eastern forested areas.

Tecumseh, the greatest Indian leader during the War of 1812, was killed at the Battle of the Thames in Ontario on October 5, 1813. (Reproduced from the Collections of the Library of Congress)

2

The War of 1812

INTRODUCTION

The War of 1812 was the last significant military conflict between Great Britain and the United States. A direct outgrowth of the Napoleonic Wars in Europe, the War of 1812 involved two and a half years of land and sea warfare; its end marked the beginning of a long period of profitable trade relations and generally cordial diplomatic relations between the two nations.

After a brief interlude from 1801 to 1803 (when the Louisiana Purchase was made), the Napoleonic Wars resumed in 1803, and by 1805, Napoleon's victories had given France control of most of the European continent, while British admiral Horatio Nelson's brilliant naval victory at the Battle of Trafalgar had ensured British control of the seas. For the United States, this meant increasing pressure from the British and the French, both quite unwilling to have Americans trading with the enemy.

British pressure began in 1805 with the *Essex* case. Prior to 1805, the British had allowed American ships to carry goods from the French West Indies to France, provided they stopped at an American port on the way. This "reexport" trade formed more than half of America's neutral trade. But in the *Essex* case, tried in a British court, it was ruled that goods could be sent on to France only if an American duty or tariff had been paid on them and if it could be shown that the West Indian goods had not been meant for France in the first place. Ships that could not show evidence of this were liable to British seizure.

In the wake of the *Essex* case, President Thomas Jefferson sent emissary William Pinckney to join James Monroe, the U.S. minister in Britain, to work out some kind of agreement. During these negotiations, Napoleon increased French pressure by issuing the Berlin Decrees in December 1806 and the Milan Decrees in December 1807, which established a blockade around the British Isles and ordered the confiscation of all ships that had visited a British port or were on their way to one. Since most neutral ships were from the United States and since most U.S. trade was with or through Great Britain, the major impact of these decrees was on the United States. To make matters worse, the British responded with the Orders-in-Council, a series of decrees that blockaded French-controlled ports and subjected to capture any ships headed to or from those ports. As a result, American merchants lost several hundred ships during Jefferson's second term, mostly to the British. Altogether something over 1,400 American ships were captured in the eight or nine years before the declaration of war in 1812. Although the ships captured represented only about one in every six ships that made the voyage and the profits earned by the other five ships more than offset the loss of the sixth, the captures were an insult to the honor of the United States and contributed significantly to the coming of the war.

Impressment, the British practice of stopping American ships at sea and taking off men alleged to be deserters from the British navy, was another serious problem after 1803. Desertion was quite common in the British navy, for it was a cruel and harsh institution, and with the expansion caused by the war with Napoleon, the navy always needed men and was eager to recapture its deserters. On the other hand, the American merchant marine was growing rapidly by means of its profitable neutral trade, and shipowners could entice British sailors by offering higher wages and better working conditions. As a result, many British deserters did end up on American ships. Many of them took out U.S. citizenship papers or even completed the process of becoming an American citizen, but the British policy was "once an Englishman, always an Englishman." Thus, sailors were often impressed despite having evidence that they were Americans; often one's accent was the determining criterion. The practice of impressment had been going on since the Revolutionary War, and it was redoubled after 1803, but the climactic event, the *Chesapeake* affair, happened in June 1807 and almost led to war.

The American warship *Chesapeake* was suspected by the British of having a certain deserter on board. Near Chesapeake Bay, the *Leopard*, a British ship, stopped the *Chesapeake*, and its captain demanded the right of search. When the captain of the *Chesapeake* refused, the *Leopard* fired on the American ship, causing 21 casualties. Members of the *Leopard*'s crew then boarded the *Chesapeake*, found the man they were looking for, and also took three American citizens who, they claimed, had once served in the British navy.

The reaction to the *Chesapeake* affair was, as expected, a loud outcry for war. But Jefferson hated war and searched for a policy that would avoid it. In December 1807, he announced a policy of "peaceful coercion," in which American vessels would be kept off the seas to avoid capture and to save the country from insults to its honor. He reasoned that Britain and France would miss American goods so much that they would come to recognize the neutral rights of the United States. Congress agreed and passed the Embargo Act on December 22, 1807, cutting off all U.S. foreign trade, even with Canada.

The effect of this act was to bring ruin to American commerce and American ports. Trade dried up, and this spread to other sectors of the economy. Although all sections of the country were hurt, the Northeast, dominated by Jefferson's political opponents, the Federalist party, was hurt worst, and the embargo became a divisive political issue. Federalists accused Jefferson of buckling under to Napoleon with the embargo and of discriminating against Federalist shipping interests. Had the Federalists been a stronger party, the embargo might have been a crucial issue in the presidential election of 1808, but Republican strength was more than enough to guarantee the victory of its candidate, James Madison, over the Federalist, C. C. Pinckney.

One of the last actions Jefferson took as president was to sign the repeal of the Embargo Act. After 14 months, even most Republicans had had it with the embargo. In its place, Congress passed the oddly named Non-Intercourse Act, which prohibited trade with both Britain and France but opened it to all other nations. If either Britain or France removed its offending decrees, moreover, the trade prohibition would continue to apply only to the other.

Neither Britain nor France chose to nibble at the American carrot, however, and U.S. economic conditions continued to worsen. In May 1810, Congress passed yet another variation of economic warfare with Macon's Bill No. 2. Under this act, trade was resumed with both Britain and France, but if either revoked their decrees, the United States would reinstitute nonintercourse against the other. Trade immediately resumed with Britain, and merchants began earning greater profits than ever. In November 1810, Napoleon announced that the French decrees were revoked, and Madison cut off trade with the British in March 1811. This was probably a trick on Napoleon's part, since he failed to abide by his announced revocation and French ships continued to prey on American commerce. Meanwhile, relations with Britain deteriorated; the British minister in Washington returned to London, and the U.S. minister there was called home.

In the West, yet another Anglo-American dispute accelerated the course toward war. This involved the resident Indians, toward whom the general policy had been to move them farther and farther west to make room for white settlers. In 1811, the great Shawnee chief, Tecumseh, decided that the Indians had been pushed around enough; they would fight further efforts to displace them. In July, he warned Indiana territorial governor William Henry Harrison that he intended to form an alliance with several southern tribes. Intended to intimidate Harrison, Tecumseh's warning only encouraged the unimaginative general into attacking Tecumseh's followers in his absence. At the Battle of Tippecanoe in north-central Indiana, Harrison's forces prevailed and burned the Indian encampment. The outraged Tecumseh promised eternal war, and many settlers fled the territory.

This became a diplomatic problem because it was universally believed that the British in Canada supplied Tecumseh and his Indians and encouraged their violence toward settlers. Thus war against the Indians was war against the British, and western congressmen demanded the conquest of Canada to remove the British menace.

The Congress that met in November 1811 was more warlike than the previous one due to a number of outspoken western representatives, dubbed War Hawks by their eastern colleagues. The Kentuckian Henry Clay was elected Speaker of the House, and under his direction, Congress passed bills to create a large army and enlarge the small navy. There was still considerable Federalist opposition to the war, and Madison was reluctant to press for it, but when the American vessel, the *President*, beat a smaller British ship, the *Little Belt*, in an impromptu naval battle, a war spirit arose in the country, and the president sent Congress a declaration of war. Congress approved it on June 18, 1812, unaware that Britain's House of Commons had repealed the Orders-in-Council on June 16.

Militarily, the war was a draw. Britain was involved in European wars and could not devote its full energy to fighting the United States. In the United States, considerable difficulties were encountered in preparing the country for war. Congress balked at raising taxes and tariffs to pay for the war, and only half of an $11 million bond issue was sold. Six months after war had been declared, Congress appropriated money to enlarge the navy and enlarge the army from 25,000 to 35,000 men. Enlistment, however, was slow; in the first two months, only 400 Kentuckians signed up, and no other state had wanted war more.

Because of the lack of preparation and poor military leadership, American efforts to conquer Canada got nowhere. On both land and sea, where the American navy fought very well, a kind of stalemate existed until April 1814, when Napoleon abdicated, freeing Britain to launch a new offensive against the upstart Americans. A blockade of the American coast was extended, and a raid on Washington in August resulted in the burning of the Capitol and White House, forcing Madison and his family to flee ignominiously into Virginia. A major British attack against Niagara and Lake Champlain in the North and New Orleans in the South stalled, but peace negotiations, which had begun in early 1814, finally resulted in the Treaty of Ghent, signed on Christmas Eve 1814.

The treaty was merely a cease-fire, which returned the status of the combatants back to the way it was before the war. Basic settlements came in the Rush-Bagot Agreement (1817), which demilitarized the Great Lakes, and in the Convention of 1818, which extended the U.S.–Canadian boundary along the forty-ninth parallel to the Rocky Mountains and established a northern border for the Louisiana Purchase. The convention also provided for a ten-year joint occupation of the Oregon Territory and included an agreement on the use of fishing areas off the coast of Newfoundland.

Politically, the War of 1812 marked the end of the Federalist party. In the election of 1812, the Federalists tried to exploit the substantial lack of sympathy for the war but failed to prevent Madison's reelection. During the war, the Federalist stronghold of New England lent little support to the effort, sending few men and little money forth in the service of the country. Worse, the Hartford Convention of 1814, a gathering of New England dissidents, championed a group of constitutional amendments designed to protect the political influence of the region and threatened secession if Congress failed to meet its demands. When the war ended shortly after the convention, the Federalist party was left with the stigma of disloyalty, which marked its doom. By 1820, the United States would have but one viable Republican political party.

INTERPRETIVE ESSAY
Sally E. Hadden

Sandwiched between the American Revolution and the American Civil War, the War of 1812 has been termed the "forgotten conflict." Descriptions of the nineteenth century frequently dismiss the impact of this war on American society, pointing out that the Treaty of Ghent, which ended the conflict, resolved none of the issues—impressment and seizure of ships on the high seas by the British navy—that Americans ostensibly entered the war to fight for. The treaty did not change British policy, and no territory changed hands between the Americans and British as a result of the conflict. So what did the war accomplish? Surprisingly, the war had a tremendous long-term impact on international law of the sea, American foreign and domestic policies, and America's plans for expansion to the south and west, which altered American-Indian relations for the rest of the century. The war elevated men like Andrew Jackson, Henry Clay, and John C. Calhoun to power in American politics; all would effect momentous decisions in the years before the American Civil War.

Although the War of 1812 made its greatest mark on American domestic policy, its influence on international law and international affairs should not be underrated. In the period before the War of 1812, Secretary of State James Madison attacked the British policy of seizing ships from neutral countries (of which the United States was one). At this time, America was a weak nation militarily, and it sought to defend itself through international law as well as by economic means like trade embargoes. As secretary of state, Madison developed a cogent theory of neutrality to combat British policies, one still in use today. The term *neutrality* appeared as early as the seventeenth century, but theories of neutrality experienced full development during the nineteenth century, in part because of the role played by Madison and the United States during this period. Madison's complaints about the impressment of private citizens and the seizure of neutral ships during wartime were elaborated most fully in his anonymously authored treatise on the doctrine of neutral trade, *Examination of the British Doctrine, Which Subjects to Capture a Neutral Trade Not Open in Time of Peace* (1806?).

Madison's ideas about the rights of neutral countries were to have a long-lasting appeal. Unfortunately, his views on neutral shipping rights were not shared by the British government in 1812, which served as one of the causes for the War of 1812. But following the war, the British stopped impressments and never used them again. More significant, Madison's ideas about the absolute sovereignty of a ship's flag have been widely adopted and are almost universally employed to the current day, giving neutral countries greater security on the high seas. Ships sailing under the flag of a given nation are under that nation's exclusive jurisdiction while at sea and may not be boarded or stopped by another nation's ships without consent. It does not matter what strength either nation's navy may have—strength alone cannot force a neutral ship to let itself be boarded, have its sailors taken away, or have its cargo seized. These ideas have significantly improved the position of neutral countries, and with the exception of the American Civil War and World War I, the United States has continued to support the rights of neutral countries to "free trade in free ships," which it first championed in the War of 1812. Madison's views on the position of neutral countries continue to hold sway even today, although they were novel and largely unpopular outside the United States in his own time. However, America's attempt to enforce the right of neutrals while remaining militarily weak had proved unworkable in the years before the War of 1812. The war's outcome demonstrated that some degree of military preparation was essential to the nation's ability to affect international affairs. Americans realized that they would have to maintain a sizable standing army and standing navy in times of peace in order to receive any international respect.

The rights of neutral countries alone, however, did not lead to America's entry into the War of 1812; territorial expansion was a crucial concern for many Americans. Maritime grievances like impressment and ship seizures hardly explain the unanimity of trans-Appalachian votes taken in the House of Representatives on war measures. What did inland congressmen hope to gain from promoting a war against England? There must have been other motives to explain their behavior. The traditional answers, according to historians like L. M. Hacker, Julius W. Pratt, and Bradford Perkins, could be found in the drive for territorial expansion to the west, including Canada to the north, in fears of uneasy coexistence with Indians in the Ohio Valley, plus southern expansionist dreams of obtaining Florida, or in the absolute necessity for war to save the Republican party and the fledgling nation from the appearance of cowardice. None of these explanations has conclusively been proved to the exclusion of the others, and most textbooks stress some combination of maritime grievances plus the other three causes. Indeed, the most popularly used explanation suggests an alliance between western and southern expansionists. Although historians have yet to prove unequivocally the existence of an alliance between congressional representatives of the West and South, the effects of the war in both areas must have been precisely what many of those congressmen had hoped for. One of the undeniable effects of the War of 1812 was territorial expansion into both the West and South.

Although we more frequently associate the term *manifest destiny* with the 1840s, the concept of territorial expansion was rooted in American history from the first settlement and reconfirmed at the time of independence. From charters that granted colonists rights to lands distant and unseen, to the Articles of Confederation and the Constitution, which set out the methods by which new states could join the government, Americans had long expected to move westward into the seemingly vacant frontier. As the population of the United States soared from 4 million in 1790 to more than 9.5 million in 1820, population pressures drove Americans west to seek new homes, and the lack of restraint from the nation's government placed few impediments in their way. By the time the War of 1812 began, families had moved into the Ohio country and were settled down the Ohio River all the way to its junction with the Mississippi River. Ohio had been home to only a few hundred whites in 1790, but by 1820, its population had grown to nearly 1 million. While marching west against the Indians, General William Henry Harrison expressed feelings shared by many other Ohio migrants when he asked, "Is one of the fairest portions of the globe to remain in a state of nature, the haunt of a few wretched savages, when it seems destined by the Creator to give support to a large population and to be the seat of civilization, of science, and of true religion?"

Other expansionist visionaries focused on moving into Florida, which with the Gulf of Mexico seemed a natural southern boundary to the United States, one that many Americans considered a simple extension of American settlement already occurring in the Deep South. One newspaper said that lands in Florida "as naturally belong to us as the county of Cornwall does to England." Desire for Florida was heightened by the sense that the lands could be easily obtained from Spain, weakened significantly in this period because of its involvement in Napoleon Bonaparte's ongoing wars. With multiple governments competing for control in Spain, the Spanish were hardly in a position to safeguard their distant

Florida colony. Because of an alliance with Spain in 1809, Great Britain was also embroiled in the Floridas. It was in Britain's interest to sustain Spanish territorial claims in Florida, and it provided military and naval support to the Spanish both before and during the War of 1812. But the combined strength of British and Spanish forces was not enough to deter American expansionist goals. Portions of West Florida were annexed by America a few weeks before war was declared in 1812, and Congress authorized President Madison to take possession of East Florida during the war, but this never happened. Instead Andrew Jackson led an attack on Spanish- and British-garrisoned Pensacola in 1814, which fell to the Americans shortly before the war's closing battle at New Orleans. Although no territory changed hands as a result of the Treaty of Ghent, America annexed parts of Spanish West Florida at the expense of neutral Spain rather than belligerent Great Britain.

In the years following the War of 1812, Americans continued to hunger for the parts of Florida that they did not already control. In December 1817, Andrew Jackson invaded Florida as part of his campaign to crush the Seminole Indians. Jackson's expansionist goals for annexing Florida were well known to President Monroe and Secretary of State John Quincy Adams, who may have disapproved of Jackson's ideas but did nothing to stop him. Indeed, Adams shared Jackson's vision of acquiring Florida, even if he did not necessarily approve of Jackson's methods. As early as 1811, Adams had written that "the whole continent of North America appears to be destined to be peopled by one *nation*." After dispersing the Seminoles, it seemed perfectly natural for Jackson's armed forces to move against and subdue Spanish forces in Pensacola. Monroe's administration then presented the Spanish with a warning that the Spanish must either control the Indians or turn over Florida to the United States. By the time the Adams-Onís Treaty was finally ratified in 1821, Spain had ceded all of Florida to the U.S. government, completing the American takeover that had begun during the War of 1812.

Elsewhere in the South, Jackson and American troops confronted the Creeks in 1813, becoming embroiled in an ongoing civil war between the elder chiefs and younger Creek warriors, commonly called Red Sticks. Jackson led incursions into Creek territory and crushed the Indians at the Battle of Horseshoe Bend in Alabama, which broke the power of the Creek nation. As a result of Jackson's continued predations, tribal elders ceded large portions of Georgia and Alabama to the United States in 1814. The younger warriors fled into Florida and continued fighting as allies of the Seminoles against the United States until well into the 1840s.

In addition to annexing parts of Florida and gaining control over portions of Georgia and Alabama, the U.S. government's participation in the War of 1812 fueled expansionist dreams of many Americans in other ways. Americans had long considered expanding beyond their northwestern territorial boundaries to acquire Canada and western lands held by Native Americans. Invasions of Canada had been tried before, in the colonial period and during the American Revolution, but none had been successful, and indeed, attempts to claim Canada militarily during the War of 1812 proved unsuccessful once again. But while forcible annexation of Canada failed, Americans were much more successful in their efforts to remove American Indians from western lands. The war provided the pretext for settling a long-burning problem: how to put an end to alleged British intrigues with Indians in the northwest Ohio Valley.

As events preceding the War of 1812 moved toward confrontation, westerners believed—incorrectly as it turned out—that British officials in Canada had used their influence with the Indians of the Northwest to deny Americans use of the Ohio Valley region for fur trading. Instead, much of the Indian hostility can be accounted for by the prewar land policies of westerners themselves. In the Treaty of Fort Wayne (1809), territorial governor (and later military general) William Henry Harrison gained Indian concessions of nearly 3 million acres, in return for a few lifetime annuities and a lot of whiskey. Outraged by this kind of treaty, many Indians claimed that the lands still belonged to the tribes, not whites. The Shawnee were particularly resistant to these treaties, and they became the focal point for encouraging other tribes to resist the incursions of whites.

In fact, although the Indians of the Northwest were commonly perceived as allies-in-waiting for the British, it took American action in the immediate prewar years to make the alliance reality. With his warriors, the Shawnee war chief Tecumseh took up arms against the American "long knives" in 1811. His efforts at the Battle of Tippecanoe in 1811 promoted the political fortunes of General William Henry Harrison. At Tippecanoe, fought while Tecumseh was away, the Indian forces were routed, leaving behind British-made weapons. The loss at Tippecanoe convinced Tecumseh that he should seek out British military assistance in 1812, something he had avoided doing earlier. Conversely, Tecumseh's loss convinced some Indian tribes, like the Choctaw and Pushmataha, that resistance to American forces was futile. Meanwhile, certain that Tecumseh's efforts were supported by the British with guns, westerners eagerly supported the approaching war with Britain. Following the Battle of Tippecanoe, congressional leader and War Hawk Felix Grundy described the alleged conspiracy between Indians and the British as one between weak, gullible natives and malign foreigners: "[The Indians] understand too well their own weakness, and our strength. They have already felt the weight of our arms. . . . How, then, sir, are we to account for their late conduct? In one way only; some powerful nation must have intrigued with them, and turned their peaceful disposition towards us into hostilities. Great Britain alone has intercourse with those Northern tribes." As war with Britain loomed, government agents circulated among the Northwest Indian tribes, urging them to remain neutral during the coming war but threatening retribution if they allied with the British.

Tecumseh represented a threat to American expansion not only because of his military activities, but also because of his attitude toward land sales to white men. Tecumseh urged northwestern tribes to stop selling land piecemeal to Americans and instead adopt a "common property" idea that would prevent further American expansion. Tecumseh realized that a never-ending series of treaties transferring land from the Indians to the government could result only in the eventual, total loss of the Indian way of life. He also tried to establish a form of tribal confederation that would prevent any further land sales by providing political unity among the various tribes. Although Tecumseh's ideas were opposed by some Indians and even divided some tribes internally, his views became a rallying point for Indians who hoped to prevent American expansion into the Northwest. Tecumseh confronted American agents and territorial governors using the same rhetoric and reasoning. He told government officials that among the Indians, land "never was divided, but belongs to all, for the use of each. . . . No part has a right to sell, even to each other, much less to strangers." In 1811 Tecumseh attempted to spread these ideas across the South by traveling among the Creek, Chickasaw, and Choctaw tribes in an effort to convince them to put aside their divisions and unify against the white men politically and militarily. He attempted to bring unity to the previously disunited tribes of the North and South, with a single goal: to prevent the spread of trans-Appalachian American settlements onto Indian lands.

Westerners used the War of 1812 as a pretext to make repeated attempts to drive the Native Americans out of Ohio and Indiana. Much of the war's impact can be measured in the fighting between U.S. forces and Indian tribes that allied with the British on the country's northwestern and southwestern borders. Here, at least, the United States won some devastating military victories over the Indians that were of lasting importance. In October 1813 at the Battle of Thames River, Tecumseh and his Indian warriors, along with an army of British troops, were overrun by General Harrison. Tecumseh died in the fighting at Thames River, leading to the breakup of the incipient Indian alliance he had forged. Probably the most important American victories came during Andrew Jackson's campaign against the Creek nation, which led to the destruction of their military power in the Deep South. At the war's conclusion, Tecumseh's death and the withdrawal of the British signaled an end to the Indians' ability to stop westward migration. The conclusion to the War of 1812 effectively left the Northwest Indians at the mercy of frontiersmen and the American government. Similarly, Jackson's defeat of the Creeks brought to a close the possibility of widespread Indian resistance to white expansion in the Southwest. Indeed, the weakness of the remaining Creek Nation made it more likely that all southern Indians would be removed from lands east of the Mississippi. The conclusion of the war also killed any hopes for a larger, pan–American Indian confederation that could forestall American expansion to the south and northwest.

In 1814, while negotiating the peace treaty in Ghent, British officials demanded that Native Americans be given a secure territory in the Northwest. Neither the British nor the Americans would be permitted to buy the lands in this "buffer state," which would be a permanent area for Indian settlement. The American negotiators rejected these proposals outright, claiming that the Indians were not independent nations but living within territory controlled by the American government as a result of the Treaty of Paris (1783), which had concluded the Revolutionary War. The creation of such a buffer area would effectively preclude American settlement in the Old Northwest and close off a major route of western expansion, and American diplomats were unwilling even to discuss the British proposals. Further efforts by the British to protect Indian interests were similarly rejected. British diplomats soon realized that curtailing American expansion to the west could not be an issue at the Ghent peace talks.

At the war's conclusion, the power of the northwestern Indians had been broken. Tecumseh's death removed their most effective leader, and the attempts of other tribes to stop the American migration into the Northwest met with failure and served to accelerate the postwar process of government-managed forced removal. In the years following the War of 1812, Indians in all of the Old Northwest were moved to lands beyond the Mississippi River. Their removal would hasten the arrival of even more settlers bent on moving westward into newly opened "frontier." Further, European powers would no longer attempt to influence or coerce Native Americans to act as their cat's-paw to prevent American expansion.

The war's impact can also be seen in domestic politics, where it led to a renewal of intense sectional squabbling and the eventual demise of the Federalist party. The Federalists relentlessly opposed the war and any effort that would boost the fortunes of the Republican-dominated army and navy. Federalists refused to support direct taxation to finance the war and did as much as they could to undermine war recruiting and public opinion on the war. Indeed, throughout the war, the Federalists claimed that the conflict was being prosecuted as nothing more than an attempt by the Republican party to grab Canadian lands by underhanded means. The commercial community, long a mainstay of the Federalist party, felt that it had little to gain from territorial expansion in the South and West and much to lose from congressionally imposed embargoes of U.S. trade. Federalist members of the Massachusetts House of Representatives urged citizens to resist the war and refused to let their state militia leave home. On the national scene, Federalists in Congress united against the Madison administration's war efforts in over 300 congressional votes.

The Federalists also took advantage of sectional tension to build opposition to the war. Their efforts had the potential for greatest success at the 1814 Hartford Convention. Dominated by delegates from New England and Federalists, the men who met in Hartford discussed their growing frustration with the war as well as the loss of New England's power within the national government. They wanted to reverse the three-fifths compromise that gave southern states greater power in the House of Representatives and sought to limit the presidency to one term in order to break the apparent hold Virginians had on that office. They considered separating from the national government if their suggestions were not acted on, although they never actually voted for secession, a step prevented by moderates in the convention. Their proposals were designed to reduce the power of the South in the national government while boosting their own political power. The activities of the Hartford Convention clearly revealed the potential for sectionalism that existed in America before the Civil War and would resurface again. The efforts of the Federalist-dominated Hartford Convention were ultimately swept away when their delegates arrived in Washington at the same time news arrived of the rousing victory at New Orleans and the conclusion to peace treaty negotiations at Ghent.

Opposition to war measures came at a cost for the Federalists. Had the war been perceived as a total failure and waste of effort by the American people, it is likely that the Federalist party would have been rewarded for its steadfast opposition to Madison and the military. But in spite of its military losses, Americans came to believe that the country had "won" the war and had triumphed in the peace negotiations: the myth of the "successful" War of 1812 became accepted across America. Following 1815, Americans viewed the war as a positive expression of national pride and identity. As a result, Federalists looked unpatriotic, and Republicans appeared heroic. Despite their repeated bungling of the war, Republicans received a major boost with news of Jackson's victory at New Orleans. And Madison's acceptance of the Treaty of Ghent, which acquired no new territory for the United States, stood as a stark rebuke to Federalists' claims that the war had been nothing but a land grab. At the war's conclusion, the Republican party was rewarded for its handling of the War of 1812, easily winning the 1816 presidential and congressional elections and eventually placing Republican James Monroe in the presidential race of 1820 with negligible opposition. The activities of the Hartford Convention, combined with their earlier antiwar criticism, spelled the end for the Federalist party and gave unlooked-for support to the Republican party, which remained the dominant party of the 1820s until the rise of Andrew Jackson.

The War of 1812 boosted the fortunes of young political War Hawks and military war heroes alike. Aggressive young Republicans who touted the war, like John C. Calhoun and Henry Clay, would play important roles in national politics for the next 30 years. Calhoun and Clay would both suffer with unrequited presidential ambitions that would ultimately lead them to diametrically opposed positions on national unity. Clay would earn his greatest fame as a political compromiser in the House of Representatives, forging temporary agreements in 1820 and 1850 in an effort to overcome the tragic effects of sectionalism. Thwarted in the 1820s in his desire to move up from the vice presidency to the presidency, Calhoun would provide the theoretical underpinning for nullification in the 1830s with his pamphlet *Exposition and Protest*, temporarily reviving the old Federalist arguments about secession. Similarly, the war would promote military figures William Henry Harrison and Andrew Jackson to the presidency, and Jackson's political fortunes would eventually lead to the creation of the Democratic party in the mid-

1820s. Indeed, we might credit the war with giving Jackson's heroism the chance to outshine the political efforts of Henry Clay, creating a stronger leader to serve as the voice of western leadership. Riding the national wave of military popularity and expansionist rhetoric generated by the War of 1812, Jackson and the rapidly growing Democratic party succeeded in holding onto power at the national level for decades preceding the Civil War.

In the immediate postwar period, the Republican party developed a new national program for the government, reversing many of its traditional political stances by calling for (and getting) a new national bank, greater spending on land and naval defenses, and the introduction of a protective tariff. In his 1815 message to Congress, President Madison said that the war had demonstrated the need for a national bank and better means of transporting men and material throughout the country. Cut off from European markets and goods, the war had made domestic manufacturers appear patriotic, to the point that even the postwar Republican party sought to reverse its long-held hostility to promoting business and other internal improvements. These new Republican programs would be dubbed the "American System" by Henry Clay. In areas beyond the bank, the military, and commerce, revitalized American nationalism was revealed; in the era following the war, America was able to negotiate the Adams-Onís Treaty and legitimate Jackson's invasion of Florida.

The War of 1812 swamped any growing sectionalism with a contagion of nationalism. Many believed the war had begun as a contest to defend the nation's honor over maritime insults, and the war concluded on the same note after the Battle of New Orleans, with an exhultation of national honor. Patriotism had been championed throughout the war. Touting national honor and the necessity of preserving a republican form of government, War Hawk Republicans and President Madison played on the patriotism of Americans to garner support for the war. If Britain continued to deal with the United States as if it were still a colony, then America must once again prove its independence from British policies. The war showed that the nation was capable of defending itself without sacrificing the republican form of government. The conflict seemed to be a second war for national independence against their old foes, the British, a conflict that America "won" a second time. Jefferson and Madison's secretary of the treasury, Albert Gallatin, believed that the war had strengthened American nationalism: "The war has renewed and reinstated the national feelings and character which the Revolution had given, and which were daily lessening. . . . [Because of the war] they are more Americans; they feel and act more as a nation; and I hope that the permanency of the Union is thereby better secured." The war revived American nationalism, born in the era of the Revolution, and gave Americans something to be proud of by creating a symbol for national unity.

Yet it was unclear what kind of nationalism Americans would support in the years immediately following the War of 1812. Would they favor internal improvements and the systematic creation of economic incentives that would help the economy flourish (and line the pockets of the wealthy at the same time), or would they prefer a more piecemeal approach to economic activities that might curb the privileges and wealth of the unpopular "aristocratic" elites? Historian Steven Watts has suggested that the nationalism revived by this war helped transform the country's values from civic-minded republicanism to more liberal values. The notion of the self-made man, the ethics of industrial capitalism that came to dominate the nineteenth century, Watts believes, were significantly strengthened in the war's aftermath. By using, as Watts puts it, "the complicated function of war in American society," he describes how liberal America was shaped from elements in society that survived the crucible of war. Although this is a suggestive interpretation, it has yet to be taken up by a majority of scholars who study the nineteenth century and must still be considered a theory in the making. Even so, historians continue to debate exactly which nationalism Americans were attracted to in the postwar era.

By creating a new pride in the Union, the War of 1812 neatly undercut the growing sectional divisions that were apparent at the Hartford Convention. Historian Samuel Flagg Bemis has suggested that the strength of American nationalism generated by the War of 1812 made it possible for the country to triumph over the growing threat of states' rights later in the nineteenth century. As he put it, "We may say that if it had not been for the War of 1812 the Union might not have triumphed in 1865." This may be overstating the importance of the War of 1812, yet the wave of nationalism that swept through the United States certainly delayed many of the divisive events that led to the Civil War, while fueling the westward expansion that ultimately threatened to undo the political ties binding together the North and the South.

SELECTED BIBLIOGRAPHY

Bartlett, Ruhl J. "Neutrality." In Alexander DeConde, ed., *Encyclopedia of American Foreign Policy*, 2: 679–687. New York: Scribner, 1978. Brief overview of the concept of neutrality as it pertains to America and developments in its uses up to the modern day.

Bemis, Samuel Flagg. *A Diplomatic History of the United States.* 5th ed. New York: Holt, Rinehart & Winston, 1965. Of the major surveys of American diplomatic history, the strongest on nineteenth-century affairs, although tinged with patriotism.

Brooks, Philip C. *Diplomacy and the Borderlands.* Berkeley: University of California Press, 1939. Still the best introduction to the Adams-Onís Treaty.

Broussard, James H. *The Southern Federalists, 1800–1816.* Baton Rouge: Louisiana State University Press, 1978. Argues that the Federalist party in the South was not destroyed by antiwar sentiment or support for the Hartford Convention but through loss of major issues dividing the party from Republicans.

Brown, Roger. *The Republic in Peril: 1812.* New York: Columbia University Press, 1964. Highlights the importance of Federalist-Republican partisan fighting as a cause of the War of 1812, making the war necessary to show the viability of the republican experiment.

Burt, Alfred. *The United States, Great Britain, and British North America from the Revolution to the Establishment of Peace after the War of 1812.* New Haven, CT: Yale University Press, 1940. Stresses the importance and complexity of impressment and ship seizure as a cause for the war.

Cayton, Andrew R. L. *The Frontier Republic: Ideology and Politics in the Ohio Country, 1780–1825.* Kent, OH: Kent State University Press, 1986. Links territorial politics to ideology and provides local background to Northwest controversies.

Dangerfield, George. *The Awakening of American Nationalism, 1815–1828.* New York: Harper & Row, 1965. Best short introduction to the impact of the war on nationalism and the ensuing debate about the type of nationalism (economic or democratic) that would be best for America.

Edmunds, R. David. *Tecumseh and the Quest for Indian Leadership.* Boston: Little, Brown, 1984. Well-written, insightful study of the Shawnee leader and his followers in the period before and during the War of 1812.

Fredriksen, John C. *Free Trade and Sailor's Rights: A Bibliography of the War of 1812.* Westport, CT: Greenwood Press, 1985. Contains more than 6000 items, published and unpublished, relating to the war.

Hacker, Louis M. "Western Land Hunger and the War of 1812." *Mississippi Valley Historical Review* 10 (1923–1925): 379–395. Although now discredited by Julius Pratt (see below), Hacker formulated the theory that westerners supported the War of 1812 to acquire Canadian lands and gain control of the fur trade.

Hickey, Donald R. *The War of 1812: A Forgotten Conflict.* Urbana: University of Illinois Press, 1989. Most recent general history of the war, focusing primarily on the military and naval campaigns and emphasizing America's political ineptitude and military unpreparedness.

Higginbotham, Don. "The Early American Way of War: Reconnaissance and Appraisal." *William and Mary Quarterly,* 3d ser. 44 (1987): 230–273. Surveys the most recent writings in military history; excellent analysis of the impact of political ideology on the issue of standing armies and citizen-soldiers.

Horsman, Reginald. *The Frontier in the Formative Years, 1783–1815.* New York: Holt, Rinehart & Winston, 1970. Describes both northwest and southeast frontiers and their expansion in concise fashion.

Merk, Frederick. *Manifest Destiny and Mission in American History: A Reinterpretation.* 1953 ed. Westport, CT: Greenwood, 1983. Chapter 1 discusses territorial expansion in the early nineteenth century, focusing on the sense of mission behind expansionism, in response to Albert Weinberg (see below).

———. *History of the Westward Movement.* New York: Knopf, 1978. Describes westward migration in American history from the seventeenth to the twentieth centuries.

Owsley, Frank Lawrence, Jr. *Struggle for the Gulf Borderlands: The Creek War and the Battle of New Orleans, 1812–1815.* Gainesville: University Presses of Florida, 1981. Brief survey of the southern theater of war, discussing the importance of removing the Creek Indians and the activities of Andrew Jackson.

Perkins, Bradford. *Prologue to War: England and the United States, 1805–1812.* Berkeley: University of California Press, 1961. Focuses on the importance of national pride and effects of repeated British insults that required a war to "vindicate the nation's character."

Pratt, Julius W. *Expansionists of 1812.* New York: Macmillan, 1925. Gives a full explanation of Pratt's thesis of the alliance between southern and western expansionists; most textbooks still rely on this interpretation.

Prucha, Francis P. *The Great Father: The United States Government and the American Indian.* Lincoln: University of Nebraska Press, 1984. 2 vols. One of many important works about Indians by Prucha, providing a sweeping review of government policy toward Native Americans from settlement to the twentieth century.

Remini, Robert. *Andrew Jackson and the Course of Empire 1767–1821.* New York: Harper & Row, 1977. One of several excellent studies by Remini tracing the rise of Jackson and the Democratic party in the early nineteenth century.

Risjord, Norman K. "1812: Conservatives, War Hawks, and the Nation's Honor." *William and Mary Quarterly,* 3d ser. 18 (1961): 196–210. Focuses on national honor as a unifying force leading to the war's onset.

Smith, Dwight L. *The War of 1812: An Annotated Bibliography.* New York: Garland Press, 1985. Over 600 full annotations of major sources on the war.

Stagg, J.C.A. *Mr. Madison's War: Politics, Diplomacy and Warfare in the Early American Republic, 1783–1830.* Princeton, NJ: Princeton University Press, 1983. Discusses domestic politics, administrative incompetence, and finance while ranging briefly beyond the war to examine its impact on American society.

Stuart, Reginald C. *United States Expansionism and British North America.* Chapel Hill: University of North Carolina Press, 1988. Gives a new twist to the

Hacker-Pratt land expansion controversy, suggesting that the war was driven by military defensive motives rather than conquest.

Watts, Stephen. *The Republic Reborn: War and the Making of Liberal America, 1790–1820.* Baltimore: Johns Hopkins University Press, 1987. Cultural history that suggests the War of 1812 served as a vehicle for the transformation of American character from republican citizenship to liberal capitalism.

Weinberg, Albert K. *Manifest Destiny: A Study of Nationalist Expansionism in American History.* 1935 ed. New York: AMS Press, 1979. Surveys variety of American ideas toward territorial expansion, including the early nineteenth century.

White, Richard. *The Middle Ground: Indians, Empires, and Republics in the Great Lakes Region, 1650–1815.* Cambridge: Cambridge University Press, 1991. Excellent introduction to the intricate relations between Indians and American settlers, explaining cultural as well as political contact and activities.

President James Monroe gives his cabinet a geography lesson during discussions leading up to the Monroe Doctrine in 1823. Note the outline of the Louisiana Purchase on the map behind Monroe. (Reproduced from the Collections of the Library of Congress)

3

The Monroe Doctrine, 1823

INTRODUCTION

During the eighteenth century, the United States and the Latin American colonies of Spain had little in common. The systems of government, the predominant religion, and the racial mixtures were all very different, and there was little trade with or travel to South America from the United States. But in 1808, when Napoleon invaded Spain during the Napoleonic Wars, Latin American revolutionaries took advantage of the disruption of their home government to lead anti-Napoleon movements loyal to ousted King Ferdinand VII. By 1812, the principal South American colonies had achieved de facto independence from Spain and looked to make contact with other nations. Great Britain took the lead in establishing trade relations, but the United States sent money to relieve victims of an earthquake in Venezuela, and two enterprising Americans established the first newspaper in Chile. To facilitate the growing American trade, consuls were sent to Caracas and Buenos Aires in 1810 and 1812, respectively.

When Ferdinand VII was restored to his throne in Spain in 1814, he tried to put his former South American colonies under Spanish rule again. He sent a sizable army and fleet and had indeed subdued all of them except La Plata (Argentina) by 1816. But the revolutionary leaders

José San Martín, Simón Bolívar, and Bernardo O'Higgins kept up the fight, and by 1818, most of the old colonies had once again secured their independence or had come close enough so that their leaders were requesting of the United States that they be extended diplomatic recognition. Chile, Venezuela, and La Plata compared their struggle for independence to that of the United States and expected U.S. recognition of their independence. In the United States, they had some strong advocates. Speaker of the House Henry Clay spoke eloquently of the "glorious spectacle of 18 million people struggling to burst their chains and be free." But, President James Monroe and Secretary of State John Quincy Adams were cautious, fearful of antagonizing Spain, which though weak itself had strong European allies, and Congress passed a neutrality act with respect to Latin America. Adams did not have much faith in the newly independent countries; he "wished them well" but saw no prospect that they could establish free governments, since they had no such tradition. Monroe and Adams were not interested enough to champion Latin American independence; they were content to let Spain fight it out with its former colonies as long as other European states did not intervene and threaten U.S. security. There was no administration desire to dominate a Western Hemisphere league or obtain exclusive trading privileges.

In 1818, Monroe did go so far as to ask his minister in Britain to propose to the London government a joint Anglo-American statement of recognition, but the British declined, torn between their desire to help maintain monarchy (and thus assist Spain) and their interest in preserving the trade advantages they had already won in Latin America. Britain tried to persuade Spain to agree to a compromise measure whereby the former Latin American colonies would retain their autonomy but stay under the shadow of the Spanish crown. But Spain was insistent on restoring the status quo before the revolutions. By 1822, Peru and Mexico had been added to the list of free republics, revolution had spread to Spain itself, and Brazil had worked free from Portugal. In Europe, the Quadruple Alliance, consisting of Russia, Prussia, Great Britain, and France, had been formed in 1815 and had held some discussions about a joint military expedition to restore Spain's former colonies to Spanish control, but Britain's objections prevented the implementation of this scheme. By 1822, Britain had left the alliance. Between Mexico and Cape Horn at the southern tip of South America, only Belize, Bolivia, and the Guianas were still under colonial rule.

In March 1822, Monroe extended diplomatic recognition to the governments of La Plata, Chile, Peru, Colombia, and Mexico, and Congress appropriated money to send missions to these countries. Britain was not yet ready to recognize rebel republican nations for fear of inciting Irish nationalists, but Prime Minister George Canning knew that if Britain did not take some sort of action, the United States might walk off with exclusive commercial advantages and possibly even a hemispheric defense alliance.

Both the United States and Great Britain had definite interests in Latin America. For the United States, there was the ideological sympathy of fellow republicans; any Latin American republic represented a blow against monarchy. And if Europe were kept outside the Western Hemisphere, there was less chance of the United States becoming entangled in a future European war. Finally, the commercial advantages, once ignored, were taking on more importance as American traders saw a sizable new market in independent Latin America. As for Britain, its commercial ties with Latin America were well established by 1822, and Britain looked to the United States mainly for help in protecting its investments in Latin America.

By 1823, France had sent troops to Spain to help halt the revolution against Ferdinand VII, and it was common knowledge in Europe that planning was underway for a joint Franco-Spanish military expedition to Latin America. Neither Britain nor the United States wanted the French to reestablish any kind of influence in the Western Hemisphere. This consideration, along with the commercial interests involved, prompted Canning to suggest to Richard Rush, the U.S. minister in London, that the two nations make a joint protest against intervention in Latin America. Rush was flattered at Canning's suggestion but aware of the traditional American opposition to entangling alliances. He responded that the United States would consider a joint declaration if Britain would recognize the newly independent Latin American nations. This idea, along with the knowledge that the proposed Franco-Spanish intervention was not likely to occur, cooled Canning's ardor for a joint statement. Nevertheless, Rush sent the idea back to Monroe, who received it in October 1823.

Another issue that entered into the Monroe administration's discussions in 1823 concerned the Russians, who controlled what is now Alaska and were attempting to extend Russian control down to the fifty-first parallel in the Pacific Northwest and Russian claims all the way to San Francisco Bay. Moreover, non-Russian ships were to stay at least 100 miles away from the coast. This conflicted with claims to that area that Adams had obtained in the Adams-Onís Treaty and dealt a blow to American shipping interests in that area. Adams told Russia in the summer of 1823 that its moves in the region were improper and that no part of the American continents was subject any longer to European colonization. This declaration found its way into the Monroe Doctrine and American diplomacy as the noncolonization principle.

In Washington, Monroe consulted with his cabinet and also with former presidents Jefferson and Madison about the joint Anglo-American declaration idea. Jefferson and Madison thought the idea a good one, but Secretary of State John Quincy Adams noted that it might cause difficulties if the United States ever wanted to acquire Cuba or Texas. Moreover, wrote Adams, Britain was clearly a stronger nation than the United States, and with a joint declaration, the United States would be seen "as a cockboat in the wake of the British man-o-war." He urged that the United States act alone in opposing intervention in the Western Hemisphere.

Another current issue concerned revolutionary affairs in Europe. The Greeks were revolting against a harsh Turkish regime in a movement that had won a great deal of sympathy (and money) among Americans, and the Spanish were staging an uprising against French occupation. Monroe was very interested in helping the rebels, especially the Greeks, and he wanted to make some mention of that fact in his annual message to Congress, but Adams convinced him that these were European matters and no business of the U.S. government. If the United States did not want European intervention in the Western Hemisphere, it should not involve itself in European conflicts.

Adams's positions on an independent pronouncement and on remaining isolated from Europe won the day, and after another month of cabinet deliberations, the policy that became known as the Monroe Doctrine was worked out and included in the annual message of the president to Congress on December 2, 1823. It presented three basic points:

1. The American continents shall be considered closed for future colonization, and any effort of European powers to establish new colonies would be considered dangerous to the peace and safety of the United States.

2. Any attempt of European powers to interfere in the political systems of American nations would be considered dangerous to the peace and safety of the United States.

3. The United States had no intention of meddling in European affairs.

In the United States, public opinion reacted enthusiastically to the nationalistic spirit of Monroe's message. The Latin American nations were disposed in a friendly way, although they realistically expected more protection from the British than from their neighbors to the north. Canning was irritated at the decision of the United States to act alone, and most of the rest of Europe did not take it seriously. In reality, the Monroe Doctrine had little immediate practical application. President James K. Polk, twenty years later, was the first to use the name "Monroe Doctrine," and it did not become a significant tenet of U.S. foreign policy until the Civil War era.

If the Monroe Doctrine was not immediately applicable, it did probably spur more interest in Latin American affairs among U.S. policymakers. In 1826, Simón Bolívar called a meeting of Latin American representatives in Panama to discuss his idea of a Latin American alliance against Spain. Bolívar disliked Americans and did not invite the United States to the congress, but he did invite the British, whom he saw as the logical European patron of his alliance. Mexico and Colombia, however, extended an invitation to the United States, and Secretary of State Adams thought it would be a good idea to have delegates in attendance. Congress was less certain and failed to appropriate money in time for U.S. delegates to reach Panama before the congress adjourned. In the end, the Panama Congress, with only four Latin American nations and Great Britain present, failed to accomplish anything, although the British delegates were able to propagandize against the United States. When Canning died in 1827, the seriousness of the Anglo-American rivalry over Latin America faded. Although British trade and investment would remain paramount in Latin America until well into the twentieth century, the United States had the freedom to use the Monroe Doctrine as it saw fit for political and security reasons without significant interference from the British.

INTERPRETIVE ESSAY
Peter G. Felten

James Monroe would have been pleasantly surprised at the centennial celebration of his most famous presidential message in 1923, when public figures around the country sang the praises of his declaration, even comparing it in importance to the Constitution. Yet there are few other subjects in American diplomacy that have been more misunderstood. The confusion has resulted primarily from how politicians have used the ideas he outlined in 1823. President Monroe established a fairly clear policy based on pressing international, political, economic, and cultural concerns. Over the years, however, others have revived his words under very different circumstances and for quite different purposes. The Monroe Doctrine expanded from a statement of principles to become both a domestic political weapon and a justification for U.S. intervention in Latin America.

In 1823 James Monroe recognized that his long and distinguished career soon would end. He had completed most of his second presidential term, and he could look back proudly on his achievements as a diplomat and politician. He had been a member of both houses of Congress during the nation's earliest days and had served as an ambassador in major European capitals, the governor of Virginia, the secretary of state, and, finally, president. Yet Monroe worried that his accomplishments paled in comparison to those of his friends and predecessors, Thomas Jefferson and James Madison. Throughout his presidency, Monroe hoped to make an indelible mark on American history, guaranteeing that he too would be remembered. He did not believe a complex crisis in 1823 presented such an opportunity, but it did.

Since declaring independence nearly 50 years earlier, many Americans considered their nation the first wave in a global republican tide. Monroe and others saw the United States as the model for freedom everywhere. They feared that hostile European monarchs planned to destroy the American experiment. The decades of international conflict since 1776, particularly bitter disputes with Great Britain and Spain, confirmed these suspicions. This combination of worries and pride mixed to produce an increasingly nationalistic culture after the War of 1812. Politicians like President Monroe, reflecting the views of the population at large, were determined to protect American interests in the world and to project American ideals around the globe.

Economic considerations reinforced these nationalist aspirations. The economy expanded rapidly following the War of 1812. Industrialization spread, protected by tariffs that excluded foreign competition for American goods. Cotton from the South blanketed the world, making trade with the textile factories of Great Britain crucial to prosperity. Farmers brought the market economy further into the center of the continent, and American merchant ships became an important presence in both Latin

America and Asia. To guarantee continued economic growth and to preserve the American republic, politicians focused on securing global trading rights while defending industrial development at home.

Economic interests led to heightened tensions between the United States and Russia in the Pacific. Both nations had vague claims to lands along the west coast of North America, and a bustling fur trade after 1800 made the competition more intense. The area also served as an important launching point for commercial expeditions to Asia. Because of this economic potential, each country coveted the area. Between 1815 and 1820, more than 100 American merchant ships visited the Northwest. A nervous Russian ruler in 1821 tried to check the growing U.S. presence by strengthening his forts in the area and by banning foreign vessels in his nation's territorial waters in the Pacific. During the summer of 1823, President Monroe's secretary of state, John Quincy Adams, bluntly warned the Russians that America would contest any new colonization in the region.

Monroe and Adams worried about European moves not only in the Far West but also to the South. The Spanish Empire had been crumbling in Latin America for more than a decade. Local insurgents, at times modeling themselves on the revolutionaries of 1776, declared independence throughout the hemisphere. Many U.S. citizens identified with the rebels and supported their cause. The United States additionally had an economic stake in the success of the new nations, since trade with them could support prosperity and growth. Finally, President Monroe and others feared that European monarchs would reestablish colonial control in the region, threatening both U.S. commerce and the American republican experiment. In 1823 the rulers of Russia, Austria, Prussia, and France, calling themselves the Holy Alliance, united to overthrow the infant republican government in Spain. The Holy Alliance then cast its gaze on Latin America.

The United States found an unlikely ally in its opposition to European expansion in the Americas. Fifty years before, the North American colonists had rebelled against Great Britain. In 1812 the two nations fought again. In 1823, however, they shared a desire to keep the Holy Alliance out of the Western Hemisphere. The British were the world's greatest trading nation, and they stood to gain the most economically from the loss of Spanish influence in the Americas. Recognizing the common interests of these once bitter enemies, British diplomats suggested to their Yankee peers that they cooperate. The marriage of America's location close to the contested territories and the powerful British navy, it was thought, would convince the Holy Alliance that an invasion of the former Spanish colonies would be ill advised.

International coordination with the British made practical sense for the United States but not political sense for important American policymakers. President Monroe was on the verge of retirement in 1823, and many of his advisers sought his office in the 1824 election. Unlike the president, they had to calculate how voters would react if they worked in tandem with the hated British.

John Quincy Adams had the most to lose in this equation. Adams had an impressive political record, and as secretary of state he held the office that had propelled both James Monroe and James Madison to the presidency. Adams had used his diplomatic position in 1819 to negotiate the popular Adams-Onís Treaty with Spain, purchasing Florida and extending the nation's border to the Pacific. But cooperation with Great Britain in 1823 threatened to undermine Adams's presidential ambitions by reinforcing suspicions that he, like his Federalist father, former president John Adams, was not sufficiently nationalistic and was too sympathetic to the British. Secretary of State Adams politically could not afford to coordinate U.S. policy with London, no matter how sensible it seemed in the international arena.

Adams's opponents in the presidential race, however, generally saw unity with Britain as good foreign policy and an effective way to undercut one of their political rivals. Besides Adams, the leading candidates in the 1824 election were Secretary of the Treasury William H. Crawford, Secretary of War John C. Calhoun, Speaker of the House Henry Clay, and General Andrew Jackson. Clay in particular used global issues to attack Adams and to boost his own chances. He called for the United States to grant diplomatic recognition to rebel governments in Greece and in Latin America, declaring the spread of republicanism to be the American national mission. Adams could not take such a step without seriously jeopardizing other U.S. interests in the world, so he resisted this popular move. More important, Clay, Calhoun, and others (including former presidents Thomas Jefferson and James Madison) encouraged President Monroe to work with Great Britain against the Holy Alliance. Their argument rested on solid international considerations, but it also had a political angle for some of those involved. Since Adams was secretary of state, his opponents could blame him if the policy failed or lost favor with the voters.

In order to preserve his political hopes while securing U.S. interests in the widening global crisis, Adams persuaded President Monroe to take a different course. Adams convinced Monroe that America could resist European moves in the region without openly cooperating with the British. This would preserve American independence in its foreign policy, something prized since George Washington's Farewell Address. It also would be as effective as a joint Anglo-American statement. The United States on its own would be declaring what Britain had proposed to do together. This unilateral doctrine, finally, would undermine the allegations that Adams was too cozy with the British.

On the advice of Secretary of State Adams, President Monroe responded to the international tensions in his December 1823 annual message to Congress. Ironically, what became known as the Monroe Doctrine was not included in one clear passage but rather appeared in two distinct parts of the president's statement. Near the beginning of his text, Monroe discussed the Pacific Northwest. He declared the American continents "are henceforth not to be considered as subject for future colonization by any European power." The United States could tolerate the existing European colonies in the region but would oppose the establishment of new ones. Later in the document Monroe returned to foreign affairs, this time focusing on the Holy Alliance's ambitions in Latin America. The president said the United States would not interfere with purely European affairs and warned European states that their intervention in the Americas would be seen as "dangerous to our peace and safety . . . [and] the manifestation of an unfriendly disposition towards the United States." In short, Europe should keep its hands off the Western Hemisphere.

Americans greeted Monroe's words with pleasure. The president's declaration appealed to nationalist sentiments by asserting that America's republican culture would dominate the area, to the exclusion of Old World monarchy. At the same time, Monroe had defended the country's economic and international interests, again popular causes, yet the president said little that was new or surprising. The warning to Russia had been issued previously by Secretary of State Adams. Monroe's hostility toward the Holy Alliance, and toward European recolonization in general, merely stated the obvious. Additionally, since the United States lacked a large military, Monroe did not have the power to support his words with deeds had he been challenged. Despite this, Monroe had neatly summarized the nationalist beliefs of his countrymen, winning their praise and ultimately securing a place in history books.

Outside the United States, the president's statement received a mixed response. Latin American rebels rejoiced, reasonably assuming that Monroe had implied the United States would protect the new nations from foreign powers. Over the next three years, these republics issued five appeals to Washington for such action, but none was forthcoming. Monroe's pledges, it turned out, had been aimed more at protecting American interests than at spreading American ideals. Europe's experienced and cynical diplomats generally recognized this, leading many to discount the significance of Monroe's words. The Holy Alliance disliked the upstart United States, but the member nations already had decided an invasion of Latin America was not practical. The British navy, not Monroe's policies, scared them away. Great Britain welcomed the declarations, which paralleled ideas they had proposed for a joint statement, although officials in London frowned on the more nationalistic portions of Monroe's message, which warned all Europeans, including the British, to stay out of the Americas.

Regardless of the national and international reaction, Monroe's doctrine soon faded into obscurity. The Holy Alliance never attacked, and Russia in 1824 offered to divide up the northwest coast, acknowledging the growing American dominance in the region. Without a crisis to give Monroe's message relevance, people in the United States turned their attention to other matters, including the upcoming election. The president's unilateral declaration guaranteed that Secretary of State Adams would not be seen as too friendly with the British, so foreign policy was not a major campaign issue. Adams had defused a potentially explosive political problem, but this alone did not win him the presidency in 1824.

The nation largely had forgotten Monroe's words when politicians in the 1840s revived them. Territorial expansion had become an increasingly important national concern over the previous two decades. President John Tyler recalled the Monroe Doctrine in 1842 when he demanded the independent Republic of Texas be brought into the United States. In 1844, James K. Polk won the presidency in part by promising to annex Texas. He also pledged to establish firm American control over the Oregon country, a huge area under joint Anglo-American occupation and bordered by Mexican California to the south, Russian Alaska to the north, the Rocky Mountains in the east, and the Pacific Ocean in the west. Motivated by an upsurge of aggressive nationalism in American culture, often called manifest destiny, Polk and his followers vowed to extend the nation across the continent. In his December 1845 message to Congress, President Polk claimed his ideas were in line with the 1823 doctrine, so his bold policies would "reiterate and reaffirm the principle avowed by Mr. Monroe."

By recalling Monroe, Polk cleverly associated his controversial stand on expansionism with a nationalist hero. This was good politics, but it obscured the very real differences between Monroe's goals and Polk's intentions. President Polk refocused the Monroe Doctrine to cover two contemporary issues. First, he narrowed its scope from encompassing all of the Western Hemisphere to concentrating primarily on the territories surrounding the United States. Polk made it clear that his concerns centered on North America. Second, he expanded the definition of the types of European interference that threatened American interests. President Monroe had warned against a military invasion by the Holy Alliance and against Russian colonization of the Pacific coast. Polk opposed any European involvement in the region. He particularly feared British and French advice that the Republic of Texas not accept the statehood offer from Washington. Monroe had spoken against concrete actions by European powers, while Polk reacted to their mere words.

With these alterations, President Polk used the Monroe Doctrine to justify territorial expansion. He argued that European meddling in Texas violated cherished American principles, requiring immediate annexation of the Republic. Polk also insisted the United States had a right to the entire Oregon Territory. He denied any British claim to the area on the grounds that it would constitute new colonization, another blow to Monroe's dictum. Allies of Polk, and at times the president himself, even stated that the United States ought to acquire Mexican California and Spanish Cuba in order to prevent potential British moves that would challenge the doctrine. What had been a defensive declaration under Monroe, warning Europeans to stay out, became under Polk an aggressive assertion of America's right to expand. Fundamentally, however, Polk's meaning remained similar to Monroe's original ideas. In 1823, President Monroe had unilaterally declared America's right to defend its interests in the hemisphere. In 1845, President Polk reaffirmed that principle, adding his conclusion that the United States must acquire new land to preserve its independence.

Although territorial expansion largely was completed during Polk's administration, his broad view of the Monroe Doctrine would be dominant in American politics long into the future. The new interpretation mirrored a growth of U.S. power. Industrialization throughout the nineteenth century transformed the country from its agrarian youth into a mature manufacturing giant. American trade around the globe grew apace, with total exports jumping from $281 million in 1865 to $1.2 billion in 1898. As the country became more influential and active in the world, Americans widened their understanding of their nation's rights and obligations in the hemisphere, expanding the doctrine. Although President Monroe lacked the military might to back up his declaration in 1823, by the end of the Civil War the United States had become the dominant force in the region. Monroe's hands-off policy now could be enforced against Europeans.

In the immediate aftermath of the Civil War, Monroe's words were recalled, again for both political and diplomatic reasons. French and Austrian influence in Mexico caused this outburst. The ambitious leader of France, Napoleon III, used Washington's distraction during the Civil War to install his Austrian ally, Ferdinand Maximilian, as ruler of Mexico. As the conflict in the United States concluded, Secretary of State William Henry Seward convinced Napoleon to withdraw his troops from Mexico, leaving Emperor Maximilian in the lurch. Rumors that Austria planned to send a small contingent of soldiers to prop up Maximilian led Seward to trumpet the Monroe Doctrine. The threat presented by the Austrian force was minor, hardly justifying the secretary's passion. Seward apparently reacted so strongly because it suited his political needs at home. In early 1866, President Andrew Johnson faced Republicans in Congress who increasingly opposed his lenient Reconstruction policies. Seward revived Monroe's principles as part of an attempt to rally nationalists around the controversial president. His effort failed both because the Austrians backed down quickly and because the differences over Reconstruction could not be obscured by Seward's smoke and mirrors. American power had deflated the crisis, but Seward was neither the first nor the last to use the Monroe Doctrine primarily for political reasons.

A more significant expression of Monroe's principles occurred a few years later, in 1870. Early in his administration, President Ulysses S. Grant tried to annex the Dominican Republic, the eastern portion of the Caribbean island of Hispaniola. Santo Domingo, as the country sometimes was called, possessed excellent harbors and lush farm lands, making it attractive as a regional base for both the U.S. Navy and American traders. The formerly independent nation, however, recently had fallen under Spanish control. When Dominican rebels drove the Spanish out,

Grant saw an opportunity to add this valuable real estate to the United States. A political uproar forced Grant to abandon his plans, but he used the hubbub to announce an addition to the Monroe Doctrine: "Hereafter no territory on this continent shall be regarded as subject to transfer to a European power." The "no-transfer" principle had roots in American diplomacy predating President Monroe, reaching back at least to an 1811 controversy concerning Spanish Florida. Grant for the first time made "no-transfer" a formal part of what Americans understood to be the Monroe Doctrine. Now the United States claimed both that Europeans could not recolonize the hemisphere and that Washington should have something to say in how empires disposed of their colonies. Under this expanded vision of Monroe's ideas, the United States exercised its new power to supervise the decolonization of the Americas.

The doctrine's growth climaxed in a series of incidents around the turn of the century. President Grover Cleveland and Secretary of State Richard Olney dramatically unfurled Monroe's banner in a conflict with Great Britain. The crisis arose out of an old dispute between Venezuela and British Guiana, both of which claimed territory along the Orinoco River that provided valuable commercial access into northern South America. The debate had been simmering for decades when President Cleveland suddenly inserted the United States into the equation in 1895. Washington had no direct interest in the affair, but Cleveland concluded that confronting London would be popular with American voters and would calm jitters about alleged British violations of the Monroe Doctrine. Cleveland sent Great Britain a note demanding international arbitration to settle the matter. When busy British diplomats ignored him, an outraged Cleveland instructed Secretary Olney to get London's attention. Olney wrote a second message with gusto, this one warning British diplomats that American "honor and interests" required a prompt and favorable resolution to the border issue. "Today the United States is practically sovereign on this continent," Olney asserted, ". . . its infinite resources combined with its isolated position render it master of the situation and practically invulnerable as against any or all other powers." London, preoccupied with more serious problems and worried about the surprising American hostility, quickly agreed to arbitration. President Cleveland succeeded in this strange affair. More important, Secretary of State Olney had extended Polk's aggressive Monroe Doctrine to cover the entire hemisphere. In essence, the United States declared the Americas to be its sphere of influence, forcefully opposing any European meddling in its backyard.

The 1898 war with Spain confirmed the new reality. When rebellion broke out in Cuba during the 1890s, the United States recognized an opportunity to exercise its growing military might against a weakened Spanish Empire, the ruler of Cuba and neighboring Puerto Rico. Assistant Secretary of the Navy Theodore Roosevelt and others urged President William McKinley to support the Monroe Doctrine with the armed forces. After tensions escalated, McKinley led the country into war in April 1898. The United States easily defeated the Spanish, and McKinley made Puerto Rico an American territory. Congress, however, contained his ambitions toward Cuba. Under the Platt Amendment, Washington established its control over Cuban affairs without taking on the day-to-day governing of the island. In the name of Monroe, the United States had moved from vocally opposing the creation of new European colonies in the Americas to waging war to oust a long-established empire. The doctrine's defensive pretext had been dropped. The war also represented a major step beyond Olney's words of just three years earlier. The United States progressed from publicly rejecting European involvement in the hemisphere to forcefully ejecting that presence.

President Theodore Roosevelt completed the doctrine's evolution. Roosevelt feared that debts Latin American nations owed European creditors might squeeze U.S. influence out of certain countries. Citing the need for order and stability, in 1904 he issued what became known as the Roosevelt Corollary to the Monroe Doctrine. "Chronic wrongdoing . . . ," Roosevelt claimed, "may in America, as elsewhere, ultimately require intervention by some civilized nation, and in the Western Hemisphere . . . the Monroe Doctrine may force the United States, however reluctantly, in flagrant cases of such wrongdoing or impotence, to the exercise of an international police power."

Roosevelt expanded Monroe's principles far beyond their original scope, creating a distinct doctrine rather than simply an addition to the original. The United States now asserted the right both to exclude European activity from the Americas and to regulate the internal affairs of regional states. Monroe had supported hemispheric rebellion because it removed European influence and fostered republican values; Roosevelt opposed such rebels because they threatened order, giving outside powers an opportunity to become involved in the Americas. By asserting the right to act as the hemisphere's policeman, Roosevelt was taking on a fundamentally new role for the United States. This position matched the country's growing economic and military power and fit with the aggressive nationalism of the times, yet it was so far removed from James Monroe's 1823 words that it represented something entirely different.

The country had changed, and politicians like Roosevelt had molded the Monroe Doctrine to fit the new realities.

Throughout the twentieth century, the process of adapting Monroe's legacy to conform to contemporary needs has continued, with the doctrine fading in and out of fashion. The 1980s witnessed its strongest revival since the days of Theodore Roosevelt. President Ronald Reagan wielded the Monroe Doctrine to rally popular support behind his policies in Central America. He opposed the government of Nicaragua, alleging that its sympathies for the Soviet Union violated the doctrine. Reagan contended that, in effect, the Soviets had established a colony in Nicaragua. The United States funded a rebellion to overthrow Nicaragua's ruling party and to restore a pro-Washington regime. Reagan's use of the Monroe Doctrine, however, had more to do with domestic politics than with international affairs. By recalling a policy that stretched back to the early days of the republic, Reagan associated his actions with the patriotic legacies of the founding fathers. Congressional opponents of White House moves in Nicaragua could point to the very real differences between Monroe's words and Reagan's deeds, but their historical arguments often were overwhelmed by the nationalist appeal of the doctrine. Once again, the Monroe Doctrine had been revived and reinterpreted to suit the political needs of a president.

With the end of the Cold War, Monroe's principles seemed to lose their practical meaning. Any external threat to the nations of the Western Hemisphere vanished. But the doctrine had evolved considerably since Monroe's times, and its more recent incarnations may keep it out of the dustbin of history. The United States remains dominant in the region. Secretary of State Olney's assertion of an American sphere of influence continues to be a reality. The United States also maintains its role as the policeman of the Caribbean, sending troops into Haiti in an effort to restore democracy to that troubled nation in 1994. Most important, the political value of the dictum endures. Politicians since John Quincy Adams have employed Monroe's words as a powerful weapon against their domestic opponents. The Monroe Doctrine's practical uses almost certainly guarantees its future relevance, even if, as in the past, its meaning is obscured or altered in the struggle to solve modern problems.

SELECTED BIBLIOGRAPHY

Ammon, Harry. *James Monroe: The Quest for National Identity.* New York: McGraw-Hill, 1971; Charlottesville: University Press of Virginia, 1990. A detailed biography.

Bemis, Samuel Flagg. *John Quincy Adams and the Foundations of American Foreign Policy.* New York: Alfred A. Knopf, 1956. A classic that some dismiss for its nationalist interpretation.

Coleman, Kenneth M. "The Political Mythology of the Monroe Doctrine: Reflections on the Social Psychology of Hegemony." In *Latin America, the United States and the Inter-American System.* Edited by John D. Martz and Lars Schoultz. Boulder, CO: Westview, 1980. A provocative interpretation of the flaws in American memory of the doctrine.

Collin, Richard H. *Theodore Roosevelt's Caribbean: The Panama Canal, the Monroe Doctrine, and the Latin American Context.* Baton Rouge: Louisiana State University Press, 1991. A strong defense of Roosevelt's policies.

Commager, Henry Steele, and Milton Cantor, eds. *Documents of American History.* Vol. 1: *To 1898.* 10th ed. Englewood Cliffs, NJ: Prentice-Hall, 1988. An easily accessible collection including the text of the Monroe Doctrine and other relevant documents.

Dangerfield, George. *The Awakening of American Nationalism, 1815–1828.* New York: Harper & Row, 1965. An insightful look at Monroe's era.

Dozer, Donald Marquand, ed. *The Monroe Doctrine: Its Modern Significance.* New York: Knopf, 1965. A useful collection of commentaries.

Johnson, John A. *A Hemisphere Apart: The Foundations of United States Policy toward Latin America.* Baltimore, MD: Johns Hopkins University Press, 1990. Explains the policymaking context of the doctrine's development.

Kaplan, Lawrence S. "The Monroe Doctrine and the Truman Doctrine: The Case of Greece." *Journal of the Early Republic* 13, no. 1 (Spring 1993): 1–21. An insightful contrast between two crucial events in U.S. diplomacy.

LaFeber, Walter. "The Evolution of the Monroe Doctrine from Monroe to Reagan." In *Redefining the Past: Essays in Diplomatic History in Honor of William Appleman Williams.* Edited by Lloyd C. Gardner. Corvallis: Oregon State University Press, 1986. A critical view of the doctrine's development emphasizing economics and spheres of influence.

Langley, Lester D. *America and the Americas: The United States in the Western Hemisphere.* Athens: University of Georgia Press, 1989. A solid introduction to inter-American relations.

———. *Struggle for the American Mediterranean: United States–European Rivalry in the Gulf-Caribbean, 1776–1904.* Athens: University of Georgia Press, 1976. A detailed but accessible examination of nineteenth-century inter-American affairs.

Liss, Peggy K. *Atlantic Empires: The Network of Trade and Revolution, 1713–1826.* Baltimore, MD: Johns Hopkins University Press, 1983. Explains the regional and historical context of Monroe's decision.

Logan, John A., Jr. *No Transfer: An American Security Principle.* New Haven, CT: Yale University Press, 1961. A thorough look at this partner to the Monroe Doctrine.

May, Ernest R. *The Making of the Monroe Doctrine.* Cambridge, MA: Belknap Press of Harvard University Press, 1975. A persuasive argument for the domestic political motives behind the doctrine.

Merk, Frederick, with Lois Bannister Merk. *The Monroe Doctrine and American*

Expansion 1843–1849. New York: Alfred A. Knopf, 1966. Explores how expansionists transformed the Monroe Doctrine to justify their goals.

Perkins, Dexter. *A History of the Monroe Doctrine*. Boston: Little, Brown, 1955. Still the place to start for the doctrine and its development over the years.

———. *The Monroe Doctrine, 1823–1826*. Cambridge, MA: Harvard University Press, 1927. A detailed examination of the doctrine's creation.

———. *The Monroe Doctrine, 1826–1867*. Baltimore, MD: Johns Hopkins University Press, 1933. A thorough look at the doctrine's early decades.

———. *The Monroe Doctrine, 1867–1907*. Cambridge, MA: Harvard University Press, 1937. A comprehensive study of the doctrine's evolution.

Russell, Greg. *John Quincy Adams and the Public Virtues of Diplomacy*. Columbia: University of Missouri Press, 1995. A complex analysis of the political and diplomatic philosophy of Adams.

Schoultz, Lars. *National Security and the United States Policy toward Latin America*. Princeton, NJ: Princeton University Press, 1987. An insightful examination of contemporary inter-American affairs.

Smith, Gaddis. *The Last Years of the Monroe Doctrine, 1945–1993*. New York: Hill and Wang, 1994. Explains the Cold War's impact on the doctrine.

Stagg, J.C.A. *Mr. Madison's War: Politics, Diplomacy, and Warfare in the Early American Republic, 1783–1830*. Princeton, NJ: Princeton University Press, 1983. A thoughtful summary of diplomacy of the era.

Valone, Stephen J. " 'Weakness Offers Temptation': William H. Seward and the Reassertion of the Monroe Doctrine." *Diplomatic History* 19, no. 4 (Fall 1995): 583–599. Stresses Seward's political motives for reviving the doctrine.

Weeks, William Earl. *John Quincy Adams and American Global Empire*. Lexington: University Press of Kentucky, 1992. Clearly links the Monroe Doctrine and the 1819 Adams-Onís Treaty.

Whitaker, Arthur Preston. *The United States and the Independence of Latin America, 1800–1830*. Baltimore: Johns Hopkins University Press, 1941. A classic study of early inter-American relations.

This engraving of Andrew Jackson suggests his determination to pursue policies in which he strongly believed. (Reproduced from the Collections of the Library of Congress)

4

Jacksonian Democracy, 1828–1840

INTRODUCTION

Named for Andrew Jackson, the noted War of 1812 veteran and Indian fighter from Tennessee who served as president from 1829 to 1837, Jacksonian democracy represented a new and different concept of the nature and responsibilities of the federal government. Jacksonian democracy was seen primarily in a greater sense of democratic participation in the government and in a reduction of federal responsibility, particularly with respect to the nation's economic system.

Andrew Jackson had lost the 1824 presidential election to John Quincy Adams in a close and controversial contest that was decided in the House of Representatives. Although Jackson had received a plurality of electoral votes in the general election, he had fallen short of a majority, and when third-place finisher Henry Clay shifted his support to Adams in the House of Representatives vote, it was sufficient to vault the former secretary of state into the White House. Although many at the time thought a secret deal had been made between Adams and Clay, especially since Clay became Adams's secretary of state, no hard evidence has ever been found to prove what was called a "corrupt bargain."

Jackson was not a man to forget or forgive, however, and he came back with a vengeance in the election of 1828. This campaign was the first in which personal attacks played a role. Jackson's campaign spread the word that Adams had installed a billiards table and a chess set in the White House and claimed that the White House now contained "gaming tables and gambling furniture." Adams's campaign retaliated with tales about Jackson's frontier brawls and, worse, Jackson's alleged premarital relations with the woman he later married. Possibly because of the stress of these personal attacks, Jackson's wife died soon after the election and never lived in the White House.

Adams had not had a very successful presidency, and that, combined with Jackson's heroic military exploits, was enough to carry the day. Jackson won states in every region of the country and, to use the present-day term, clearly won a national "mandate" to govern. And with Jackson's highly personalized presidency came that which is known as Jacksonian democracy.

The process of democratization that is central to Jacksonian democracy was clear in the election itself. Between 1810 and 1820, six new states had entered the union with constitutions that contained no property qualifications for voting; other states liberalized their qualifications. The result was that the number of voters increased from just 355,000 in 1824 to 1.16 million in 1828. Over the next 20 years, the number voting jumped to nearly 3 million, an increase far greater than can be accounted for by population growth.

In more general terms, other changes were accomplished in the political system. The increase in population in the West, along with the economic distress that followed the panic of 1819, showed the need for electing officials who would represent the true interests of the majority. Through the growth of free public education and a cheap press during this time, the common man became much more aware of the political system and what it could do to protect or advance his opportunities in society.

One immediate result was the scrapping of the old system of nominating presidential candidates through a congressional caucus, a process that the public now viewed as remote and aristocratic. Additionally growing sectional conflicts made it more difficult for the caucus to achieve consensus on a single candidate. Consequently, parties turned to the national party convention during this time, a move that allowed far more democratic participation and deliberation. By the time Jackson left office, all parties were holding conventions on a regular basis.

Although Jackson was not nominated at a party convention, he nevertheless personified the democratic movement. He was the first president from outside the Virginia or Massachusetts aristocracy. Born on the Tennessee frontier, he was of humble origins, and the people loved him for it. His military victory at the Battle of New Orleans in 1815, moreover, had made him a kind of folk hero, a symbol of American valor and nationalism. And he looked the part—tall and lean, with a hawklike frontier face and a thatch of thick white hair. He was quick to anger and slow to forgive, and he had been in more than one duel. He was known for his chivalrous attitude toward "the fair," and his excellent manners, provided he kept his temper.

Jacksonian democracy would not allow for class distinction, so all were invited to the White House inauguration party, and some 10,000 people showed up, standing on chairs with muddy boots, fighting for the limited refreshments, and breaking glass and porcelain. Jackson escaped the mob by climbing out a window, and the guests were induced to leave the White House by the ploy of placing large tubs of punch out on the lawn.

More serious events during the early months of Jackson's presidency contributed to the idea of Jacksonian democracy. One issue was the nature of bureaucratic appointments and the spoils system, the process of replacing public servants from the previous administration with loyal supporters of the new administration. Although the spoils system had been common practice at the state level for some time, Jackson is particularly identified with it. He was the first to discard bureaucrats on a wide scale at the national level for no other reason than to reward deserving Democrats, and the haste with which he did it was alarming. In the end, he removed only 252 of 612 presidential appointments, but the Adams people were shocked, and Adams charged that it made government "a perpetual and unintermitting scramble for office."

Jackson, however, considered it a positive good—a reform. To him, it was the rooting out of a permanent office-holding class. He felt that most bureaucratic jobs were simple and routine enough that any citizen with average intelligence could adequately perform them and that the country gained more from the rotation of bureaucrats than it did from having experienced people in the offices. Thus, old and able Jeffersonians were replaced by young and often disreputable Jacksonians, the worst of whom was one Samuel Swartout, who became the collector of customs of the port of New York. He managed to steal over $1 million before he was caught. The spoils system endured on a large scale until the 1880s, when civil service reform was introduced, and it still continues to some degree.

Jackson's belief in greater democracy became apparent in his dealings with Congress. He conceived of himself as a national leader responsible to the people as a whole. Presidents before him had been content simply to administer laws Congress passed; Jackson, however, vetoed more legislation in his two terms than all his predecessors combined. He was also the first to take advantage of the pocket veto: the provision that permits a president to kill a measure passed fewer than ten days before the adjournment of Congress simply by withholding his signature. In reply to charges of presidential usurpation of power, Jackson maintained that he needed to use his office as a bulwark against aristocratic establishments and powerful monopolies. He favored what he called a "plain system" of government, "void of pomp—protecting all and granting favors to none—dispensing its blessings, like the dews of heaven, unseen and unfelt save in the freshness and beauty they contribute to produce."

In the 1832 presidential election that matched Jackson, running for his second term, against Henry Clay, the Bank of the United States was the major issue. The bank had been chartered in 1816 for a 20–year period to handle federal finances, issue national bank notes, and maintain financial stability in the country, but many were critical of the bank for its refusal to honor the paper money of state banks, which often was overissued relative to the real value of the bank's assets. Jackson had at first favored the Bank of the United States, but by 1832, he had come to doubt both its constitutionality and its value to the country. He believed it operated in the spirit of monopoly, and he hated monopolies. Nevertheless, he was reluctant to attack the bank because several of its supporters sat in his cabinet and because the bank did provide certain useful services for the country. Jackson instead contented himself with pressuring Nicholas Biddle, the bank's president, to place more administration people on the bank's payroll. Biddle resisted, fearing that the bank would fall under the spoils system, and instead he tried to influence key members of Congress by offering them advances on their salaries or low-interest loans. Among the bank's friends in Congress were Henry Clay, who saw political advantage in siding with the institution, and Daniel Webster, who earned a handsome fee serving as the bank's legal adviser.

Biddle's lobbying efforts only made the stubborn Jackson more determined to get rid of the bank when its charter came up for renewal in 1836. In early 1832, the bank's supporters in Congress decided to make the renewal of its charter a central campaign issue by bringing forward a bill for renewal four years early. They reasoned that the bank was so popular in the country that Jackson would have no choice but to sign the renewal if he expected to be reelected. But Jackson told his vice president, Martin Van Buren, "The Bank, Mr. Van Buren, is trying to kill me, but I will kill it." And so he vetoed the renewal bill, concluding in his veto message that the bank was neither necessary, nor proper, nor constitutional. Biddle thought Jackson's message was so outrageous that he circulated it as pro-bank propaganda during the campaign, but Jackson was an easy winner in the election, which he took as a mandate to carry on against Biddle's "Hydra of corruption."

Over the next four years, Jackson and Biddle battled over the status of the bank. Biddle thought that Jackson might withdraw government funds from it and so used a good part of those already on deposit to make even more loans and publicize the bank's virtues in the press. Jackson became convinced that federal funds were not safe in the bank and, after some political infighting with his cabinet, succeeded in placing most government money in selected state banks.

Biddle responded by launching a campaign to restrict credit and create enough financial distress in the country to force the president to change his policies. Although Biddle did manage to create some distress, Jackson was able to turn the blame on Biddle, who in 1834 was forced to retreat from his campaign at the urging of his friends in the business community. But by this time, it was too late; the battle between Biddle and Jackson had caused irreparable damage to the economy. Two years of unrestrained land speculation on the part of the state banks, fat with federal funds, followed. To try to halt this, Jackson issued the Specie Circular in 1836, requiring that all land payments to the government be in specie, or gold and silver. This decision made the paper money that state banks issued virtually worthless, and almost overnight land sales collapsed, followed in 1837 by a disastrous fall in stock and commodity prices and the worst economic downturn of the century. Jackson left office two months before the onset of the economic crisis and thus escaped most of the blame for the troubles, which fell on the administration of his handpicked successor, Martin Van Buren. Hoping to lead people out of oppression, Jackson led them into depression.

Van Buren entered office in March 1837 riding the crest of Jackson's popularity, but the depression that began later in the year dominated his single term. Van Buren's solution to restore confidence in the banking system and the crippled economy was something called the Independent Treasury System, whereby federal funds would be taken from banks and placed in subtreasuries around the country. Receipts from customs duties and federal land sales would also be deposited in the subtreasuries, and government expenditures would be made in cash. The idea would have protected government funds and discouraged speculation, but it would have taken much specie out of circulation, which would have hurt business. Still, Van Buren managed to push the measure through Congress in 1840, and it, along with the depression, cost him reelection in November of that year. The next administration did away with the Independent Treasury System, the economy recovered mostly on its own, and one of Jackson's legacies passed from the scene. Not until the Civil War would the nation see another centralized national banking system.

Jackson's was a flawed presidency, but it was a significant one. He reshaped the whole character of the office by his belief in greater democracy and by his own autocratic and imperious style. As Van Buren and many others who followed him discovered, Jackson was a hard act to follow.

INTERPRETIVE ESSAY
Thomas C. Mackey

Of the portraits on the currency of the United States, President Andrew Jackson's image on the $20 bill is the most dashing. George Washington, on the $1 bill, will always be the marble, unmoving man; Abraham Lincoln, on the $5 bill, appears strained yet redeemed—ever the Old Testament patriarch "Father Abraham." Alexander Hamilton, on the $10 bill, appears haughty and aloof from the real world. Then there is Andrew Jackson's unabashedly stirring romantic portrait. With his tousled hair, his high prominent forehead, his cape pulled firmly but not tightly against him, shielding him from the elements, Jackson appears firmly in control. As he peers past his right shoulder staring down the elements, Jackson's portrait exudes the qualities attributed to him by his loyal legions of supporters: strength and confidence. Jackson's image on the $20 bill suggests an uncommon man who, ironically, loomed over a time when Americans hailed the common man as the ultimate American. No other president's name has become identified with the key changes and developments of his era as Jackson with "Jacksonian America." Although Jackson (affectionately nicknamed "Old Hickory") himself did not personally bring about the numerous changes of his times, his struggle for the presidency, his election, and his administration occurred during a time of profound change in American social, economic, and political cultures, changes that he came to symbolize. Ironically, although Jackson became the leader of the era, he was as much a follower of the larger social, cultural, and political trends of his times as he was the leader of those trends. His influence on the United States can be suggested through analyzing the changes wrought in American politics and democracy when Jackson's name and presence hung heavy in the air. It is these changes in American political and civic culture from 1824 until 1840 (and beyond) that provide the topics for this chapter.

Just as Jackson the person came to symbolize all the changes of his era, so too has an event in Andrew Jackson's presidency come to be seen as a symbol of the social and political changes sweeping the land. That event occurred on March 4, 1829, the day of Jackson's first inaugural as president. After being sworn into office at the capital, Jackson and his friends returned to the White House (then called the Executive Mansion) in order to greet his supporters. And his supporters turned out en masse. In fact, so many "common people" turned out to greet the new president that they crowded the rooms of the Executive Mansion to overflowing proportions. They stood on the furniture to get a peek at the new president, turning over the tables by their sheer numbers. Jackson escaped the press of people by leaving the mansion by a side exit, but in order to encourage the crowd to leave the mansion, aides had to move the punch bowls out on to the grounds of the house. This near riot and breach of public decorum led one commentator to write in his diary that "King Mob," not Jackson, now governed in America. This scene at the Executive Mansion can be seen as a symbolic takeover of the presidency by the people, represented by Jackson, and the turning out of the "interests" and aristocrats who had dominated the presidency from George Washington to John Quincy Adams. By taking over the building and grounds of the Executive Mansion, the crowds announced the end of the old republic and the arrival of popular democracy in the United States.

With Jackson's presidency, a new era in America's history had begun. Just as in any other age, most of the reforms of the Jacksonian era sought to fix problems inherited from an earlier time. What the Jacksonians opposed from this earlier period was the perceived dominance of the federal government by the "interests," the "privileged," and the Northeast states. Most of Jackson's supporters and political strength came from the South and such newly emerging western areas of the nation as Jackson's own Tennessee and Kentucky. These supporters believed that the established (and wealthier) areas of the country, especially the political leaders and cities of the Northeast, held an unwarranted stranglehold on the nation and its economy and, through their dominance, corrupted the federal government. President John Quincy Adams, son of John Adams, the second president, and perhaps the quintessential New Englander, came to represent for the Jacksonians everything that was wrong with the country. His education, his ties to trade and commerce, his support of the national bank (the ultimate symbol of "special privilege"), his encouragement of commerce and manufacturing rather than farming, his historic name, together with his aloof personality, all combined to make him appear distant and out of touch with the rising masses of the country. Add in Jackson's allegation of a "corrupt bargain" between Adams and Henry Clay in the presidential election of 1824 to swing the election away from Jackson and to Adams, and the stage was set for Jackson and his supporters to paint Adams as the personification of northeastern corruption. Such an image was an unfair and inaccurate depiction of Adams, but at the dawn of mass politics in America, the political technique of putting own's opponent in the wrong and keeping him there already operated.

Special privilege especially interested, irritated, and motivated the Jacksonians. To that era, special privilege entailed almost any sort of governmental largesse or favoritism to one person or a group of persons that was not available to all persons. By "person," Jacksonian spokesmen almost always meant white males over 21 years old, and although this definition of political persons did not mean universal suffrage (women and most blacks, for example, were not included), still it was a broader definition of suffrage than previously existed. For example, part of the resentment against special privilege came to focus on the privilege of voting, which many localities and states had restricted to property owners only. But in an era that proclaimed the equality of white males, property requirements for voting appeared unequal, unfair, and a special privilege of an elite few. Therefore, when Jackson's supporters, organized in the nation's first truly national political party, the Democratic party of 1828, held majorities in the state legislatures, one of their first tasks and accomplishments was to drop the property requirement for voting and to move toward universal white male suffrage.

Also, when the Jacksonians came to dominate state governments in the late 1820s and 1830s, they reapportioned the electoral districts in their states. These new political majorities, drawn from the more western and rural parts of the states, altered the election district lines so that the older, more well-established, and wealthier sections of the states lost political power relative to the newer, more westerly, and rural parts of the states. In this fashion, then, universal white male suffrage changed the face and composition of the state legislatures and, in time, even Congress.

Jacksonians aimed their crusade against special privilege against more than just the suffrage requirements; they also attacked the ties between the social and economic elites and the government. A good example of this resentment against elites was the movement in the states and localities to lower the requirements to enter the professions. Traditionally, if someone wanted to become a doctor or a lawyer, he (almost never she) would apprentice with a practicing doctor or lawyer, emulate his actions, and read and study his books. Local or state boards of experts in the professions, such as the local bar association or the local medical association, oversaw the examination of those students who wished to enter the profession, although occasionally local judges decided when an apprentice was ready to enter the law on his own. In some instances, these private associations of professionals had the power of issuing licenses to their members. Through licensing, the profession oversaw the quality of its members and it could limit the numbers of people in the profession, thereby maintaining the social standing of its members and a shortage of practitioners and keeping fees up. In other words, this power to license practitioners of a profession constituted a special privilege for these key social groups. Jacksonians argued that such elitism constrained the market for professional services and violated the fundamental principles of the country that "all men are created equal." If that proposition were true, Jacksonians reasoned, then anyone, regardless of skills or training, ought to have a chance to become a doctor or a lawyer. They attacked professional associations as examples of elite and special privilege, unfairly limiting the economic ability of the common man and his chance in the market. As a result of these attacks on the professions, by the 1840s, all anyone who wanted to become a doctor or a lawyer had to do was hang out a sign and start practicing. Numerous states had dropped their licensing and education requirements in the 1820s and 1830s under the weight of criticism of their medical and bar associations. Although the quality of services the average doctors and lawyers delivered declined during the Jacksonian era, the lowering of professional standards nicely fit and reflected the general mood of the country against special privilege for special groups.

But such social and legal reforms did not happen overnight or magically. Social and political reforms need a structure to channel reformers' energies, and the Jacksonians created just such an organization. What propelled Andrew Jackson into the Executive Mansion was a political creation he helped to build and manage: the nation's first truly national political party. His party differed from earlier political organizations such as the Federalist or Jeffersonian-Republican factions in that his party was built to endure. Factions formed around prominent political figures and lasted only as long as the political figure remained prominent and important. Political factions lacked the internal structure, such as party discipline and party dues, which later political parties developed. What Jackson set about doing after he lost the 1824 election to the alleged "corrupt bargain" between Adams and Clay was to build a permanent political organization with loyal members, a central treasury to support candidates, common party policies described in a party platform, and organized from the most local, grass-roots level up. Jackson used this political organization to appeal not to the local elites and the northeastern elites who had dominated politics and policy from the founding of the Constitution until the late 1820s but to the masses. Jackson, a southerner and a westerner, used his political organization to motivate and inspire the electorate in ways not previously seen in America. Through party newspapers, parades, barbecues, and rallies (all adequately supplied with spirited liquid refreshments), Jackson's Democrats swept into office in 1828 from local courthouse to the Executive Mansion. Although control of political parties might be dominated by cliques of powerful persons, for Jackson's era the political theory held and people believed that the party embodied and represented the people. And through the party, the people governed. Jackson's party and his appeal through mass politics were something new in the country that changed the country then and have since become American traditions.

A sure sign that political appeals to the masses and the use of political parties were ideas whose time had come was the reaction of Jackson's opponents. In order to counter Jackson's claim to the loyalty of the people and with the hope of capturing some offices for themselves, Jackson's opposition found it necessary to copy his methods and form their own permanent political organizations. Jackson's opponents called themselves the Whigs, as had the American revolutionaries, a group with whom the anti-Jackson forces wished to be identified with as the true inheritors of the Revolution. They discovered that to remain viable politically, they needed an equally organized party to battle the Democratic party for votes and the right to set state and national policies. Two-party politics, by the 1830s an American tradition, emerged and crystallized because of Jackson's Democrats.

As parties sought to organize to attract the attention of voters to select national candidates, the Jacksonian era witnessed the start of another American political tradition, the party-nominating convention. Prior to this time, men interested in serving in a political office let their desire be known to powerful people in Congress, in the states, and in their localities. Then a political caucus consisting of members of the faction decided which candidates to support. Party conventions theoretically changed that selection process. Instead of the leadership of the party huddling together and announcing the party's candidates, delegates to a party convention would nominate and vote on who would lead the party in the upcoming election. In this way, the "people," the common men, of the party chose their leaders, who then ran against the other party's candidates in the general election. To a minor third party of the period, the Anti-Masonic party, goes the distinction of holding the nation's first political convention; the Democrats and Whigs quickly followed suit. In September 1831, the Anti-Masonic party held a convention to select its candidate to run in the 1832 presidential race. Not only did the party set the model for party conventions, but it also adopted the first party platform, which served to tell the voters where candidates stood on the pressing issues of the day. Adherence to one's party platform became the requirement if a candidate wanted money, advice, and support from his party. Party platforms made public what the party stood for and stood against, and party platforms became one standard for judging whether a particular party lived up to its stated goals. This political innovation continues to be an important document for parties' publicity and legitimacy, and often some of the fiercest political battles are waged within parties over the language and content of their platforms. Too often dismissed as self-serving puffery, political party platforms form another American heritage and tradition inherited from the age of Jackson.

Political parties are extraconstitutional, meaning that the Constitution does not explicitly provide for them. Parties formed to serve immediate political needs and in time became legitimate. So too did another extraconstitutional political body, the president's cabinet. In order to discuss policy and to decide on party strategies, President Jackson relied on a series of unofficial advisers. Although Jackson had a formal cabinet composed of the heads of prominent federal departments, he preferred informal groups for discussion. In time, his opponents labeled these informal groups the "Kitchen Cabinet," as opposed to the more formal "Parlor Cabinet." As historian Donald B. Cole has argued in his important book, *The Presidency of Andrew Jackson*, "More than any president before him, [Jackson] needed men who could offer ideas, writing skills, organizational ability, and political contacts—in addition to loyalty." Jackson always insisted on making any final decision himself, and he occasionally did not consult anyone, including the Kitchen Cabinet, before he made important decisions, but it is also true that he usually relied on friends and colleagues for discussion and help in running the government. Among the most important of the Kitchen Cabinet were Martin Van Buren, secretary of state in the first administration and vice president in the second, as well as one of the few Parlor Cabinet heads who served also in the Kitchen Cabinet; Amos Kendall of Kentucky and postmaster general in the second administration; Duff Green, the editor of the important pro-Jackson newspaper the *United States Telegraph;* Thomas Hart Benson and James K. Polk from Congress; and Frank Blair, Sr., the editor of another pro-Jackson newspaper, the *Globe.* Reliance on unofficial and informal groups of advisers began with President Jackson and became a tradition as numerous later presidents continued the practice.

One of the most important topics for discussion among President Jackson and his Kitchen Cabinet was political patronage. Although it would be incorrect to say that Jackson and his administration started the spoils system, he strongly supported the awarding of political offices to faithful party workers. This system formed the reason that a person might support a particular candidate: if the candidate won the election, the loyal party worker hoped to receive appointment to a government office (in addition to the wages and benefits of the office). Democratic senator William L. Marcy of New York summed up the idea of the spoils system in an 1832 speech defending the practice when he stated that in America "politicians followed 'the rule, that to the victor belong the spoils of the enemy.' " In practice the rule meant that when one political faction or party took over from another political faction or party, then most (if not all) of the appointed positions in the government ought to be taken by persons loyal to the new political majority. In that way, the new ideas, programs, and policies of the new political majority could be carried out without interference from partisan officeholders of the previous administration. Although this system ran the risk of placing undeserving or unqualified persons into jobs, the Jacksonians did not view the issue in that manner. Instead, they saw the spoils system as a solution for the aristocratic dominance of the federal government and as another way to attack and limit special privilege. Through the spoils system, the state and federal governments could be made more accountable to the masses as plain people, and not elites, received the offices and jobs. Jackson defended the spoils system by pointing out that such turning over of officeholding, from one political officerholder to another, was common in the states and that all he sought to implement was the same system on the federal level. In this way, then, the democratization of the republic could advance; the federal government would become more truly of the people.

Jackson and his administration defended and certainly used the spoils system, but Jackson never used it to the extremes his critics claimed or his successors did. Some of his opponents claimed that up to 20 percent of the federal workforce (mostly treasury and post office employees) were turned out of office in favor of loyal Democrats, but that number was far too high. Studies have shown that only about 9 percent of federal workers lost their positions for political reasons during Jackson's years. In fact, later presidents would remove and replace more workers than Jackson, but the term and its usage came to acceptability at the federal level during his times.

Jacksonians brought about still other reforms and changes in state and federal politics, which further signaled a shift in the country from an elite-led republic to a mass democracy. Jackson and his followers believed in frequent rotation in officeholding. This political value was both new on the American scene and a ripple effect of the spoils system. If the people governed, then no one should hold office, especially high office, for very long. A high turnover in officeholding was to be encouraged as a sign of the vitality of the democracy—of the people governing and sharing the responsibility of governing. Also, through rotation in office, government could be held accountable to the people of the country. Since no one would serve for long, no one could amass undue influence and power; each officeholder would have to act in the best interest of all since each would soon be out of office and just another one of the masses. Further, in a political democracy, the theory ran, anyone ought to be able to fill any office. If, as the Declaration of Independence states, "all men are created equal," then any and all offices ought to be available to anyone wishing to serve. Although this political faith, like the spoils system, could result in unqualified persons seeking office for the glory (and salary) of the position and thereby potentially abusing the system, to the Jacksonians rotation in office formed another technique to diminish what they perceived to be an overly elitist government. Only when anyone could hold any office would democracy exist in the United States.

As a direct result of the political value of frequent rotation in office, numerous previously appointed offices and even administrative positions became electable by the people. So-called long ballots developed. Voters sometimes faced extended lists of offices and candidates running for those offices. It became common to elect administrative department heads and their assistants in local elections; even city dog catchers and their assistants stood for election by the people. Although electing dog catchers might appear inefficient and even silly to modern voters, electing such officials made perfectly good political sense to the Jacksonians as a method for making democracy a reality.

Further, the Jacksonians broadened the logic and value of rotation in office and selection by the people not only to administrative officials but also to the judiciary. Law must be made accountable to the people in a political democracy, and one way to make sure law stayed close to the people was through frequent rotation of legislators and executive officers. But legislative lawmaking was only one side of the coin; administration of the law was the other, and the administration of the law fell to the judges. Prior to the Jacksonian era, judges, even local ones, received their appointment to the bench from executives such as governors, who appointed state judges, and mayors, who appointed some city judges and justices of the peace. In theory, this selection process would protect judges from popular pressures and local prejudices and thus ensure fair administration of the law. Yet to the Jacksonian, appointed judges were another form of special privilege for a select few elites in the community. Because the Jacksonians could not stand that privilege—the people must rule—the practice of appointed state and local judges came to an end. Though highly controversial then (and even now to some degree), the popular election of state and local judges became another lasting political reform of the age of Jackson. Mississippi led the way in 1832 when its legislature adopted legislation requiring not only the election of lower court judges but also of appellate and even state supreme court judges. Beginning in the 1840s, numerous other states followed Mississippi and changed the selection process of their judges from appointive to elective.

Jacksonians believed that the law must stay close to the people and reflect the values of the mass of the people; law must not be a tool of the elite or the wealthy. Their hope for electing judges even to high appellate courts was an increased accountability to the masses. Since law could be used to protect special privileges such as monopolies, the democratization of the nation generally called for the democratization of the law as well. Make the judges accountable to the people in scheduled elections and the judges will think twice before rendering opinions contrary to the will of the majority of the people, the argument went. It worked well in theory, but in reality, the election of state judges actually changed very little because of the law's own internal rules and standards. Although some talked of making federal district judges electable, the federal judiciary was not affected, and federal judgeships remained appointed positions. The symbolic change of electing state judges was enough to signal the new political values on the American scene.

In keeping with these same values and parallel to electing judges, a movement began in the Jacksonian era to simplify the common law systems of the states. Instead of relying on a common law system made up of a jumble of statutes, social and legal customs, judicial opinions, and mysterious rules, reformers argued that in a political democracy, the law had to be accessible and understandable to plain people. Therefore, what was needed was the codification of the common law. Codification offered the hope of simplicity and accessibility of the law, its rules, and its procedures to plain people; it also offered the hope of avoiding a specially privileged group, lawyers. Some reformers argued that the common law had become too inflexible and too technical for most people, especially the poor, to understand; as a result, the law offered little fairness.

Other legal reformers stressed that the common law provided too many exceptions and too few clear and concise rules for even the lawyers to follow. In particular, this second group of law reformers wanted to clarify the rules of the law in order to create a more stable and hospitable climate in which businesses could operate. Providing a clear code of the rules of contract, for example, would create a legal climate in which businessmen would be willing to risk investment since they could know their potential liabilities before investing. Codification went furthest in New York, which authorized lawyer and reformer David Dudley Field (brother of Stephen Field, who became a U.S. Supreme Court justice, and Cyrus Field, who invented and laid the first transatlantic cable) to design a law code for that state. His code, which he presented to the legislature in 1848, dramatically simplified civil and criminal procedure and generally streamlined the state's law. Although New York chose not to adopt Field's code, Missouri (in 1849) and California (in 1851) adopted variations of it. Codification, like the election of state judges and the rotation in office, reflected the values of the era in its anti-elite appeal to the masses' values. But unlike elected state judges, codification never caught on widely, which left the common law and its system of case-by-case, statute-by-statute analysis in place.

In this dramatic period of reform, yet another important political alteration can be linked to Andrew Jackson and his era: a strengthening of the presidency. Although Jackson's immediate successors did not follow up on his style of strong presidential leadership, in time presidents built on and added to the strengthened presidency Jackson forged. Abraham Lincoln, for example, used the expanded powers of the presidency in his struggle to hold the nation together during the Civil War and to protect constitutional government. Presidents Theodore Roosevelt, Woodrow Wilson, and Franklin D. Roosevelt regularly relied on the strengthened presidency first achieved or foreshadowed by Andrew Jackson.

In particular, Jackson changed the popular perception of the presidency. Prior to Jackson, Americans thought of the presidency as simply the administrative branch of the federal government, with the real political power located in the Congress. Congress, not the president, best represented "the people." But Jackson changed that popular perception, as well as political theory. He saw himself as not merely someone carrying out the wishes of Congress but rather as the keystone in the formation of federal public policy, as the leader of his political party, and at least as important a representative of the people as Congress was. For Jackson, the presidency represented the people and, largely through his own forceful personality and the good press stimulated by the *United States Telegraph*, Jackson sold the image to the American people.

The seeds of his arguments and his dramatic popular image would have failed to take root, however, if Jackson's ideas about the importance of the presidency were not in keeping with the general mood of the country. Jackson's arguments for an expanded presidency reflected the popular will of the times, and his ideas exactly fit the needs of the times. Jackson was both benefactor of the new mood in the country and beneficiary of the new era. As one of the most important Jackson historians, Robert V. Remini, argues in *Andrew Jackson and the Course of American Democracy*, "Jackson had become [the people's] spokesman and symbol; they were quite prepared to accept him as their representative at the seat of government." Jackson understood that large numbers of people in the country wanted to bring to bear their political will on the federal government and, through the president, to see their political will reflected in the nation's policies and decisions. Jackson was the right man at the right time to assist in moving the country from its old republican origins to political majoritarian democracy.

And the people loved Jackson for his actions and for what he represented. He was the head of the government, carrying out the will of political majorities; by turning majority will into public policy, the people governed. By relocating some of the southeastern Indian tribes west of the Mississippi River, Jackson's actions reflected the anti–Native American fears of those who elected him. This bond of respect and empowerment between the president and the people was something that earlier presidents had not experienced and only a few later presidents built upon. This popular bond, combined with Jackson's strong personality and military background, made him a force to be reckoned with for political friends and foes alike. On issues that mattered to Jackson, such as the destruction of the premier example of special privilege, the Bank of the United States—which Jackson referred to only as "the monster"— or turning back the South Carolina nullifiers, who sought to nullify or invalidate disagreeable federal laws within their state, in 1832–1833, Jackson used strong leadership to keep his party united behind him and to separate himself from the Whigs. By establishing a strong presidential presence in the federal government and thereby shaping public policy decisions, Jackson represented the rising tide of democratic sentiment in the country. He stood for the sometimes subtle and sometimes dramatic changes occurring in the presidency specifically and in the country generally.

During the era of Jackson's presidency, the people not only invaded the Executive Mansion (literally and figuratively), but political majorities came to dominate the political scene as never before. Leading the common people was an uncommon man, Andrew Jackson. It is no wonder, then, that Jackson's portrait on the $20 bill shows him confidently facing the winds of change. He knew (and the country was about to find out) that the will of political majorities, organized in mass political parties, constituted an unstoppable wave of political change, which Jackson both directed and rode. From the $20 bill, Jackson stares into the future, challenging his political enemies to run counter to the times and his supporters to upset the conventional wisdom of the times and follow him in remaking the country from a republic into a democracy. That road to political democracy was not always even or certain, yet Jackson and the Jacksonians succeeded in changing the country, the government, and thus themselves and all Americans who followed.

SELECTED BIBLIOGRAPHY

Cole, Donald B. *The Presidency of Andrew Jackson.* Lawrence: University Press of Kansas, 1993. An impressive and important biography of Jackson suggesting that Jackson was not quite the "man of iron will" as he is usually portrayed. In fact, argues Cole, events controlled Jackson as much as he controlled events during his presidency. As a result of this interpretation, a more human and less deified Jackson emerges.

Latner, Richard B. *The Presidency of Andrew Jackson: White House Politics, 1829–1837.* Athens: University of Georgia Press, 1979. An intriguing account of the politics, power struggles, and disputes within Jackson's Kitchen Cabinet and national politics generally during Jackson's administrations.

Pessen, Edward, ed. *New Perspectives on Jacksonian Parties and Politics.* Boston: Allyn and Bacon, 1969. A collection of essays that surveys the ongoing areas of discussion and dispute between historians of Jackson and his times.

Reid, John, and John Henry Eaton. *The Life of Andrew Jackson.* M. Carey and Son, 1817; reprint, Frank Lawrence Owsley, Jr., ed., Tuscaloosa: University of Alabama Press, 1974. A good example of a primary source promoting and advertising Andrew Jackson and his personal qualities and military successes.

Remini, Robert V., ed. *The Age of Jackson.* Columbia: University of South Carolina Press, 1972. A useful compilation of important primary sources necessary for understanding Jackson and his times.

———. *Andrew Jackson and the Course of American Empire, 1767–1821.* Vol. 1. New York: Harper & Row, 1977. The first volume of Remini's important multivolume biography of Andrew Jackson; describes the United States in the late eighteenth century during Jackson's formative years and follows Jackson's life and development through his governorship of the Florida Territory.

———. *Andrew Jackson and the Course of American Freedom, 1822–1832.* Vol. 2. New York: Harper & Row, 1981. The second volume, which interprets Jackson's life from his return to Nashville in 1822 after serving as the territorial governor of Florida through his first administration as president.

———. *Andrew Jackson and the Course of American Democracy, 1833–1845.* Vol. 3. New York: Harper & Row, 1984. The third volume, examining Jackson's life, influence, and accomplishments from his second term as president through his death on June 8, 1845.

———. *The Legacy of Andrew Jackson: Essays on Democracy, Indian Removal, and Slavery.* Baton Rouge: Louisiana State University Press, 1988. Brings together the Walter Lynwood Fleming Lectures delivered at Louisiana State University in 1984 by one of the most important Jackson scholars. In this volume, Remini seeks to assess and weigh the lasting importance of Jackson on these three key issues: democracy, Indian removal, and slavery.

Schlesinger, Arthur M., Jr. *The Age of Jackson.* Boston: Little, Brown, 1945. Emphasizes the expansion of democracy and the struggle for power between the people and the interests in the Jacksonian era. Later historians have revised some of Schlesinger's arguments, but this work remains a powerful interpretation favoring Jacksonian reforms.

Sellers, Charles. *The Market Revolution: Jacksonian America, 1815–1846.* New York: Oxford University Press, 1991. An impressive and satisfying overview of the economic and social changes sweeping the country before, during, and after Jackson's presidency. This work demonstrates how the rising economy paralleled the rising movement in the country for the people to govern more directly as they assumed greater prominence in the economy.

Ward, John William. *Andrew Jackson: Symbol for an Age.* New York: Oxford University Press, 1955. Argues that Jackson, the symbol of the rising democracy, was as important as (if not more important than) Jackson the man or Jackson the president. One of the most widely read and influential books on Jackson.

The abolition movement was frequently marked by outdoor rallies, such as this one in Massachusetts in 1832, featuring Wendell Phillips as the principal speaker. (Reproduced from the Collections of the Library of Congress)

5

Abolition, c. 1820s–1860

INTRODUCTION

The movement to abolish slavery in the United States was the most significant reform movement in an era of reform that swept the country between 1825 and 1850. The many other reforms ranged from the beginning of the women's rights movement to improvements in prisons and mental health facilities to various health-oriented reforms, such as Sylvester Graham's promotion of the nutrient value of the type of flour that came to bear his name. The abolition movement nevertheless transcends all of these, and its impact on the country was seen in its contribution to the sectional hostility that produced the Civil War.

The history of abolition divides into three periods. From about 1817 to 1830, the movement was dominated by the American Colonization Society, which worked to colonize former slaves in a new African nation called Liberia. During the 1830s, the movement was centered in the American Anti-Slavery Society, which helped sectionalize abolition and laid out some of the basic tenets of the drive to rid the country of slavery. After 1839, the formal structure of the movement was more political, focused first in the Liberty party, a single-issue party, and later in the Republican party, a sectional party that developed in the 1850s in opposition to the extension of slavery into newly acquired territory.

By 1808, the year prescribed in the U.S. Constitution for the end of the foreign slave trade, all of the northern and none of the southern states had abolished slavery. Over the next two decades, the industrialization of the North further sectionalized the slavery issue, especially since the South continued to be almost completely reliant on an agrarian economy. The situation was worsened by the migration of some prominent southerners north during this time. They freed their slaves and became abolitionists, making the dividing line between the sections still sharper by depriving the South of voices of moderation.

The American Colonization Society was founded in 1817 by people who believed in the biological inferiority of the Negro race and did not think that whites and blacks could ever live freely together in harmony. Thus they urged the expatriation of consenting "free persons of color," who, with aid from the federal or state governments, would go to Africa. But Congress was not willing to subsidize this migration, nor were most state governments, and, in the end, only about 400 emigrants traveled to Liberia. Many in the South feared that even discussing the financing of black migration would lead to debate about the nature of slavery itself and, quite possibly, governmental interference into the private business of slave owners. But it is important to note that the colonization movement was a perpetuation of the idea of racial inferiority; no one wanted to admit the possibility of racial equality or in any other way raise the status of black people.

In the early 1830s, a distinction between antislavery and abolition developed. While antislavery was seen as a reform movement designed to bring an end to a particular social problem through colonization, gradual or compensated emancipation, or some other way, abolition involved loftier values. Abolitionists believed that not only was colonization impractical and economically unsound, but also it was philosophically flawed because it was based on racial prejudice. Moreover, sending free blacks to Africa would strengthen the institution of slavery. Abolitionists were convinced that slave owners would never consent even to gradual emancipation and thus saw their struggle in more apocalyptic terms. To them, it was a struggle not just for a specific reform but part of the loftier fight for human rights and dignity. Out of this line of thinking came the American Anti-Slavery Society, founded in 1833 with a doctrine of immediate emancipation.

Within the American Anti-Slavery Society, an extremist group developed, led by William Lloyd Garrison, who had begun publishing the abolitionist tract, the *Liberator*, in 1831 and had helped found the New

England Anti-Slavery Society in 1832. That group was folded into the American Anti-Slavery Society at its founding two years later. Garrison's views were more extreme; he denounced the Constitution as a proslavery document and repudiated the federal government by refusing to vote, hold office, or in any other way recognize a government that recognized slave owners.

The mainstream membership of the American Anti-Slavery Society suffered financially in the depression that followed the panic of 1837 and joined in the creation of the Liberty party in 1839, a political organization based on the single principle of hostility to slavery. A Kentucky lawyer, James G. Birney, was its leader. He was inflexibly antislavery and piously Christian. Although Birney and the Liberty party received only 67,000 votes in the 1844 election, it may have made the difference in a very close election between James K. Polk, the Democratic candidate, and Henry Clay, the Whig. Polk won the popular vote by just 38,000 votes; most of Birney's votes would have been cast for Clay had he not run. But the election convinced Birney that a single-issue party could not succeed in American politics. The Liberty party faded from the political landscape, and its followers joined with former Whigs in 1854 to form the Republican party, which soon became the principal national rival to the Democratic Party.

After its experience with the Liberty party, the American Anti-Slavery Society was reluctant to become directly involved in national electoral politics. Rather, it became the base of a widespread social reform organization in the North that worked hard to persuade northerners that slavery was a national disgrace and should be eliminated.

One of the most persuasive of the abolitionist spokesmen during this time was Frederick Douglass, who became the best-known black person in nineteenth-century America. Douglass was born a slave but escaped in 1838 to Massachusetts, where he met Garrison and became associated with the Massachusetts abolitionists. He was a superb orator, and his lectures about his own experiences as a slave were particularly compelling. During the 1840s, he made lecture tours throughout the northern states and Great Britain, and he also published a periodical, the *North Star*, which served as a platform for black and reformist writers. Douglass was also involved in other reform movements of the time, most notably the women's movement, prohibition, and the campaign to end capital punishment.

The abolitionists had many arguments against slavery, and different abolitionists opposed slavery for different reasons, but most arguments centered around a religious and moral base or focused on legal and political questions. Many theology students and preachers joined the movement because they saw slavery indicated as a sin in the Bible, and noted that humans were created in the image of God and therefore should not be reduced to a piece of merchandise to be bought and sold. Others stressed the moral deficiencies of slave owners, castigating them for failing to establish a common school system in the South, for resorting to murder under the dueling code, for their propensity for drinking and gambling, and for their frequent immoral sexual liaisons with female slaves. For the slaves, their dependence on their owners impaired their manliness, crushed their souls, and destroyed their ability to distinguish right from wrong. Slavery cultivated immorality, placed a premium on deception, and made lying and stealing acts of self-deception.

Other abolitionists pointed out how slavery was contrary to the fundamental principles of the American way of life and plundered slaves of the inalienable rights guaranteed them as Americans. Abolitionists were concerned that slaves had no protection against the arbitrary power of their owner, who had nothing to restrain his behavior toward his slaves except his own conscience and will. Indeed, a slave had no legal rights whatsoever; he could not testify in court against a white man, could not make contracts, and could not own property. Finally, abolitionists hit on the well-known southern fear of slave insurrection and called it a national weakness. The South, they asserted, was dependent on the entire nation for protection from outside interference or internal combustion.

In the South between 1830 and 1860, a proslavery argument permeated regional writing and oratory. Newspapers, periodicals, sermons, essays, and lectures all touched on the general theme. Although historians once thought that the proslavery argument was a direct response to abolitionists, more recent research suggests that it was probably intended as a device to reassure and unify southerners, since little writing from either side was seen in the other. What southern writing did make its way to the North was not likely to have been thought credible in any case.

The keynote of the proslavery argument was that slavery was a national benefit, not a national evil. This feeling resulted in the suppression of slavery criticism in the South; prices were even put on the heads of northern abolitionists, and mail from the North was seized and censored. Proslavery writers tried to demonstrate classical and biblical sanction, referring to Aristotle's insistence on an orderly and functional society and to biblical evidence that slavery had existed in early times and that God had designated the darker races to be the "hewers of wood and the drawers of water." Science, such as it was in the early nineteenth century, provided additional justification for slavery, based on purported evidence that blacks were physically and intellectually inferior to whites. Indeed, some scientists refused to consider blacks as members of the human species. Many of these scientific arguments were not convincingly refuted until the twentieth century.

Other proslavery advocates raised the specter of the horrors of life in a society without slavery. A few slave insurrections, such as that led by Nat Turner in 1831, were ample evidence that black people could not be expected to live peaceably in a society of laws. Even worse was the specter of miscegenation (the intermarriage of blacks and whites). Almost all southerners believed unquestioningly that racial intermarriage would degrade the white race while doing nothing to improve the black race. So strongly held was this notion that laws forbidding miscegenation remained on the books in most southern states until the 1960s.

During the 1850s, events began to overtake the abolitionists. While they worked hard to persuade people to ignore the provisions of the fugitive slave law that was part of the Compromise of 1850, the issue of the extension of slavery into territories such as Kansas and Nebraska and the rise of the Republican party engaged politicians at the national level and meant that abolitionism was no longer the defining sectional issue. By the outbreak of the Civil War, abolitionism was just one of many problems dividing North and South.

The abolitionists fanned the passions that led to the Civil War, but the argument that had they kept silent, emancipation would have come peacefully, does not ring convincingly. Abolition was an irresistible force in a Christian world and was not confined to the United States. But the trouble with the abolitionists was that they spent all their compassion on the slave and had none for the southern white who was so involved in the system and could see no way to get rid of it. Although abolition doubtless created its share of hatred, in view of southern resistance to any limitation on the institution of slavery as well as southern insistence on acquiring more slave territory and more guarantees of protection of slave property, it is unlikely that emancipation could ever have come any other way than through civil war.

INTERPRETIVE ESSAY
Thomas Clarkin

One of the many reform movements that developed in nineteenth-century America, abolition refers to the abolishment of slavery. Although the term generally encompasses any antislavery sentiment, it is typically used to refer to the radical abolitionist movement that appeared in the 1830s. Not merely opposed to slavery, the radical abolitionists called for the emancipation of all slaves and the guarantee of some political and legal rights for freedmen. Despised in the South and shunned by many northerners as extremists, abolitionists nonetheless influenced and intensified the national debate over slavery in the years before the Civil War.

For almost 150 years after the first slaves arrived in Jamestown in 1619, there was no significant opposition to the institution of slavery in North America. Most Europeans disdained African societies and cultures as inferior to their own; they regarded dark skin as further proof that Africans were not their equals. Moreover, slaves provided the labor necessary to make the British colonies economically viable. Southern colonies depended on slaves to work the fields and harvest the crops, especially tobacco and rice. Colonies that did not rely directly on slave labor profited from the lucrative slave trade. The combination of these factors, the assumption of African inferiority and the need for workers who could be controlled, created an acceptance of slavery as a natural feature of colonial life.

Quakers made the first attacks on slavery in America. Although many Quakers owned slaves, they found slavery difficult to reconcile with their belief that all men are brothers. Individual Quakers such as Benjamin Lay and John Woolman denounced slavery as a sin. Antislavery Quakers in America received support and encouragement from their counterparts in Britain, who were actively protesting slavery in the West Indies. Quaker opposition to slavery slowly mounted until 1758, when leaders at the Yearly Meeting in Philadelphia condemned both the slave trade and slavery. Quakers in other northern states followed suit, and the few Quakers who refused to free their slaves were banned from positions of authority within the Society of Friends.

At first the Quakers gained few converts outside their religion, but the growing conflict with England raised new questions about the legality and morality of slavery that contributed to the growing unease with the institution. Many supporters of the American Revolution saw a fundamental contradiction between their own demands for liberty and the ownership of other human beings. In addition to concerns over the morality of slavery, many Americans feared that their slaves would rise in rebellion or support the British war effort. The rhetoric and idealism of the Revolution and anxieties about the response of slaves to the war prompted leaders such as Benjamin Franklin, John Adams, and Patrick Henry to denounce slavery.

The abolitionist sentiments generated by the American Revolution had a tremendous impact on American slavery. Abolitionist societies organized in many states and agitated for the end of slavery. Free and enslaved blacks in the North circulated petitions calling for emancipation. In 1777 the constitution of the new state of Vermont banned slavery. The following year a Pennsylvania law required the gradual emancipation of all slaves. In 1783 a Massachusetts court outlawed slavery on the grounds that it conflicted with state's constitution, which contained a clause declaring that all men were free and equal. A census taken seven years later reported no slaves in the state. By 1784 all northern states except New York and New Jersey had enacted emancipation laws. Resistance from powerful slaveholders slowed the cause of abolition in those states but could not stop it; by 1804 both states had enacted abolition laws.

The newly freed slaves in the North nevertheless encountered racial prejudice and discrimination. They were often denied the protection of the law, could not vote or serve on juries, usually held only the poorest-paying jobs, and lived in segregated neighborhoods. In addition, the gradual emancipation laws enacted by several states left thousands of men and women in bondage. Nonetheless, northern abolitionists had scored a tremendous victory in the years after the Revolution.

Unlike the North, the South considered slavery an essential economic and social institution, and the southern states had not responded enthusiastically to the calls for emancipation. For a brief time the egalitarian spirit of the Revolution encouraged some liberalization of laws regarding slaves, but most southern states had laws that made manumission, the freeing of slaves, illegal. In 1782 Virginia permitted slave owners to free their slaves voluntarily, and soon all southern states except North Carolina allowed some private manumission. However, these changes were short-lived. A successful slave revolt on the Caribbean island of Santo Domingo frightened southerners, who responded with stricter slave laws. The growing demand for slaves to work the fields of the new states of Alabama and Mississippi also contributed to the waning influence of abolitionism in the southern states. Southern abolitionism foundered on fear, racism, and profit.

The success of abolitionism in the North and its failure in the South calmed most abolitionist agitation. The urge to ignore regional differences in the interests of nationalism, economic ties with the South, and racism all blunted the desire of northerners to carry the cause of emancipation to the southern states. By the end of the first decade of the nineteenth century, abolitionism had little force in American society and politics.

Although abolitionism faltered, anxiety over slavery continued. One outlet for those concerned about slavery was the American Society for Colonizing the Free People of Color of the United States, commonly referred to as the American Colonization Society. Founded in 1817, the society was in no sense an abolitionist organization. Although it advocated the voluntary emancipation of slaves by their owners, its true aim was to send all free blacks to Africa. The sheer expense of transporting thousands of men and women across the Atlantic Ocean made the goal of the society impossible; nonetheless, it attracted many supporters, including prominent leaders such as Thomas Jefferson, John Marshall, and Henry Clay. Free blacks recognized the racism inherent in the transportation proposal and vigorously condemned the scheme. They rejected the argument that Africa was their homeland and proclaimed themselves Americans. Despite its failure to condemn slavery, the American Colonization Society attracted a number of young men who remained doubtful of the morality of slavery, men motivated by ideals that would lead them to radical abolitionism during the 1830s.

The new idealism that spurred the future abolitionists to condemn slavery had its roots in a wave of religious revival that swept across the United States in the early nineteenth century. Referred to by historians as the Second Great Awakening, this great outpouring of religious enthusiasm exposed thousands of Americans to new ideas about themselves and their society. Revivalist lecturers exhorted their listeners to strive for perfection here on earth while awaiting the Kingdom of God. They preached the virtue of "disinterested benevolence," the value of doing good merely for the sake of doing so without receiving any reward. These ideas inspired thousands of American men and women to join reform movements dedicated to improving American society. Among the more popular movements were temperance, education and prison reform, and abolitionism.

Most antislavery appeals in the early nineteenth century advocated a gradual approach to emancipation. It was argued that if slavery were to end too quickly, the resulting economic and political disruption would be far worse than the evils of slavery. In addition, advocates of gradualism argued that slaves were not prepared for freedom and that a long process of education and preparation was necessary before slaves could become free. Gradualism seemed a reasonable and balanced method of solving the problem of slavery. However, it quickly became apparent that gradualism offered no real solutions and that slavery was becoming more entrenched and problematic. As the nation grew, the institution of slavery spread across the lower South. Controversy over the expansion of slavery had sparked a national crisis in 1819, a crisis resolved by the Missouri Compromise. Fearing that education would spark rebellion, southerners rejected any programs for improvement of the slaves. Freed blacks also opposed gradualism, demanding a more strident response to the slavery problem.

Gradualism conflicted as well with the high ideals of the reformers, who saw it as an unacceptable tolerance of evil and sin. In 1824 the British abolitionist Elizabeth Heyrick had composed a pamphlet condemning gradualism and defending immediate emancipation. By the early 1830s American antislavery advocates raised the cry of immediatism, an ambiguous and confusing term. Immediatism did not mean the immediate emancipation of all slaves, an act that even the most ardent abolitionists recognized would cause dislocation and turmoil. Rather, it referred to the personal commitment of reformers to the abolition of slavery. The immediatists condemned slavery as sinful and immoral and called for immediate action to begin the end of slavery. In addition, the immediatists maintained that blacks deserved not only their freedom but full rights as citizens. The turn to immediatism marked the radicalism of abolitionism and its return as a social and political force in American society.

The appeal of abolitionism to American blacks is easily understood. Whether enslaved or free, blacks had experienced the burdens of racism. However, most blacks were dependent on whites for employment, so it took exceptional courage for blacks to call openly for emancipation. Most black abolitionists had personal experience with the Protestant religious revivals that inspired the reform movements. They also tended to be highly educated. Black participation served to keep abolitionism, with its aim of equality for blacks, from degenerating into an antislavery movement, which would oppose slavery but ignore the needs of free blacks.

Historians have puzzled over the attraction of abolition for white reformers and have attempted to create personality profiles of prominent abolitionists in order to understand their motivations. Most abolitionists came from religious households that placed great emphasis on moral behavior. They also had at least one parent who was very strong-willed. Many abolitionist leaders were ministers or deacons in their churches. Although the leaders of the movement tended to come from cities, most followers lived in farming communities. These attempts to identify particular features common to abolitionists have created debates among historians that have not been resolved. It can only be said that abolitionists were highly moral individuals who recognized in slavery a great moral evil.

Historians point to the year 1831 as a major turning point in abolitionist activity. That year the British government enacted a program of gradual emancipation in the West Indies. In America, an influential new abolitionist periodical, the *Liberator,* first appeared. William Lloyd Garrison, its publisher, had been a supporter of colonization in the 1820s. Association with the Quaker antislavery leader Benjamin Lundy led him to a more radical stance. In the *Liberator,* Garrison denounced both colonization and gradualism and called for immediate abolition. Garrison was one of many prominent abolitionists, but his publications and activism served to place him in the forefront of the cause. His pronouncements energized opponents of slavery in the North who were drawn to his calls for action and condemnation of slavery as a sin.

In the South, however, Garrison's message was taken as a threat. Slaveholders considered gradualism and colonization as mild but inconsequential critiques of slavery; immediatism, with its accusations of sin, was taken as an attack not only on slavery but also on southern morality. Southerners charged that immediatism fostered rebellion among slaves, who took its message as a call to arms. They pointed to Nat Turner's 1831 slave rebellion in Virginia as evidence that abolitionist pieties led to dead southerners. Although it was only coincidental that Turner's rebellion came just months after the first edition of the *Liberator* was published, southerners remained convinced that there was a connection between the two events. The Georgia legislature offered five thousand dollars to anyone who would kidnap Garrison and bring him to Georgia to stand trial. Any expression of antislavery sentiment in the South was met with hostility or even violence. Southern advocates of abolition either kept their opinions to themselves or moved to the North.

Like their southern counterparts, most northerners also considered abolitionism an extremist and dangerous position. They regarded slavery as a southern problem, one that might be disgraceful but that nonetheless was not their concern. Antislavery agitation caused conflict between the two regions of the nation that might disrupt commerce. Moreover, most northerners correctly perceived that abolitionism might ultimately result in equal rights for freed blacks. Most northerners were profoundly racist in their views and had no desire to mingle socially with blacks or to compete with them for employment. In the 1830s abolitionists were regarded with disdain in both the North and the South.

Despite the hostility and criticism, abolitionists continued to organize and agitate for an end to slavery. In 1833 they founded the American Anti-Slavery Society, an organization with members in the northern and western states. Although dominated by white men, the founding members included both blacks and women. William Lloyd Garrison wrote the group's Declaration of Sentiments, a document that spelled out both strategies and goals. The declaration, which denounced colonization, called for nonviolence in the struggle to achieve emancipation, required members to reject all racial prejudice, and sought equal opportunity for both blacks and whites to enjoy the benefits of education and prosperity, offering a vision of a racially integrated society completely at odds with life in America. Abolitionism had become more than an attack on the institution of slavery; it now called for the complete reform and revision of society in both the North and the South. In order to achieve such a goal, the American Anti-Slavery Society hoped to use moral suasion, the appeal to the consciences of slavery supporters. Political campaigns might change laws, but the key to ending racial prejudice lay in changing attitudes.

Although the abolitionists undertook their cause with great fervor and enthusiasm, they met with significant opposition. When Prudence Crandall opened a boarding school for black girls in Canterbury, Connecticut, the townspeople poisoned the school's well, attacked the building, and had Crandall jailed. That same year a mob of fifteen hundred antiabolitionist New Yorkers rushed a chapel in search of Garrison and Arthur Tappan, another prominent abolitionist. Another mob paraded Garrison through the streets of Boston with a rope around his neck in 1835. Elijah Lovejoy, an abolitionist printer in Illinois, was murdered by a crowd in 1837 while he defended his printing press. Mob violence was a common occurrence in America in the 1830s, and abolitionists often found themselves confronted by angry and even violent crowds.

Abolitionists did score some victories. In 1834 the wealthy abolitionist Arthur Tappan sent Theodore Weld to Lane Seminary in Cincinnati, Ohio. An advocate of immediate abolition, Weld so greatly influenced the students and faculty at Lane that eighteen days after his arrival, they voted to endorse abolition. When the people of Cincinnati demanded that the student antislavery organization disband, a group of 40 students left the seminary. They founded Oberlin, the first American college open to both blacks and women.

If the abolitionist cause met with little success in the North, its efforts in the South were complete failures. In 1835 a man caught with abolitionist literature in Tennessee was given 20 lashes. The few southern converts to abolitionism such as James G. Birney and Sarah and Angelina Grimké moved to the North. Southerners remained intransigent, and abolitionists risked life and limb if they journeyed south with their crusade. In response, the American Anti-Slavery Society organized a postal campaign to flood the South with abolitionist literature. A fine example of moral suasion, the postal campaign began in May 1835. The abolitionists hoped, naively, that exposure to abolitionist arguments would persuade southern ministers and politicians to turn their backs on slavery. By 1837 over 1 million antislavery tracts had been distributed through the mails. The campaign led to violence and repression throughout the nation. In the North, angry crowds confronted the abolitionists. Several states considered legislation to limit antislavery activism. In the South, a mob broke into the Charleston post office and burned the mail from New York. Throughout the region, mail was searched for abolitionist literature which was then destroyed. In response former president Andrew Jackson, himself a slaveholder, called for a ban on the mailing of antislavery literature. The postal campaign failed to convert any southerners or change attitudes toward slavery.

Yet the campaign was not a total failure. The uproar in the North served to bring the abolitionist cause to the attention of the public, and the abolitionists used the publicity to spread their message and seek new converts. Angered by the censorship of the mail, abolitionists began sending petitions denouncing slavery to the U.S. Congress. Southern representatives demanded that the petitions be ignored. In 1836 the Congress adopted the gag rule, which allowed for abolition petitions to be tabled without consideration. Abolitionists correctly charged that the gag rule violated their constitutional right to petition Congress, but Congress refused to repeal the rule. Still they continued to send the petitions; by 1838, over 415,000 had arrived at the Capitol. The censorship of the mail and the gag rule in Congress prompted many northerners uninterested in the abolitionist cause to wonder if the South, in its zealous defense of slavery, was not willing to sacrifice the civil liberties of all Americans. Although the postal campaign failed to achieve its goal of converting southerners, it raised doubts in the minds of many northerners about the intentions of slaveholders in the South. As a result, membership in antislavery societies rose significantly in the last years of the 1830s.

The stresses of continuing the abolitionist campaign and disagreements over strategy caused factions to develop within the American Anti-Slavery Society. By 1837 many abolitionists argued that moral suasion had failed and that political strategies would best serve the cause. They advocated aligning with political parties, endorsing candidates, and changing laws. Opponents charged that a political strategy would require compromise and that any compromise was an unconscionable bargain with the sin of slaveholding. They also maintained that political strategies might end slavery but would not bring about equality for the freedman. This could be achieved only through moral suasion.

Divisions within the society were deepened when Garrison and his followers embraced a radicalism that many conservative abolitionists could not support. Garrisonians, as they were known, adhered to an extreme form of Christianity that rejected all forms of authority as coercive. They called for a total reform of all social institutions, a position that conservatives claimed not only detracted from the goal of abolition but was also unattainable. Garrisonians also championed women's rights, another controversial issue that conservatives refused to support.

Women had been active in the American Anti-Slavery Society since its founding. They generally served in all-female organizations and worked to convert other women. However, as they became more active in the movement, conflicts arose. Revealing a deep-seated racial prejudice, some men worried about sexual contact between the female abolitionists and the black men they insisted were their equals. Women also spoke to groups that included men, which was considered improper by the standards of the day. The issue became a serious problem when the Congregationalist churches circulated a pastoral letter condemning Sarah and Angelina Grimké for speaking to audiences of men and women. Although the pastoral letter troubled many abolitionists, the Garrisonians shrugged it off as yet another example of authoritarianism. The conflict caused irreparable damage to the already divided American Anti-Slavery Society. When at the 1840 convention, Garrisonians managed to elect a feminist, Abby Kelly, to the executive committee, angry conservatives abandoned the society and formed the American and Foreign Anti-Slavery Society. The split marked the decline of abolitionism as a social movement in the United States.

Garrison and his followers continued to agitate throughout the 1840s.

In 1842 Garrison presented a series of resolutions that called for peaceful dissolution of the United States. He condemned the Constitution as a proslavery document, argued that slavery could not continue to exist in the South without the military and economic support of the North, and said that if the northern states left the Union, slavery in the South would be doomed. At first Garrison's suggestions were met with shock, but within two years the American Anti-Slavery Society had adopted disunion. The disunion strategy garnered public attention and reflected the highly moral and religious origins of abolitionism, the absolute refusal to tolerate sin and evil.

The political abolitionists formed the Liberty party, devoted to the single issue of the abolition of slavery. Political abolitionists realized that the party would not win elections, but they wished to keep the abolition campaign in the public eye. They also hoped that the Liberty party would gain enough votes to worry the major political parties, which in turn might adopt antislavery measures to attract Liberty votes. Originally dedicated to equal rights for freedmen, the party's lack of success by 1846 led several leaders to abandon the fight for equal rights in the hope of gaining votes from northerners who opposed slavery but also disliked blacks. Garrison had been correct: the political strategy required compromises that ultimately destroyed the abolitionist agenda. After the 1848 presidential election, the Liberty party virtually ceased to exist.

Black abolitionists were not as troubled by the abolitionist schism. Although they too experienced some conflict over differing strategies, they were willing to work as a group and use a variety of methods to achieve their goals. As the goals of abolitionism gave way to mere antislavery during the 1850s, blacks showed a greater interest in militant responses, including the validity of violence in certain circumstances. Some blacks argued that the only reasonable response to the racism of American life was to leave; they advocated emigration to Canada and, ironically, even Africa.

Abolitionism declined as a force not only because of the factional split of 1840 but also because events outpaced the abolitionist movement. Northern suspicions of southern intentions spawned fears that a conspiracy of slave owners and sympathetic northern politicians was attempting to control the federal government. The growth of antislavery sentiment in the North during the 1840s and 1850s was born out of hostility toward the South and had little to do with concern for the fate of blacks, as reflected in the platforms of the Free Soil and Republican parties. The abolitionist commitment to nonviolence could not withstand the tensions generated by the slavery conflict, and a bloody civil war was necessary to end the institution of slavery on American soil.

Although abolition had ceased to exist as a movement, the abolitionists lived on. During the war abolitionists such as Frederick Douglass pressured Lincoln and the Republicans to make abolition a war aim, and after the release of the Emancipation Proclamation they pressed for a constitutional amendment banning slavery. The passage of the Thirteenth Amendment achieved the abolitionist goal of ending slavery but did nothing to ensure that blacks would be treated as equals in American society. Although many antislavery societies disbanded after the war, several abolitionists, including Douglass and Lewis Tappan, Arthur Tappan's brother, turned to black education and improvement of black standard of living. Their efforts never attracted the attention of the abolitionist movement of the 1830s, and by the 1870s the last remnants of abolitionism had faded away.

Historians debate the impact and the importance of abolitionism in American history. Abolitionists clearly failed to achieve their aims. They inspired few southerners to abandon slavery; on the contrary, the abolitionist crusade inspired the South to defend slavery as a beneficial institution for both masters and slaves alike. In the North, abolitionists remained a tiny minority. Historians estimate that abolitionism attracted less than 2 percent of the North's population. Both the strategies of moral suasion and political abolition had little influence over the fate of the nation's slaves and freedmen.

These criticisms have drawn vigorous responses from defenders of the abolitionists. Although the abolitionists failed to achieve any of their stated objectives, they nonetheless made slavery an issue of national debate. They attracted enormous public attention, though not always positive, and their influence far outweighed their numbers. Most important, they attacked the racism prevalent in nineteenth-century America and raised significant questions about the roles of minorities in American society that have yet to be resolved.

A far more serious criticism contends that abolitionists heightened regional tensions and contributed to the coming of the Civil War. Motivated by unresolved social and economic tensions within their own lives, abolitionists freely criticized a feature of American society far removed from their own neighborhoods. Their shrill and even hysterical condemnations of slavery and the South forced southerners to defend and bolster an institution that might have eventually faded away for economic and social reasons. This argument places the blame for the Civil War squarely on the very advocates of nonviolence.

These criticisms have also received attention from historians. Recognizing abolitionism as part of the larger reform movement in the United States, they argue that abolitionism was a natural response to a glaring social problem of the time. The fact that abolitionists were confined to the North, far from the institution that they criticized, ignores the fact that southerners reacted to abolitionism with a far more violent response than did unappreciative northerners; it was prudent to criticize slavery from a distance. Moreover, the abolitionists were just as quick to condemn the North for profiting from the labors of slaves and for accepting the existence of the institution anywhere on American soil. To blame the abolitionists for the Civil War is to ignore the serious social and economic tensions generated by the existence of slavery in a nation that was becoming increasingly modern in its outlook and its economy. Regardless of its failures, abolition remains a movement that articulated beliefs in equality and liberty that still resonate in the American political dialogue.

SELECTED BIBLIOGRAPHY

Absuz, Robert H. *Passionate Liberator: Theodore Dwight Weld and the Dilemma of Reform.* New York: Oxford University Press, 1980. A biography of an important abolitionist that includes material on the Grimké sisters.

Barnes, Gilbert Hobbs. *The Antislavery Impulse.* New York: Harcourt, Brace & World, 1934. A classic study that drew attention to the work of Weld.

Bartlett, Irving H. *Wendell Phillips, Brahmin Radical.* New York: Greenwood Press, 1961. A portrait of a wealthy intellectual and active abolitionist.

Berlin, Ira, and Ronald Hoffman, eds. *Slavery and Freedom in the Age of the American Revolution.* Charlottesville: University Press of Virginia, 1983. Includes several articles on the Revolution's impact on slave societies.

Bracey, John H. Jr., ed. *Blacks in the Abolition Movement.* Belmont, MA: Wadsworth, 1971. Articles profiling black leaders and their roles as abolitionists.

Curry, Richard, ed. *The Abolitionists.* Hinsdale, IL: Dryden Press, 1973. Includes articles very critical of the abolitionists.

Davis, David Brion, ed. *Ante-Bellum Reform.* New York: Harper & Row, 1967. Contains several brief articles on antislavery.

Dillon, Merton L. *Elijah P. Lovejoy, Abolitionist Editor.* Urbana: University of Illinois Press, 1961. A biography of the abolitionist printer murdered in 1837.

Filler, Louis. *The Crusade against Slavery.* New York: Harper & Row, 1960. A general survey of abolitionism.

Friedman, Lawrence J. *Gregarious Saints: Self and Community in American Aboli-*

tionism, 1830–1870. Cambridge: Cambridge University Press, 1982. Focuses on immediatism in the abolitionist campaign.

Hersh, Blanche Glassman. *The Slavery of Sex: Feminist-Abolitionists in America.* Urbana: University of Illinois Press, 1978. Examines the lives of 51 women in the abolitionist movement.

Kraditor, Aileen S. *Means and Ends in American Abolitionism: Garrison and His Critics on Strategy and Tactics, 1834–1850.* New York: Pantheon Books, 1967. Includes chapters on religion, politics, and the women in abolitionism.

Kraut, Alan M. *Crusaders and Compromisers.* Westport, CT: Greenwood Press, 1983. Essays about party politics and abolitionism.

Lerner, Gerda. *The Grimké Sisters from South Carolina: Pioneers for Woman's Rights and Abolition.* New York: Shocken Books, 1971. A fascinating biography of two southern sisters who became prominent reform leaders.

Lumpkin, Katharine Du Pre. *The Emancipation of Angelina Grimké.* Chapel Hill: University of North Carolina Press, 1974. A readable biography of the younger Grimké sister.

Magdol, Edward. *The Antislavery Rank and File.* Westport, CT: Greenwood Press, 1983. Offers social profiles of people attracted to abolitionism.

McFeely, William S. *Frederick Douglass.* New York: W. W. Norton, 1991. A biography with illustrations and photographs.

Merrill, Walter H. *Against Wind and Tide.* Cambridge, MA: Harvard University Press, 1963. Casts William Lloyd Garrison as the central figure of the abolitionist movement.

Nash, Gary B. *Race and Revolution.* Madison, WI: Madison House, 1990. Considers the impact of the American Revolution on slavery.

Perry, Lewis. *Radical Abolitionism: Anarchy and the Government of God in Antislavery Thought.* Ithaca, NY: Cornell University Press, 1973. Focuses on the Garrisonians within abolitionism.

Perry, Lewis, and Fellman, Michael. *Antislavery Reconsidered: New Perspectives on the Abolitionists.* Baton Rouge: Louisiana State University Press, 1979. Articles that synthesize the historical interpretations produced during the 1970s.

Quarles, Benjamin. *Black Abolitionists.* New York: Oxford University Press, 1969. Studies the motivations and methods of the black abolitionists.

Sorin, Gerald. *Abolitionism: A New Perspective.* New York: Praeger, 1972. Offers a brief but useful overview of abolitionism influenced by the civil rights movement of the 1960s.

Stampp, Kenneth M. *The Imperiled Union: Essays on the Background of the Civil War.* New York: Oxford University Press, 1980. Contains Stampp's essay "The Irrepressible Conflict," which examines the claim that abolitionists caused the Civil War.

Stewart, James Brewer. *Holy Warriors: The Abolitionists and American Slavery.* New York: Hill and Wang, 1976. Perhaps the best general introduction to abolitionism.

Walters, Ronald G. *American Reformers, 1815–1860.* New York: Hill and Wang,

1978. Contains useful chapters on the origins of reform movements and antislavery.

———. *The Antislavery Appeal: American Abolitionism after 1830.* New York: W. W. Norton, 1978. Examines abolitionism in the contexts of family life, religion, and other topics.

Wyatt-Brown, Bertram. *Lewis Tappan and the Evangelical War against Slavery.* Cleveland: Press of Case Western University, 1969. A biography that contrasts Tappan's roles as abolitionist and capitalist.

Zilmersmit, Arthur. *The First Emancipation: The Abolition of Slavery in the North.* Chicago: University of Chicago Press, 1967. A detailed discussion of abolitionism in the last decades of the eighteenth century.

6

The War with Mexico, 1846–1848

INTRODUCTION

Westward expansion had been occurring in America since the earliest colonial days. The purchase or annexation of new territory, the impulse or economic necessity to move on, the improved facilities for migration provided by canals and railroads in the early nineteenth century all stimulated the idea of expansion. Land hunger, especially in the South where soil depleted rapidly, was another strong force for westward movement.

In the 1840s, an editor, John L. O'Sullivan, gave a label to the spirit of expansionism, manifest destiny, which encompasses the idea that the United States was preordained to occupy and control all of North America, if not even a greater area. This was not something that persons willed, but rather the product of greater forces, and seen through geographical, cultural, and historical evidence. In a sense, manifest destiny, an expression of American nationalism, was a rationalization for expansionism.

Americans thought their culture and institutions were better than those of other nations and therefore they had a right, even an obligation, to impose these better ways on less fortunate peoples. They pursued this obligation with a conviction that took the form of a mission to demonstrate to all the world the virtues of democracy. Another reason for

VOLUNTEERS !

Men of the Granite State!

Men of Old Rockingham !! the

strawberry-bed of patriotism, renowned for bravery and devotion to Country, rally at this call. Santa Anna, reeking with the generous confidence and magnanimity of your countrymen, is in arms, eager to plunge his traitor-dagger in their bosoms. To arms, then, and rush to the standard of the fearless and gallant CUSHING----put to the blush the dastardly meanness and rank toryism of Massachusetts. Let the half civilized Mexicans hear the crack of the unerring New Hampshire rifleman, and illustrate on the plains of San Luis Potosi, the fierce, determined, and undaunted bravery that has always characterized her sons.

Col. THEODORE F. ROWE, at No. 31 Daniel-street, is authorized and will enlist men this week for the Massachusetts Regiment of Volunteers. The compensation is $10 per month----$30 in advance. Congress will grant a handsome bounty in money and ONE HUNDRED AND SIXTY ACRES OF LAND.

Portsmouth, Feb. 2. 1847.

This recruiting poster attempted to stir the patriotism of the men of New Hampshire so that they would enlist in the army being assembled to fight Mexico. (Reproduced from the Collections of the Library of Congress)

American expansion was the fear of a powerful rival blocking further growth. Usually this power was Great Britain, and American expansionist desires were often directed against areas where British influence was high. Other reasons were more crass. The United States desired, in the case of Oregon, to control the northern Pacific waters and the shorter route to the trade of the Orient.

The first major outlet for American expansion after the Adams-Onís Treaty (1819) was Texas. U.S. claims to Texas had been transferred to Spain by the treaty, but ratification had been delayed partly by the objections of senators interested in the Texas territory. After Mexico won independence from Spain in 1822, the government asked Americans to settle there, hoping that the new Texans would provide a buffer between the United States and its Indians and the rest of Mexico, as well as build up the economy and tax receipts of the province. By offering land grants to settlers and promoters, Mexico attracted about 20,000 Americans with 2,000 slaves to Texas by 1830. In fact, Texas-Mexican relations steadily deteriorated. In 1830, to combat growing bitterness, Mexico tried to exert control by stopping further immigration of Americans, sending occupation troops in, and asserting other laws, such as those prohibiting slavery and those requiring Texans to become Catholics and to settle only in certain areas not reserved for Mexicans. The result was to increase Texans' irritation. In 1832, a revolution in Mexico put Santa Anna in power, and in 1836, the Texans revolted, first for reforms, and then, when Santa Anna threatened to exterminate them, for independence on March 2, 1836. The war was short and ended at the Battle of San Jacinto on April 21, when Santa Anna was taken prisoner. The treaty brought Texan independence and established a vague boundary between Texas and Mexico.

The Republic of Texas had little desire to remain independent. Texans wanted to obtain U.S. recognition, followed by annexation, and for good reason: protection against Mexico. With 50,000 people, Texas was not big enough to maintain a national government; moreover, most Texans were Americans and thus had a natural affinity for the United States. Between 1836 and 1844, pressure for annexation increased. Britain was wooing Texas but demanding the abolition of slavery. Northern businessmen and southern planters both feared this development would injure American commerce, and southerners worried that abolition of slavery in Texas might cause a great slave insurrection throughout the South. Sam Houston, who had led Texan forces in their fight for independence, propagandized effectively for Texas's annexation, and ex-President Andrew

Jackson warned that Texas must be annexed, "peaceably if we can, forcibly if we must." President John Tyler worked hard for it, and finally, in February 1845, the Congress passed a joint resolution favoring annexation. Texas became a state on December 29, 1845.

By the time Texas became a state, James Knox Polk was president. The election of 1844 had featured expansionism as the major issue. The Democrats had nominated Polk, a former governor of Tennessee, and put together a platform that stood for the annexation of Texas and the reoccupation of Oregon up to 54°50'. The Whigs nominated Henry Clay and tried to evade the issue by saying nothing at all in their platform about Texas. Clay had first opposed Texas annexation, but when the sentiment for it became apparent, he said he would not object to annexation if it could be done "without dishonor, without war, with the common consent of the Union, and upon just and fair terms." This equivocal statement angered both southern and northern supporters and may have cost Clay victory in a close election.

The first major problem Polk had to deal with after taking office was the Oregon question. Both Britain and the United States had occupied this territory since 1818 and had been unable to resolve ownership. Indeed both countries had good claims to the territory. British traders had been there since the late eighteenth century and Boston traders since 1788, buying furs to sell in China. Americans controlled the coastal trade, but the British had a stronger hold on the interior. The area most in dispute was the area in between the Columbia River and the forty-ninth parallel. The British claimed that the mouth of the river was essential; the Americans were eager to have a port at Puget Sound. Three times the British had refused to compromise by extending the forty-ninth parallel to the Pacific.

Neither Britain nor Polk was willing to go to war over the issue, and in fact Britain's interest in the area was declining as the fur trade declined and as American settlement increased. Moreover, British-American commercial relations were good, and both countries wanted them to stay that way. Polk and the Congress were on the brink of war with Mexico and were naturally reluctant to fight Britain and Mexico at the same time. Polk's advisers, furthermore, had told him that the land north of the forty-ninth parallel was unsuitable for farming, and the real plum was the harbor at Puget Sound. America's gateways to the Pacific, they said, were the Pacific harbors. On both sides of the Atlantic, calmer voices prevailed, and on June 15, 1846, the Oregon Treaty was signed, with benefits for both sides. It extended the U.S.-Canada boundary at the forty-ninth parallel to the Puget Sound and then out the Strait of Juan de Fuca. The territory between there and the Columbia River fell to the Americans, but England got navigation rights on the river and possession of Vancouver Island. Although northwesterners felt that Polk had sold out on them by not getting all of Oregon, the Senate ratified the treaty over their objections.

Polk's ideas of expansion went beyond just Oregon and Texas. He had designs on California and New Mexico (the land between Texas and California), and possibly more of the northern part of Mexico as well. Although he hoped to fulfill his desires peaceably, he was not opposed to war, an increasingly likely prospect since Mexico was not at all happy about the Texas annexation. It had broken off diplomatic relations with the United States upon the Texas annexation, and with that, a dispute over the Texas-Mexico boundary cropped out. Texas claimed that its territory extended to the Rio Grande; the Mexicans claimed the boundary was at the Nueces River out of Corpus Christi. Polk, of course, recognized the Texas claim and sent General Zachary Taylor to the Nueces line, ostensibly to protect Texas against Mexico. Polk doubtless thought he needed to support the Texans, but the Mexicans thought it was an act of aggression. Also at this time, Polk brought up the issue of several million dollars that were due American citizens from Mexico for various losses and damages. To Mexico, Polk seemed in a terrible hurry to collect the debts.

Meanwhile, California was becoming an issue. California, like Texas under Mexico, was distant from the capital and only loosely governed. American whalers had been stopping at California ports for 25 years before the 1840s, and fur traders, deserters from ships, and occasional emigrants from the east had bought land in California and were of great influence in the commerce of the province. Expansionists urged Polk to take over California before the British did, and Polk himself dreamed of a transcontinental railroad to link California with the Mississippi Valley. Besides, the ports of San Francisco, Monterey, and San Diego were valuable.

The problem was that the United States had no claims to California as it had to the Oregon Territory, and Mexican-American relations, being what they were over Texas, did not allow for the purchase of California from Mexico. But Polk decided to make one last try at acquiring California by diplomacy. He sent John Slidell, a politician from Louisiana, to Mexico City to try to settle the differences between the two nations with American money. If Mexico would acknowledge the Rio Grande border, the United States would assume the damage claims against Mexico. For the cession of New Mexico, the United States would pay $5 million, and for California, up to $25 million.

But Slidell unfortunately arrived in Mexico just at the time the government was about to be overthrown by another revolution. The government falling out of power did not dare weaken itself further by talking with him, and the one coming into power had done so by denouncing the United States, so it could hardly deal with him as well. Slidell notified Polk that his mission had failed, and with this news Polk ordered Taylor's army to move from the Nueces to the Rio Grande.

Polk's reason was again to protect Texans from a Mexican attack, but he hoped that the show of force might cause Mexico to reconsider its refusal to negotiate. Failing this, Polk perhaps hoped that the presence of American troops on disputed soil might provoke an incident that would provide an excuse for war. For several months, nothing happened, and when Slidell returned from Mexico in May 1846, Polk decided to send a war message to Congress based on the damage claims and other past grievances. Just as he was preparing this message, news arrived that Mexicans had crossed the Rio Grande and attacked U.S. troops stationed near what is now Brownsville, causing several casualties. Polk then changed his war message, calling for war to avenge "American blood shed on American soil" and sent it on to Congress, where it was passed by wide margins. Despite the congressional approval of the war (the vote was 40–2 in the Senate and 174–14 in the House), there was quite a lot of opposition. In the Northeast, people objected on moral and political grounds, and even in the South, fear surfaced that the acquisition of that much territory would cause sectional tension. As the war costs and causalities mounted, Whigs in particular denounced "Mr. Polk's war" and its aggressive origins. The greatest support came from the Mississippi Valley and Texas; they sent 49,000 of 62,000 volunteers.

The war was quickly won. General Taylor marched south of the Rio Grande to capture Monterrey in September 1846 and then defeated a Mexican army of 15,000 led by Santa Anna at Buena Vista near Monterrey the next February. Politically sensitive about the popularity of his Whig generals, Polk tabled Taylor after Buena Vista, and sent General Winfield Scott to lead an expedition against Mexico City, which was taken in September 1847. California was handled by Colonel Stephen W. Kearney, who led an overland expedition from Missouri, captured Santa

Fe, and moved into California where he joined with John Frémont and established American rule in early 1847.

After the Buena Vista victory and capture of Vera Cruz at the beginning of Scott's expedition, Polk decided to make a try for peace. For this mission, the secretary of state, James Buchanan, chose Nicholas P. Trist, a former consul at Cuba and a Spanish speaker. Trist was instructed to insist on the Rio Grande boundary and the cession of New Mexico and California; in return the United States would assume the Mexican damage claims and pay an extra $15 million—what some have called conscience money. At first, Santa Anna refused the terms, and when Trist became too friendly with General Scott, Polk ordered him back to Washington. Then he and the cabinet began contemplating more severe terms, such as cession without payment and an occupation of Mexico. Some superexpansionists thought fondly of taking over all of Mexico, justified by manifest destiny. Oddly, the South was largely against it, for fear that northern free-soilers would insist on the prohibition of slavery if the territory became states and that this would cause an irreparable sectional split.

Trist also recognized this problem. Although he had been recalled, he stayed at his diplomatic post and resumed negotiations with the new, more moderate government that had just assumed power in Mexico. He had great success and on February 2, 1848, signed the Treaty of Guadalupe Hidalgo, securing the Rio Grande boundary and gaining for the United States upper California, including the port of San Diego, and New Mexico (including present-day Arizona, Utah, Nevada, and parts of Colorado, Oklahoma, and Texas). He agreed that the United States would assume Mexican claims up to $3.25 million and would pay an additional $15 million.

The signing of the treaty by what amounted to an unauthorized negotiator gave Polk something of a problem, for the treaty's conditions met those that Polk had given Trist. If Polk repudiated the treaty, it would seem inconsistent, would certainly perplex Mexico, and would stir up all kinds of trouble in Congress, where the Whigs controlled the House. With all this, Polk accepted it and sent it to the Senate, which ratified it, 38–14, gaining majorities in both parties. The treaty added 500,000 square miles of territory to the United States and was an excellent diplomatic achievement. Five years later, in 1853, the continental expansion of the United States was completed with the Gadsden purchase— 54,000 square miles in what is now southern Arizona—that was purchased for another $10 million because through it ran the best route for the southern railroad to the Pacific.

INTERPRETIVE ESSAY
Donald A. Rakestraw

Few other events in U.S. history have produced greater effect—both immediate and over the long term—than the war with Mexico in the 1840s. Coming as the climax to an expansionist quest, the war was the product and the reflection of a unique and critical stage in the development of the nation. Woven within the pull and tug of a people whose diverse and often incompatible interests defied national identity, the Mexican War's significance rests on its positive contribution to American unity and national growth as well as its ominous portents for national disaster and fragmentation. The war's place in the course of American civilization is located within the mundane calculations of miles and acres and the grand reckoning of consequences and legacies.

As America approached midcentury, it continued to grapple with questions of identity, world context, and direction. Societal changes that were the consequence of a young nation in transition to adulthood generated a certain amount of tension and insecurity. Thomas Jefferson's agrarian ideal seemed threatened by a society following in Britain's industrial footsteps. Writer Washington Irving observed that the "march of mechanical inventions is driving everything political before it." Farm was challenged by factory, rural commonwealth by urban oligarchy. A romantic season of nationalist introspection and pride yielded to a shallower and more materialistic age committed to trade and industry. In this atmosphere, Americans strained to find a mooring. The memory of revolutionary progress had faded and with it, some feared, the rationale for the American experiment. The growth of the American population and a series of financial calamities undercut the personal independence and self-sufficiency of the Jacksonian "common man." His redemption lay in the active pursuit of what Andrew Jackson aptly called the "area of freedom."

At the same time a reactionary Europe seemed determined to contain the liberal principles of republican government and to squelch democracy with monarchical rule. Rumors were rife that France had designs on a throne for Mexico and that abolitionist Europeans were set to pounce at the first sign of weakness to cordon off America's slave system and to lock the United States behind its current restrictive borders. There, they hoped, slavery (dubbed the "peculiar institution") would die and democracy would decay. If, however, Americans could break that containment and revive their fervor for patriotism and republican virtue, a new era would be theirs. Expansionism seemed the perfect vehicle for such a revival. Rooted in the colonial tradition and encouraged by the vision of Thomas Jefferson and the continentalism of John Quincy Adams, territorial expansion could unharness the energy of America's burgeoning population, spark nationalist pride with images of western vistas, and transform an insulated and parochial people into a hemispheric power. It was, according to the journalist, John L. O'Sullivan, their "manifest destiny."

The concept was made a cause célèbre in the 1840s by newspapermen who found that technology had supplied them with the ability to broadcast their enthusiasm for expansion throughout the country. Northern editors from east to west tirelessly heralded America's geographic calling. Many were driven by the belief that farm surplus and packed warehouses could be relieved only by the continued cultivation of new markets. To them, territorial expansion would create the markets and at the same time temper the ardor for industrialization and urbanization by opening new land for rural living.

Equally essential was another type of cultivation, that of liberty and freedom. The Mexican War affirmed a sense that the United States was on a divine mission, the course of which could not be altered even if it meant the forcible appropriation of another nation's land. The zeal with which America pursued the accession of the Southwest demonstrated what some students of the period have dubbed exceptionalism—that feeling that the United States was uniquely positioned to elevate humanity to the next stage of development. What had previously been scorned as vulgar imperialism when undertaken by other nations was somehow different when effected by the United States. Washington's energies were driven, leaders would argue, not by greed or animus but by a noble desire to disseminate benevolent American institutions.

There was no better evidence of this thinking than the war of conquest in the American Southwest. Although an unintended consequence of U.S. determination to follow the hand of providence to the shores of the Pacific Ocean, alleged Mexican intransigence opened the door for an awesome and glorious means to the expansionist end. Supplanting the tedious prodding of American settlers along the Oregon Trail, armed conflict offered the expansionist movement intangibles like heroism, patriotism, and the chance to showcase America's military prowess.

Communities from across the nation dispatched their young heroes to the battlefields under the banner of God, country, and retribution for the alleged shedding of the blood of their brothers at the Rio Grande. The war made manifest destiny, previously the preserve of editors and pioneers, real to the entire population. American soldiers would return having experienced more than war and victory: a wide and exotic world where people spoke, ate, worshipped, and generally behaved differently. Never again would Americans be the insular and at times ingenuous citizens that they once were. The war would expand more than the territorial limits of the republic. It would expand America's perspective and, as predicted, awaken the nationalist pride of a unified people. Volunteers from one end of the United States to the other stood together in crisis and in battle for the United States of America. It is small wonder that the July Fourth festivities following the victorious end to the war in 1848 seemed charged with excitement and promise.

In Washington the celebration of American Independence Day seemed to herald the opening of a new and prosperous era in the development of American civilization. As celebrants in the nation's capital commemorated the date by laying the foundation stone for a monument to George Washington, they were captivated by the magnitude of their accomplishment. Before the day ended, Polk received news of the Mexican government's ratification of the Treaty of Guadalupe Hidalgo. Coinciding with word that the French had thrown off the yoke of monarchy and rekindled the spark of liberty in Europe with another revolution, the news of the treaty confirmed for the crowd that their republic had indeed inaugurated a new order: it had secured its manifest destiny to extend liberty across the continent and simultaneously proved the value, ability, and stamina of democracy. To many Americans, the war was a test of their democratic institutions. Not only had the test been passed, but the reputation of republicanism had been elevated even in the eyes of Europeans, who considered no better gauge to success than a victorious war. Even the Whig party leaders in Congress, skeptical of any expansion beyond the limited addition of Pacific harbors, hoisted their own valiant generals in celebration.

The Mexican War provided a proving ground where the U.S. Army could demonstrate its capabilities and where national reputations could be shaped. In fact, the war produced seasoned leaders for the American

Civil War, among them future Confederate commander Robert E. Lee and his Union counterpart, Ulysses S. Grant.

The conflict with Mexico also produced, to the chagrin of Democrat James K. Polk, the next two Whig presidential candidates. President Polk provoked the war by dispatching American forces to the Rio Grande under the command of Whig general Zachary Taylor. Winning immediate affection at home by suffering the first casualties of the war—on American soil, according to Polk—Taylor quickly led his outmanned troops into Mexico. The general shortly reported a series of victories at such soon-to-be-immortalized places as Monterrey and Buena Vista. In the process he ensured for himself an esteemed reputation throughout the country from which he could later transpose military campaigns into a successful political campaign for the White House. In tandem with Taylor's successes was a brilliant move by another Whig General, Winfield Scott. Demonstrating sagacity and daring, Scott used the first landing craft in U.S. military history to deploy an amphibious operation at Vera Cruz. From there, in defiance of the opinions of the best European military strategists, he marched an army overland to Mexico City to press the Mexican government to come to terms. Even the duke of Wellington, Britain's famed conqueror of Napoleon, was impressed.

The Mexican War added to the U.S. military's thin resumé an impressive list of firsts, not the least of which was the successful landing at Vera Cruz. The war experience transformed internal military communications as the army became increasingly dependent on the electric telegraph and effected external reporting with the introduction of war correspondents to ensure that the folks back home were appropriately informed of the heroics of their native sons and the advance of the troops. Field hospitals in future conflicts would be far more humane thanks to the army's adoption of ether for anesthesia. Among the other novel experiences credited to the Mexican War were the military occupation of an enemy's capital, the institution of martial law on foreign soil, and the U.S. army's first successful offensive war. These firsts combined with the success of a volunteer army deployed by a true (some would say *the true*) republic against a professional army fielded by a dictatorship to impress Europeans. The military performance won new respect for the United States and the "Napoleon of the backwoods," as the British press dubbed Polk, among the community of nations.

The successful prosecution of the war had a tremendous impact on U.S. security and international status. Victory in the war with Mexico established the ability of a republic to engage in foreign war without jeopardizing its democratic values, mobilizing both its people and its resources. Although the war did not elevate the United States to great power status in the European sense, it did draw the nation considerably closer to that rank and made it the undisputed bully of the Western Hemisphere. Even Britain would concede America's preeminence in the hemisphere two years after the war in the Clayton-Bulwer agreement that compromised British influence in Central America. After the Mexican War, the great powers would not again seriously challenge the United States by force in the Western Hemisphere. When Spain helped to usher the United States across the divide to major power status in the Spanish-American War at the end of the nineteenth century, it did so not by choice but because Washington's assertion of U.S. interests in the Caribbean left them no alternative.

Polk's revival and expansion of the Monroe Doctrine, which had decreed the hemisphere off-limits to European imperialists, left little doubt that the United States had adopted a sort of paternal obligation to the Americas. Unlike earlier intrusions, such as Britain's appropriation of the Falkland Islands and French bombardment of Mexico in the 1830s, Europeans moved more gingerly in America's neighborhood after Polk's Mexican adventure. The United States, now a continental power, could justifiably claim leadership as the world's most successful and powerful republic, and it could press its economic interests in the Western Hemisphere and perhaps even consider an isthmian canal.

Although a small affair when measured against the yardstick of similar wars of conquest, to the patriotic zealots in the United States, "Mr. Polk's War" was the most laudable event since Jackson's defeat of the British at New Orleans in 1815. At a cost of just over $100 million, including both military expenditures and the treaty award to Mexico, and a loss of about 13,000 American lives, the United States had acquired over 500,000 square miles of territory, including the Rio Grande boundary for Texas and all contiguous land from the river to the Pacific. And if the cost was not adequately balanced by the acquisition of millions of acres, the soon-acknowledged wealth of upper California went far to pacify even the most frugal citizen. In the four years following the war, the value of gold extracted from that newly annexed territory more than doubled the fiscal expense of the war. Augmenting the natural wealth of the territory, the addition of San Francisco and San Diego to the harbors of Puget Sound in the Oregon territory gave the United States control of virtually the entire Pacific coast of North America, allowing Washington to cast more than an avaricious eye on Asia. It could now work to advance America's influence on Pacific commerce. With the capture of the Pacific coast through diplomacy in Oregon and war in the Southwest, Asia had been drawn closer to the United States than ever before. There was little doubt that Americans would pursue its exploitation in their typically dogged fashion. Within a decade, Washington had negotiated treaties in the Far East, and American ships carried approximately one-third of China's trade with the Western world.

In purely military terms, the administration's efforts had been a resounding success that established a number of important precedents. By developing limited war aims and holding to them against pressure from some to annex all Mexico, Polk managed to secure peace without the necessity of maintaining a postwar occupation force and firmly established an executive prerogative to wage war on foreign soil. Subsequent presidents and diplomats such as Theodore Roosevelt would find Polk's example of bold executive leadership in foreign policy an appropriate model for a much different America of the twentieth century.

Beneath the euphoric surface, however, the war had exposed dangerous fault lines that would ultimately rearrange the political landscape and fracture the republic. When the war started, the opposition Whig party found it expedient to straddle a fine line between criticism of the war and patriotic support for the troops. The vote on the war resolution—174–14 in the House of Representatives and 40–2 in the Senate—thus deceptively conveyed overwhelming support for the war. Arguing that the conflict was a fait accompli presented to Congress rather than a declaration requested of Congress, the Whigs focused their attack on the method more than the conduct of the war. They feared that an executive war jeopardized the federal government's balance of power. In their attack, Whigs found that they had paradoxically switched constitutional postures with the Democrats. In previous partisan squabbles over such issues as the tariff, bank projects, and internal improvements, the Whigs had broadly interpreted the Constitution in order to gain latitude in pressing their agenda. But in the case of the war, they reversed themselves. Contending that the president had circumvented the letter of the Constitution, they aimed to rein in the executive, which was not strictly empowered to pursue a war of conquest bent on the acquisition of territory. John Quincy Adams, elder statesman from Massachusetts and author of early American expansion, found it impossible to support this executive usurpation of power. Adams cautioned that Polk had "established as an irreversible precedent that the President of the U.S. has but to declare that War exists with any Nation upon Earth and the War is essentially declared." He asserted that it was simple "to foresee what the ultimate issue will be to the people of Mexico, but what it will be to the People of the United States is beyond my foresight, and I turn my eyes away from it."

What Adams could not know was that the unseen specter for both Mexico and the United States would be the most ominous legacy of the Mexican War: fragmentation and civil war. Suffering tremendously in a war on its own soil, Mexico lost 50,000 lives and forfeited more than half of its national territory—arguably the most valuable half. In addition, Mexico forfeited everything from food to livestock and any part of its artistic culture not nailed down. There was little hesitation in ravaging Mexico since there was near consensus in the United States that Mexicans, like Native Americans, were an inferior people who should be brushed aside. According to prominent American journalists, the Mexican people were incapable of self-government and required Washington's supervision. An egocentric question arose concerning the likelihood that the native population of Mexico could be regenerated. In early 1848, John C. Calhoun volunteered that the United States had "never dreamt of incorporating into [the] Union any but the Caucasian race—free white race." Attitudes reflected in such remarks relegated the Spanish-speaking Californios, Tejanos, and Nuevo Mexicanos to a heritage of racism at the hands of their new masters. Already straining at the tremendous influx of immigrants into the United States in the 1840s, nativist sensitivities would not warmly extend citizenship to non–Anglo-Saxon Catholic peoples absorbed along with the territory. American politicos, some would argue, did not want Mexicans, only Mexico. This attitude presaged America's later treatment of Latin Americans and Asians at the close of the century.

The war doomed Mexico to approximately 25 years of political turmoil and civil war plagued by factional strife, authoritarian rule, and, ironically, the turn toward monarchy as perhaps the most feasible solution to Mexican instability. While the United States heralded the end to European intrigue in North America, the war it waged on Mexico actually invited foreign intervention to cure the "sick man of America." Also, not surprisingly, the war wrought a lasting legacy of bitterness among Mexicans toward the invader from the North. As Mexico receded to a national territory of 760,000 square miles, it found it was contained on the north by a United States that, at Mexico's expense, had swelled to over 3 million square miles and on the south by Central America. It was more than the concession of valuable territory to the United States that fueled the resentment and ensured its perpetuity. The United States would perpetuate an arrogant tendency to intrude in the affairs of all countries from Mexico southward, reminding them of American superiority. To many Americans, the Mexicans should have considered themselves fortunate to retain any of their country after 1848.

When the war began, Polk had hoped for a short military exchange with a quick and favorable diplomatic settlement. He had wanted territory, not war, especially since Mexico's professional army outnumbered that of the United States by five to one. In fact, he was sensitive about any commentary that presented the conflict as a "war of conquest." It was, he argued, a war prosecuted to "conquer the peace." But all efforts at securing peace through diplomacy failed, and the war dragged on. Polk did not seem to fathom that any Mexican government that relinquished California would itself be lost. As Mexico's practical dilemma prolonged the war, many of Polk's advisers including his secretary of state, James Buchanan, and his treasury secretary, Robert J. Walker, began to press for an enlargement of U.S. goals to include the procurement of the entire nation of Mexico. Polk knew that such a change contained unknown consequences for both the war and American politics. A move to take all of Mexico might protract the conflict into a guerrilla war and agitate his political rivals. He was right. But despite his more conservative decision to withstand the pressure from the "all-Mexico" movement in favor of retaining his limited aims, political agitation materialized nevertheless. Polk's decision angered many members of his own party, especially in New York and in the western states, where expansionism had become a second religion, and failed to assuage northern leaders. The all-Mexico talk, disgruntled party members contended, proved that the slaveholding South meant to capture more territory for plantation agriculture. Few seemed to realize that Mexican soil and climate were not amenable to the plantation system and that many southern leaders had already satisfied their territorial ambitions with Texas. The all-Mexico movement therefore contributed to the shake-up of the parties and their sectional realignment.

Underneath the partisan banners of the 1840s were sectional cracks that stood ready to widen into irreparable crevices at the proper time and with the proper issue. Northern politicians had been most apprehensive about the war because they assumed that new territory in the southwest would invite the expansion of the South's slave economy. Although there was adequate evidence that this would not be the case, antislavery Whigs would not run the risk. And considering the later reclamation of land in the southwest through irrigation and the emergence of cotton as a staple, perhaps they were correct to be cautious. Their skepticism at the time prompted the introduction of the topic to the war debate. A freshman Democrat from Pennsylvania who favored expansion, David Wilmot, tried to dissociate slavery from the issue of territorial indemnity. Shortly after the war began, Wilmot attached an addendum to an appropriation request from Polk for $2 million to purchase peace (and California) from Mexico. His so-called Wilmot Proviso amounted to a disclaimer that slavery would be barred from any territory ceded by Mexico to the United States as a result of the conflict. Wilmot unwittingly rerung the "firebell," signaling the awakening of the dormant and potentially disastrous debate over slavery. His ten-minute presentation had won for him instant notoriety and a prominent place in the most onerous legacy of the Mexican War.

The motion exposed the frailty of party cohesion among both Democrats and Whigs. For years, the Democratic party had exhibited surprising homogeneity, but the issues resulting from the war proved that it had been little more than an illusion. Northern Democrats were disenchanted with the Polk administration, believing that he was driven by his southern cousins to pacify their promotion of their economic system. Democrats as well as some Whigs saw Wilmot's proposal as the perfect opportunity to express their discontent and oppose slavery without being classified among the zealot abolitionists. In fact, some had determined that support for the maintenance of Mexican territorial spoils as "free soil" could work to preserve the West for white farmers and restrict blacks to the South.

Although Wilmot's suggestion could never garner enough support to pass both houses, it opened the way for political realignment on the basis of section over party. When a New York congressman revived the notion, it exposed the fracture in the Democratic party as Martin Van Buren's "Barnburners" moved to join with antislavery forces of the North while southern Democrats tagged Wilmot and his associates as traitors. Whigs too broke by section. Mostly northern "Conscience Whigs" heralded the proviso as if sent down from heaven; southern or "Cotton Whigs" condemned Wilmot and their northern Whig associates as troublemakers. Democrats and Whigs both crossed lines and began to vote with one another as sectional division prevailed over party unity.

Thus, members of both parties in the South condemned the proposal, although not for the same reasons and not out of a particular zeal for conquest. The Whigs in the South still preferred expansion by proxy on the orthodox Jeffersonian model, whereby independent republics would spring up in emulation of the United States. Democrats in the South, like John C. Calhoun, had their appetite satisfied with Texas and had no desire to add Mexican land, especially if Mexicans came with it. Southern Democrats were already on poor terms with many of their western associates, who felt betrayed by Calhoun and company for their compromise on the Oregon Territory that led to its partition with Britain in 1846. This, the western Democrats believed, was a breach of an alleged 1844 campaign promise that combined the goals of Texas and Oregon.

Astute politicians recognized the danger and worked to find a solution. After Calhoun argued that Wilmot's proposal was a violation of property rights under the Constitution, Missouri senator Thomas Hart Benton warned that the Calhoun/southern position and the Wilmot Proviso were two blades that together could shear the bonds of the Union. Polk's first reaction was denial, contending that slavery was a domestic issue that had no business in foreign affairs and that it had merely been injected into the war debate to undercut him and his party. When he faced the seriousness of the problem, his attempt at a solution was to extend the Missouri Compromise line, which had resulted from the last debate over slavery and territory a quarter century before, across the new territories to the Pacific. Michigan senator Lewis Cass introduced a concept that would be one of the mainstays of compromise in the volatile 1850s: squatter's or popular sovereignty. This notion, primarily subterfuge, would have left the question to the people who settled the territories.

In the 1848 presidential campaign, both parties, appreciating its disruptive nature, tried to set the slavery issue aside. The Democrats chose Cass, who hoped to remain silent on the subject. The Whigs, to Polk's dismay, chose General Zachary Taylor, a slaveholder who would run on his battlefield laurels and sidestep the controversy. But this was wishful thinking. There was no avoiding the matter. Antislavery Whigs and rebellious northern Democrats joined with Van Burenites to put forward former president Martin Van Buren as the candidate of the Free Soil party in 1848. By splitting the Democratic vote in New York, the free-soilers ensured the Whig victory. More important, they spelled the beginning of the end of political stability. The sections were going their separate ways. The shears were at work. National parties that had forged national institutions based on common interests and beliefs that overcame sectional bias were breaking apart. The issues created by the war had produced the ingredients of a new party, one that was almost entirely sectional, the party of Abraham Lincoln.

The generation of the Mexican War would witness Republican victories that so alienated the South and stratified the nation as to make the dissolution of the Union nearly certain. The Mexican War had laid bare the incompatibility of an expansionist policy proclaiming the goal of liberty while insisting on the progress of slavery. The bitter contest over the Wilmot Proviso foreshadowed the tragic course that the nation had unwittingly plotted toward hardening sectional lines and ultimate disintegration.

In the years immediately following the war, the prospect of dissolution of the Union was unthinkable. The "Young America" movement seemed capable of tapping the nationalist enthusiasm generated by the war and preserving unity. In fact, apart from the wrangling of politicians over the extension of slavery, most Americans rejoiced in the victory over Mexico. It ushered in several years of prosperity, satisfied the fetish common to Americans that there should always be land to own, and brought under the stars and stripes several future and resource-rich states.

The final chapter in U.S. expansion was not written in 1848. Blocked by popular sovereignty in the West, southerners in the 1850s co-opted manifest destiny and refocused it southward toward the Caribbean and Central America. The Mexican War may have satisfied some expansionist appetites, but the de facto restriction of slavery to many meant the restriction of their political power. The only hope was to reach out to the South. Over the years following the Mexican War, southern newspapers and secret societies applauded private attempts by military adventurers known as filibusters to forcibly capture the tropical states for America. One southern congressman self-servingly offered that the inhabitants of Central America awaited "our coming, and with joyous shouts of 'Welcome! Welcome!' will they receive us." By the end of the nineteenth century, the expansionist quest would go global with a new manifest destiny that relied on many of the old attitudes but would not be hindered by geographic contiguity.

Over the decades since the Guadalupe Hidalgo treaty, the war has rarely been exalted by the American public as one of the highlights of its history. The war's omission from such a list seems curious considering its many ramifications for American civilization. The American Revolution, the Constitutional Convention, the Louisiana Purchase, even the

War of 1812 customarily arouse more familiarity with the general reader. This is partly due to the Mexican conflict's proximity to the Civil War, which tends to obscure all other topics in its vicinity. But this is only part of the explanation. Although the topic of a plethora of books and articles, the Mexican War fell out of favor because of a certain sense of guilt. Despite the salving of conscience at the time with the acceptance of Polk's rather lame argument that *they* started it, an uncomfortable feeling emerged that the United States had engaged in an old-fashioned war of conquest—a feeling that did not seem compatible with the principles of the republic. This judgment, however, is perhaps too harsh. Assessed within the confines of America's idealist opinion of its model republic, the war earns ignominy. Evaluated within the reality of the nineteenth-century world, however, Polk's accomplishments, despite the dreadful residue, set the United States on track to become first a continental, then a hemispheric, and ultimately a global power.

SELECTED BIBLIOGRAPHY

Bauer, K. Jack. *The Mexican War, 1846–1848.* New York: Macmillan, 1974. Devoted to an examination of the military operations and occupation of Mexico that draws heavily from military sources.

Bergeron, Paul H. *The Presidency of James K. Polk.* Lawrence: University Press of Kansas, 1987. Contains a useful chapter on Polk's handling of the Mexican War.

Bill, Alfred H. *Rehearsal for Conflict: The War with Mexico, 1846–1848.* New York: Knopf, 1947. Stresses the military and assesses the performance of future Civil War officers seasoned in the Mexican War.

Brack, Gene M. *Mexico Views Manifest Destiny, 1821–1846: An Essay on the Origins of the Mexican War.* Albuquerque: University of New Mexico Press, 1975. Examines Mexican attitudes toward U.S. expansionism in the period before the war.

Collins, John R. "The Mexican War: A Study in Fragmentation." *Journal of the West* 11, no. 2 (1972): 225–234. Discusses the partisan and sectional schisms that developed during the war.

Connor, Seymour V. "Attitude and Opinions about the Mexican War, 1846–1970." *Journal of the West* 11, no. 2 (1972): 361–366. A short but very helpful attempt to quantify 766 works concerning the war according to their perspective and bias.

Connor, Seymour V., and Odie B. Faulk. *North America Divided: The Mexican War, 1846–1848.* New York: Oxford University Press, 1971. A concise volume that examines the causes of the war and provides a comprehensive annotated bibliography arranged by topic.

DeVoto, Bernard. *The Year of Decision 1846*. Boston: Little, Brown, 1943. Focuses on the extension of American civilization and addresses both the acquisition of Oregon and the siege of Mexico City.

Eisenhower, John S. D. *So Far from God: The U.S. War with Mexico, 1846–1848*. New York: Random House, 1989. A very readable work that chronicles the war by military campaign from the annexation of Texas to the Treaty of Guadalupe Hidalgo.

Garrett, Jenkins, and Katherine R. Goodwin, eds. *The Mexican-American War of 1846–1848: A Bibliography of the Holdings of the Libraries of the University of Texas at Arlington*. College Station: Texas A&M University Press, 1995. An extensive annotated bibliography that is indispensable for research on the war from almost any conceivable angle.

Goffin, Aivin M. "Nationalism and Mexican Interpretation of the War of the North American Invasion, 1846–1848." *Canadian Review of Studies in Nationalism* 19, nos. 1–2 (1992): 129–138. Suggests that the war was seen in Mexico as an imperialist move by the United States that encouraged an evolving Mexican nationalism.

Graebner, Norman A. "How Wars Begin: The Mexican War." In David H. White and John W. Gordon, eds., *Proceedings of the Citadel Conference on War and Diplomacy*, pp. 15–25. Charleston, SC: Citadel Development Foundation, 1979. Surveys the various interpretations of the causes of the war.

———. "Lessons of the Mexican War." *Pacific Historical Review* 47, no. 3 (1978): 325–342. An insightful article that examines President James K. Polk's struggle to balance the opposition to the war, territorial indemnity, and the all-Mexico proponents.

Hale, Charles A. "The War with the United States and the Crisis in Mexican Thought." *Americas* 14, no. 2 (1957): 153–173. Discusses the dilemma faced by Mexican liberals who, having lauded U.S. institutions before the war, found themselves struggling for reconciliation once the war began.

Harstad, Peter T., and Richard W. Resh. "The Causes of the Mexican War: A Note on Changing Interpretations." *Arizona and the West* 6, no. 4 (1964): 289–302. A concise article that traces the varying interpretations on the causes of the conflict; especially useful for the historiography of the war.

Johannsen, Robert W. *To the Halls of Montezuma: The Mexican War in the American Imagination*. New York: Oxford University Press, 1985. An artfully written volume that does not deal with the war directly but analyzes the factors that shaped Americans' attitudes toward the war and the effects of the war on American society.

———. "America's Forgotten War." *Wilson Quarterly* 20, no. 2 (1996): 96–107. An enlightening article that continues Johannsen's efforts to provide a balanced view of the United States and the war.

Lambert, Paul F. "The Movement for the Acquisition of All Mexico." *Journal of the West* 11, no. 2 (1972): 317–327. Suggests that the scope of manifest destiny grew to include all Mexico in spite of the strife over slavery and the disdainful view Americans generally had of the Mexican people.

Lander, E. M., Jr. *Reluctant Imperialists: Calhoun, the South Carolinians, and the*

Mexican War. Baton Rouge: Louisiana State University Press, 1980. Examines the southern position on the war and substantiates that the so-called slaveocracy of the South was not behind the war.

Merk, Frederick. "Dissent in the Mexican War." In Samuel Eliot Morison, Frederick Merk, and Frank Freidel, *Dissent in Three American Wars*, pp. 35–63. Cambridge, MA: Harvard University Press, 1970. An interesting and useful survey of American opinion as reflected in the antiwar press.

Merk, Frederick, with Lois Banister Merk. *Manifest Destiny and Mission in American History: A Reinterpretation.* New York: Knopf, 1963. Argues that American expansionism drew on two themes: an oppressive and manifest destiny that runs contrary to American principles and mission that depicts the American idealism.

Morrison, Michael A. "New Territory versus No Territory: The Whig Party and the Politics of Western Expansion, 1846–1848." *Western Historical Quarterly* 23, no.1 (1992): 25–51. Offers a useful examination of Whig attitudes toward the war: party members feared that the acquisition of any territory would resurrect the slavery issue, sectionalize the party, and fracture the Union.

Pletcher, David M. *The Diplomacy of Annexation: Texas, Oregon, and the Mexican War.* Columbia: University of Missouri Press, 1973. An exhaustive treatment of U.S. expansion in midcentury that is a mainstay for understanding the broad context of American territorial acquisition and the complex issues that were involved.

Robinson, Cecil, ed. *The View from Chapultepec: Mexican Writers on the Mexican-American War.* Tucson: University of Arizona Press, 1989. Attempts to illustrate the impact of the war on Mexican attitudes toward the United States by exhibiting the works of a variety of Mexican writers from different times and perspectives.

Schroeder, John H. *Mr. Polk's War: American Opposition and Dissent, 1846–1848.* Madison: University of Wisconsin Press, 1973. A concise volume that is essential for an understanding of the opposition to the war in the United States.

Silbey, Joel H. "The Consequences of Manifest Destiny, 1846–1849." In Archie McDonald, ed., *The Mexican War Crisis for American Democracy.* Lexington, MA: D. C. Heath, 1969. Analyzes congressional voting behavior and argues that the sectional division that would lead to secession after another decade had not solidified in the late 1840s.

Singletary, Otis A. *The Mexican War.* Chicago: University of Chicago Press, 1960. Stresses partisan politics and the difficulties created by interservice rivalry in the war.

Smith, Justin H. *The War with Mexico.* 2 vols. New York: Macmillan, 1919. An exhaustive treatment of the war that is extremely favorable to the United States.

Tutorow, Norman. *The Mexican-American War: An Annotated Bibliography.* Westport, CT: Greenwood Press, 1981. A useful and extensive annotated bibliography of the war.

Weems, John Edward. *To Conquer a Peace: The War between the United States and Mexico.* Garden City, NY: Doubleday, 1974. A thorough treatment of the Polk administration's prosecution of the war that chronicles the numerous considerations that occupied the president and prolonged the war.

The Civil War,
1861–1865

INTRODUCTION

After years of political compromises, agitation by antislavery and pro-slavery groups, and weak presidential leadership during the 1850s, the nation moved closer to civil war in 1860. The presidential election that year pitted Abraham Lincoln of the Republican party against two candidates from a sectionally divided Democratic party and a candidate from a fourth party whose purpose was to find a way to avoid war.

Southern leaders had warned that the election of Lincoln would mean secession; as the governor of South Carolina put it, his election would "inevitably destroy our equality in the Union and ultimately reduce the Southern states to mere provinces of a consolidated despotism . . . fatally bent upon our ruin." Most southerners saw Lincoln as a die-hard abolitionist, and their attachment to the Union had been weakened over the past decade as they felt that northerners scorned them and that the balance of political and economic power had turned permanently against them.

Few in the South anticipated the aftermath of secession. Not many believed the North would go to war, and fewer still believed that if war came, the outcome would be so disastrous for the South. With these thoughts in mind, delegates came to a convention in South Carolina in

The Civil War was the first war to be photographed extensively. This shot, by T. H. O'Sullivan, shows the dead at Gettysburg, July 4, 1863. (Reproduced from the Collections of the Library of Congress)

December 1860 and formally repealed that state's ratification of the Constitution, thus seceding from the nation. By February 1, 1861, six other states had followed suit. Four more states seceded after the war began in April.

All hope of compromise failed when delegates from the seceded states met in Montgomery, Alabama, in February and formed the Confederate States of America. Thus, when Lincoln was inaugurated in early March, secession was an accomplished fact; a rival government was now in control of important Union property.

Lincoln's most immediate problem was what to do about this property, mostly federal forts and other military installations. The critical site was Fort Sumter, in South Carolina's Charleston Harbor, one of the few Union outposts not yet seized by Confederates. Lincoln had to decide the difficult question of whether to reinforce and supply Fort Sumter. If he retreated from a confrontation, he would lend credence to the power and legitimacy of the Confederate government; if he tried to use force to deliver supplies to Sumter, he would risk a violent response and possibly look like an aggressor. He attempted a moderate course of trying to supply Sumter peaceably, notifying South Carolina of his intentions. This placed the burden on the Confederates, who would be branded the aggressors if they provoked a confrontation. Deciding to take that risk, they attacked the fort with artillery on April 12 and brought about its surrender the following day. The country was at war.

As the war began, the North had tremendous material advantages. The population of the North numbered 23 million; of the South, 9 million, including nearly 4 million slaves, whose function in the Confederate military was unclear at best. The North had ten times the number of industrial workers, more than twice the railroad mileage, and almost twice as many horses and mules. In the end, the North raised an army of just over 1.5 million men; the South claimed almost 1.1 million. By and large, the northern armies were better armed, clothed, and fed than their southern counterparts. The southern advantage lay in the greater motivation of fighting for its independence.

When the war began, neither side had a prepared war plan. There was hardly a Confederate government at all, and no agency in the federal government to do such a thing. But clearly the northern strategy had to be offensive: to try to restore the Union by force through invasion and occupation of large parts of the South. The Confederate strategy could be defensive; victory could be theirs if they could stave off defeat until the North tired of the war and accepted the reality of southern independence. The strategy of both sides was much influenced by the dominant geographical feature of the Appalachian mountains, which split the war into western and eastern theaters.

The northern strategy at first was simple: a northern army would march south and capture Richmond, which had replaced Montgomery as the Confederate capital. After a military disaster at the First Battle of Bull Run, however, Lincoln and his advisers developed a more complex plan, which called for a naval blockade of southern ports, a splitting of the Confederacy at the Mississippi River, and the building of a new army to invade Virginia. The South also settled on a defensive strategy early on, using its armies, led by the capable Robert E. Lee, to wear down the northern will to fight by putting up a strong defense while working hard to obtain foreign recognition and the aid that would come with it.

In the West, General Ulysses S. Grant led northern troops toward the goal of capturing control of the Mississippi River. Here the key battles were at Shiloh (April 1862), a two-day struggle in which the North repulsed a southern attack but failed to follow up on its advantage, and Vicksburg (May–July 1863), where a siege of several weeks finally resulted in the northern capture of the last southern point of control on the river.

In the East, Lincoln's first general, George B. McClellan, took an army into eastern Virginia, but his excessive cautiousness stalled any action until the spring of 1862, when Lee's armies met McClellan in the Peninsular Campaign. The cautious McClellan was no match for Lee, whose troops inflicted thousands of casualties and forced the northern army back toward Washington and finally into Maryland, where the critical battle of Antietam was fought in September. Neither side won this battle, but the result was worse for the South, whose advance into the North was stalled at a time when a decisive victory might have prompted recognition from the French and British. The result was just as bad for McClellan, whose lack of aggressiveness had frustrated Lincoln long enough. He was replaced by General Ambrose E. Burnside.

If McClellan was too cautious, Burnside was just the opposite. He rushed his northern army back into Virginia and met a well-entrenched Confederate force at Fredericksburg in December. When the North suffered a stinging defeat there, Burnside was replaced by General Joseph "Fighting Joe" Hooker. He rebuilt the army, marched it again into Virginia, and, in April 1863, met Lee's forces at Chancellorsville. Hooker fared no better than Burnside, and the North lost once again.

At this point, Lee took the offensive and marched his troops north into

Pennsylvania, still seeking the dramatic victory that would bring foreigners to the side of the Confederacy. In early July, his troops reached
the town of Gettysburg, where they encountered the northern army, now
led by General George Meade. In a climactic three-day battle that was
the turning point of the war, Meade turned back Lee's offensive and sent
the Confederate army retreating back into Virginia. His victory might
have been overwhelming had he pressed his advantage and pursued Lee
southward. Nevertheless, the tide of the war had turned. In the same
week, the North split the Confederacy at the Mississippi River and
blunted the last southern offensive in the east.

In the west after Vicksburg, northern armies shifted their attention to
Chattanooga, captured in November 1863, and Atlanta, which fell in Sep-
tember 1864. By this time, Grant had been brought back to Washington
as general-in-chief (and commander of the eastern forces), and General
William T. Sherman led the northern troops at Atlanta and then on a
notorious and highly destructive sweep through central and eastern
Georgia, culminating in the capture of the coastal town of Savannah in
December 1864.

In 1864, however, the real focus of the war was in Virginia, as Grant
and Lee fought a series of bloody battles. These battles were different
from those earlier in the war, as Grant never fell back but kept continuous pressure on Lee. Gradually northern troops inched toward Richmond, and although casualty figures on both sides were staggering, the
North by this time was much more able to replace its losses than the
South. After more than three years of often intense fighting, the resources
of the Confederacy were running out. Its economy was a shambles, its
currency was virtually worthless, and its troops were suffering the effects
of poor rations and not enough ammunition.

The fighting in Virginia continued through early 1865, with the southern forces continuing to weaken in the face of Grant's pressure. When
Richmond fell on April 3, Lee realized the game was up. He surrendered
to Grant in a private home in the small town of Appomattox, west of
Richmond, on April 9.

This was a very costly war in term of lives: more than 360,000 Union
deaths from battle, disease, or other causes and more than 250,000 Confederate deaths. Since virtually all of the war had been fought in the
South, its property losses were massive. Some two-thirds of southern
railroad mileage had been destroyed, and agricultural output was so
disrupted that prewar levels of production were not reached until 1880.

What had been accomplished? Negro slavery was dead, but racial injustice was hardly forgotten. The concept of secession was likewise dead, and national unity was ensured, although sectional animosity would become a cultural staple. Over the long term, the war resulted in a better-balanced economy for the South, including a productive technological and industrial base.

Militarily, the Civil War stands as the first total war, in which massive armies, using the output of economies dedicated to the war, fought each other in a conflict where there could be no compromise. The South had to fight for independence or quit; the North had to restore the Union or quit. At the same time, the Civil War was the last of the old-style wars, with massed armies charging across open fields, generals making inspirational speeches to their troops, all wrapped in the idea that war was something fought by gentlemen. In this respect, the Civil War was two wars in one.

Although the fighting ended in April 1865, the conflict did not end for another 12 years. The years from 1865 to 1877 are known as Reconstruction, a period during which native white southerners struggled to reclaim regional political power. Reconstruction might have been a much less contentious era had Lincoln not been assassinated just five days after Appomattox. Lincoln, who was given to political compromise, was replaced by his vice president, Andrew Johnson, the living incarnation of stubbornness.

The problem lay in the manner in which Reconstruction was to be effected. Lincoln and Johnson envisioned a lenient policy under the direction of the executive branch, but congressional leaders wanted to punish the South for the war. While Lincoln would probably have found a middle ground with Congress, Johnson went into open warfare with the legislature, and when the midterm election of 1866 created a veto-proof Congress, its version of Reconstruction policy was bound to prevail. This included the military occupation of the South to prevent lawlessness and protect former slaves from white retribution. Although President Johnson was rendered powerless by the midterm election, vengeful congressional leaders tried to remove him from office through impeachment. They failed by just one vote to win conviction in the Senate trial.

In its Reconstruction policy, Congress also stripped most native white southerners of their civil rights, and local and state government in the South fell to a mix of carpetbaggers, or northerners who came to the South for a variety of reasons, and former slaves. These governments, loyal to the Republican majority in Congress, quickly wrote new state constitutions that barred slavery and secession and included ratification of the Fourteenth Amendment, which guaranteed civil rights to all Americans. By the early 1870s, all the states of the former Confederacy had been readmitted to the Union, and native southern whites were gradually winning back their rights. During the decade, a process historians call "redemption" took place; in state after state, southern whites recaptured political control through the ballot box, redeeming their state from the hated carpetbag-black governments. Following a disputed presidential election in 1876, the last federal occupation troops were removed from the South in early 1877, marking the end of Reconstruction.

Most of the former slaves, now freedmen, ended up working on the same plantations where they had been slaves. The federal government discouraged migration and set up agencies called Freedmen's Bureaus to assist blacks in arranging labor contracts or sharecropping agreements with their former masters. Black families received legal recognition for the first time, black churches and schools were quickly established and became the center of community life, and some blacks began dreaming of full equality. But that was not to come for a century; white rule in the South became more and more oppressive beginning in the 1890s, creating a racially segregated society that proved to be very difficult to break down.

INTERPRETIVE ESSAY

Carl E. Kramer

With the exceptions of the American Revolution and the framing of the Constitution of the United States, no other event has played so defining a role in American history as the Civil War. By simultaneously preserving the Union, ensuring the supremacy of the national government, and destroying chattel slavery, the northern victory resolved issues that had confounded the nation's political leaders since the Constitutional Convention. By the same token, the Civil War opened a broad array of new issues, and in so doing played a critical role in shaping the nation's political, social, and economic agenda up to the present time. Not surprisingly, the Civil War has fascinated Americans since the guns fell silent in 1865.

The causes of the Civil War are a subject of debate that may never be resolved. During the postbellum decades, some suggested that it was a moral struggle between northern abolitionists and southern slaveholders. In the early twentieth century it often was depicted as an economic conflict between a modernizing industrial North and a traditional agrarian South, in which slavery had limited relevance. More recently, as a result of research prompted by the Civil War centennial and the modern civil rights movement, it has become apparent that the war's causes were much more complex than either of these broad interpretations suggested.

The Civil War is perhaps best viewed as a conflict between two opposing ways of life within the context of a constitutional-ideological struggle over the issue of expansion of slavery into the territories. By the mid-nineteenth century the North was characterized by a dynamic capitalist economy built on small shops, factories, and independent farms and embodying a belief in the dignity and worth of free labor and free agriculture, and the ideal of social mobility. To many northerners, slavery represented a serious threat to their ability to advance socially and economically.

The South, on the other hand, had a predominantly plantation, staple crop economy, which was based on a slave labor system and supported by a sense of romanticism that equated this way of life with an idealized version of medieval feudalism. Cotton was the chief cash crop, and in the eyes of most southerners, the region's survival depended on the Cotton Kingdom's ability to expand westward. The Treaty of Guadalupe Hidalgo, which ended the Mexican War in 1848, gave the United States all or part of the present states of California, Nevada, Utah, Arizona, New Mexico, and Colorado and immediately raised the question of whether this vast area would be open to slavery.

About the only point on which all parties agreed was that the issue had to be resolved in a manner consistent with the Constitution, but the Constitution lacked a clear solution to the dilemma. Thus, three broad constitutional doctrines emerged, each combining elements of historic constitutional argument and regional self-interest: free soil, popular sovereignty, and state sovereignty. As tensions mounted, Americans gravitated toward the doctrine that best fit their views on the issue, regardless of their traditional partisan identification. This process eventually destroyed the established party alignment and with it the ability of the constitutional political order to achieve a resolution that was morally acceptable across sectional lines.

The prevailing northern view was free soil, based on the constitutional provision giving Congress exclusive authority to "make all . . . rules and regulations respecting the territory . . . belonging to the United States."

Free-soilers argued that this language empowered Congress to prohibit the introduction of slavery into any territory acquired from Mexico. The central expression of this doctrine was the Wilmot Proviso, introduced in the House of Representatives in August 1846 by David Wilmot, a Pennsylvania Democrat, as an amendment to a military appropriations bill. Wilmot's provision stipulated that "neither slavery nor involuntary servitude shall ever exist in any part of . . . [any] territory" acquired from Mexico. The proviso twice passed the northern-dominated House but died in the Senate. Although the proviso failed in Congress, it embodied the northern sentiment that the West should be left open to free white workers and farmers and eventually became a core component of Republican party ideology and a powerful expression of opposition to the expansion of slavery.

Popular sovereignty, most commonly associated with Democratic senators Lewis Cass of Michigan and Stephen A. Douglas of Illinois, found favor primarily in the Old Northwest. Its proponents agreed with the free-soilers that Congress had exclusive authority to legislate for the territories, but they reasoned from that position that Congress could allow the people of the territories to decide the issue of slavery's expansion for themselves. Popular sovereignty had a strong appeal because it seemed consistent with the democratic value of self-determination. Douglas used popular sovereignty as a cornerstone of both the Compromise of 1850 and the Kansas-Nebraska Act, but both efforts at compromise broke down, the former when many northerners defied the fugitive slave law and the latter when civil war broke out in Kansas between antislavery and proslavery forces attempting to control territorial organization. The failure of compromise contributed directly to the collapse of the Whig party, the growing sectional division of the Democratic party, and the emergence of a new Republican party based on free soil.

State sovereignty, favored by the South, was formulated largely by South Carolina senator John C. Calhoun and was rooted in the compact theory of the Constitution, enunciated in 1798 by Thomas Jefferson and James Madison in the Kentucky and Virginia Resolutions. They argued that the Constitution was a voluntary compact among sovereign states to create a central government that would perform certain functions on behalf of all the states that they could not carry out effectively on their own. Inherent in the doctrine was the idea that no state would voluntarily consent to actions by the central government that were destructive to its people's fundamental interests. Therefore, any state had an implicit power to judge the constitutionality of acts of the national government within its boundaries and to nullify legislation it judged unconstitutional. An essential corollary was that the national government also had the positive responsibility to protect each state's interests beyond the state's boundaries, if necessary. Calhoun and his followers argued that slavery was fundamental to the southern way of life and that any attempt by the national government to block its expansion into the territories was unconstitutional. Indeed, not only could Congress not attempt to block slavery's expansion, it also was obliged to protect slaveholders who were attempting to move into federal territories. While southerners failed to obtain congressional legislation to this effect, the Supreme Court translated state sovereignty into constitutional law in 1857 when it ruled in the *Dred Scott* decision that Congress lacked power to regulate slavery in the territories.

Sectional divisions hardened over the next three years, aggravated by events such as President James Buchanan's endorsement of the proslavery Lecompton Constitution for Kansas in 1857 and John Brown's Harper's Ferry raid in 1859. Northerners became increasingly convinced of a southern slave power conspiracy to destroy their liberty. And more and more southerners were certain that northern abolitionists were unwilling to let them live in peace with their "peculiar institution." With each section increasingly wedded to its position and persuaded that the other intended to destroy its way of life, compromise became politically unfeasible and morally unacceptable.

The intensity of sectional feelings was highlighted in the 1860 presidential election. Four candidates represented competing constitutional and sectional positions. Republican Abraham Lincoln carried the free-soil banner; Stephen A. Douglas represented the northern Democrats, who hoped to stave off permanent division through popular sovereignty; Vice President John C. Breckinridge of Kentucky was the southern Democratic standard-bearer, running on a state sovereignty platform that included a national slave code; and the Constitutional Union party, composed primarily of conservative Whigs, nominated John Bell of Tennessee on a platform supporting "the Union, the Constitution, and the Enforcement of the Laws."

With the Democrats split and the Constitutional Unionists appealing to the border states and upper South, a Republican victory was all but inevitable. Before the election, South Carolina politicians promised that if Lincoln were elected, their state would secede. When Lincoln won, South Carolina kept its word, withdrawing from the Union in December. Six other states of the lower South followed, and in February the seven seceded states formed the Confederate States of America. Meanwhile, conservative Unionists attempted to convince the South that it could live with Lincoln. The most prominent of these efforts was a compromise introduced by Senator John J. Crittenden of Kentucky. It took the form of a thirteenth amendment to the Constitution, which would reestablish the Missouri Compromise line and extend it to California. During the territorial phase, slavery would be prohibited above the line and protected below the line. Moreover, this would be an unamendable amendment, so any future attempt by the American government to abolish slavery would be unconstitutional. Lincoln took no public position on the Crittenden compromise, but he privately considered it constitutional blackmail and passed the word to his senatorial allies that his opposition to expansion of slavery into the territories was firm. The amendment died in the upper chamber.

With Lincoln's inauguration on March 4, 1861, and his subsequent decision to reinforce Fort Sumter, the divided nation hurtled toward war. To South Carolina and the Confederacy, Fort Sumter represented a symbolic threat to southern nationhood. In the early morning of April 12, 1861, after the fort's commander, Major Robert Anderson, refused a surrender ultimatum, Confederate batteries in Charleston Harbor opened fire. Thirty-four hours later, the battered fort's garrison surrendered. The next day, President Lincoln called 75,000 state militia into federal service. The northern states responded enthusiastically, but Virginia, Arkansas, North Carolina, and Tennessee refused to answer the call and joined the Confederacy. Less than six weeks after Virginia seceded, Richmond became the Confederate capital.

The four years of bloody warfare understandably have been the primary focus of both scholarly and popular interest in the Civil War, a preoccupation that has often obscured the war's broader political and diplomatic objectives and long-term social and economic consequences. To overlook these aspects is to lose perspective on what the war was about and why each side acted as it did.

As the war began, President Lincoln had one stated aim: to restore the Union. This required that the North win the war militarily. Because northern opinion was sharply divided on numerous issues, especially the future of slavery, Lincoln had to perform a delicate balancing act to maintain public support for the war effort. This helps explain his seemingly contradictory actions at many points. A dramatic example involves his dealings with the border states. While radical abolitionists wanted to end slavery quickly, the president recognized that to do so would alienate those loyal states where slavery was protected by the Constitution. Instead, he dealt with each state in a manner that reflected its strategic importance to the Union. Maryland lay to the north of Washington, and its loss meant that the nation's capital would be surrounded by enemy territory. When pro-Confederate units began organizing and drilling, Lincoln sent troops to Maryland and suspended the writ of habeus corpus, allowing the government to detain people without charging them with a crime for an indefinite length of time. Kentucky was critical because it controlled access to western rail routes and shipping on the lower Ohio and Mississippi rivers. But the state legislature proclaimed its intention to remain neutral. Consequently, rather than take forceful action, Lincoln outwardly respected the state's "neutrality" and waited for the Confederates to make the first move. His patience was rewarded in early September when Confederate General Leonidas Polk invaded Columbus, on the Mississippi River. General Ulysses S. Grant occupied Paducah, and the Kentucky legislature declared for the Union. In Missouri, after months of vicious fighting between pro-Union and pro-Confederate forces, Lincoln relieved General John C. Frémont from command and issued an emancipation order that infuriated slaveholding Unionists in all border states.

Meanwhile, Lincoln struggled to hold the support of Republican abolitionists. Radicals like William Lloyd Garrison argued that freeing the slaves was more important than preserving the Union or defending the Constitution. But more moderate abolitionists soon advanced the notion that emancipation could be justified as "military necessity." Noting that slaves performed much labor for the Confederate army, they argued that emancipation of slaves in Confederate territory captured by Union troops constituted legitimate confiscation of enemy property. Accepting this argument, Lincoln signed the Acts of Confiscation in August 1861 and March 1862. He unsuccessfully encouraged border state leaders to support a plan for gradual, compensated emancipation. But as the war moved into its second year, it became increasingly apparent to Lincoln that it would be impossible to preserve the Union without destroying slavery. The issue became one not of goals but of timing and approach.

Whereas the North had to achieve a decisive military victory to restore the Union, the Confederacy's primary aim was to secure its independence and thus preserve slavery. In short, the South did not so much have to win the war as to prevent the North from winning. Many southerners believed that if they could achieve a military stalemate and gain European diplomatic recognition, then northern voters might demand that the South be allowed to go in peace. From this perspective, southerners began the war with several advantages, including superior military leadership and a high level of morale that resulted from fighting in defense of their homeland. The South also benefited from its geography, which included a large, heavily wooded territory and poor, often unmapped roads and railroad tracks that were vulnerable to cavalry and guerrilla attacks. These conditions would make it difficult for an invading army to protect its supply lines. The Confederacy also had many sympathizers among British and French aristocrats who considered southern planters their kindred spirits. Similarly, many planters believed they could pressure textile manufacturers in England and France to support their cause because of a need for cotton.

These advantages were offset by some significant disadvantages with which Confederate President Jefferson Davis had to contend. A major weakness was the lack of an established central government capable of waging full-scale war. In addition, many of the South's best political leaders sought military commands. Consequently, many Confederate cabinet members and congressmen were mediocrities. This resulted in poor legislative performance, high leadership turnover, and terrible administrative inefficiency. Compounding these problems was a southern tradition of political obstructionism aimed more at blocking Yankee attempts to destroy slavery than at crafting positive legislative programs.

Davis himself was a target of considerable criticism. Although a reasonably able administrator, he interfered too much in the operations of cabinet departments and often became bogged down in administrative detail. A West Point graduate, he fancied himself a grand strategist and spent too much time trying to conduct military affairs. But Davis's chief problem was a humorless personality that enabled him to make enemies quickly. He quickly fell out with Confederate Vice President Alexander Stephens, Georgia governor Joseph Brown, and North Carolina governor Zebulon Vance, all strong states' rights advocates who challenged Davis at every step in his efforts to fashion an effective national government. Complicating the situation was the Confederacy's nonpartisan political culture, which made normal conflicts all the more personal and divisive. This contentious atmosphere made it harder to overcome fundamental economic weaknesses such as limited manufacturing capacity, inadequate revenue, and excessive diplomatic and economic dependence on cotton.

By mid-1862 it was clear to both sides that the war would be a long one and that their war aims had to be reassessed and strategies adjusted accordingly. These adjustments had important diplomatic, social, and economic as well as military implications. For Lincoln and the Union, the question of slavery's future was critical. The president had exercised caution for fear of alienating border state loyalists and War Democrats, but Republican abolitionists continued to demand action to free the slaves, and Lincoln could not afford to lose their support. The issue also had a diplomatic side. Southern sympathizers in the British and French governments had taken numerous actions on the South's behalf, and vessels built by British shipyards for the Confederate navy were taking a heavy toll on Union shipping. In both countries there was talk of diplomatic recognition for the Confederacy. European antislavery leaders opposed intervention but felt it could not be prevented unless abolition became a Union war aim. On July 22, 1862, after border state leaders again rejected Lincoln's plan for compensated emancipation, he revealed to the cabinet his intention to issue an emancipation proclamation. The proposal won nearly unanimous support, although Secretary of State William H. Seward urged that the president postpone the proclamation until the military situation and northern morale improved.

Meanwhile, the war on the battlefield, particularly in the East, was going the South's way. But it was taking a large toll on rebel manpower and ravaging the land. In addition, the South had not obtained the European recognition it so desperately needed. In September General Robert E. Lee decided to take the offensive. He moved his Army of Northern Virginia into Maryland, hoping that a victory would gain diplomatic recognition and persuade the neighboring state to join the Confederacy. On September 17 he met George McClellan's Army of the Potomac at Antietam Creek. The bloody battle there was a military draw but strategically decisive. By stopping Lee's invasion, it all but eliminated the South's hopes of diplomatic intervention and gave Lincoln the "victory" he needed to issue the Emancipation Proclamation.

Six days after the battle, Lincoln announced his preliminary proclamation and stated that slaves in states still in rebellion on January 1, 1863, would be "forever free." In truth, the Emancipation Proclamation did not immediately free a single slave. It did not affect slaves in the border states or those in parts of the South already under federal control. From a legal-constitutional standpoint, it was a conservative measure based on the doctrine of military necessity. A constitutional amendment would be necessary to abolish slavery permanently, and that could not occur until the war was won. In the meantime, the proclamation encouraged thousands of slaves to desert their owners and gave Union generals the power to liberate slaves in Confederate territory captured after the document took effect. Most important, the proclamation made abolition a formal war aim, giving the Union the moral advantage not only at home but in the court of world opinion. In short, the war's purpose was transformed from restoring the Union as it had been to creating a new nation without slavery.

Emancipation was one of many social and economic changes that helped transform American society as civil war became total war. As casualty lists lengthened, both sides resorted to the draft to replenish their ranks. The Confederate Congress enacted its first conscription law in April 1862, and the federal Congress passed its own draft law in March 1863. The primary motive for the Union draft law was to encourage enlistments, and to a large degree it succeeded, but draft laws on both sides were riddled with loopholes that led to charges that the conflict was "a rich man's war and a poor man's fight."

Although this charge has been largely refuted, opposition to the war and the draft certainly had elements of class warfare. Northern Democrats opposed to the Emancipation Proclamation charged that the draft would require working-class whites to fight a war to free the slaves, who would then move North and take their jobs. Several antidraft riots erupted during the summer of 1863, the most violent in New York City, where in mid-July mobs of mostly Irish Americans lynched blacks, burned draft offices, and destroyed the homes of Republican leaders. It took city police and regiments of the Army of the Potomac four days to quell the violence. Class warfare of a different sort broke out in the South. By the summer of 1862 several areas were suffering from severe inflation and food shortages as a result of destruction of croplands, demands for food by the army, and a shortage of manpower to cultivate crops. By the spring of 1863 civilian food supplies were almost gone, and bread riots broke out in several cities. In Richmond, hundreds of women and boys looted stores before the militia brought the violence under control. Better crops that summer improved the situation for a time, but food shortages were a recurring problem in the South throughout the war.

Almost as controversial as conscription in the North was the issue of enlisting blacks as soldiers. Some abolitionists had proposed such a move during the summer of 1862. Lincoln believed in the concept but rejected it for the moment for fear of losing the support of the border states and of giving the Democrats an issue for the fall congressional races and the 1863 gubernatorial contests in Ohio and Pennsylvania. But the Emancipation Proclamation and passage of the 1863 Conscription Act gave the idea of allowing blacks to fight for their own freedom powerful logic. Lincoln openly endorsed the recruitment of black troops in March 1863, and by late spring numerous regiments had been organized. Led by white officers and paid less than their white counterparts, these black troops were initially expected to perform labor, supply, and garrison duties, but when given the opportunity to fight, they performed well. Their courage not only torpedoed Democratic opposition to use of black troops but helped abolitionists obtain legislation in 1864 to give them equal pay. By the war's end, at least 179,000 troops had been enlisted. Their performance played a vital role in passage of Reconstruction legislation and constitutional amendments to abolish slavery and give blacks equal citizenship status.

The Civil War had a profound impact on the American economy. The years before the war witnessed many modernizing tendencies, particularly the application of new technologies in agriculture, transportation, and manufacturing, but the benefits of these changes were concentrated in the North. On the eve of the war, southern cotton remained the nation's dominant export commodity and the most expansive force in the American economy. The drive by planters to protect King Cotton and promote its expansion blocked other improvements sought by northern businessmen, such as a national banking and currency system, a transcontinental railroad, federal assistance to higher education, and distribution of public land to farmers.

Secession made it impossible for southerners to block the forces of modernization any longer. The effects were not long in coming. As a result of the Union blockade and European crop failures in the early 1860s, northern grain and other foodstuffs displaced cotton as America's chief export, helping also to cement diplomatic relations with England and France. Large-scale demand for food to feed the troops, at a price acceptable to government purchasing agents, also stimulated output while driving down production costs.

Meanwhile, the need to move goods and troops stimulated improvements in transportation. Soaring traffic volume on the internal waterways, along with a need for more naval and merchant vessels, triggered a boom in production of both river and seagoing craft. Even greater expansion occurred in the railroad industry. To handle vastly increased traffic, northern railroads laid thousands of miles of new track, double-tracked busy corridors, built new bridges across rivers and valleys, standardized rail gauges, and built union terminals in major cities. The Confederacy too struggled to expand its rail system, but it faced the added burden of rebuilding tracks and bridges destroyed by invading Yankees or by Confederate cavalry and guerrillas to prevent their use by Union troops. As Union armies occupied large sections of the South, Confederate railroads came under control of the United States Military Railroads (USMRR), a branch of the War Department. To supply advancing troops, the USMRR rebuilt wrecked tracks and facilities, laid new lines, and acquired new locomotives and cars. By the end of the war, the USMRR operated the largest rail system in the world.

For American industry, the Civil War was a mixed blessing. Industries that made a direct contribution to the war effort, such as firearms, leather, explosives, wagon building, clothing, iron production, and coal mining, experienced significant growth. Particularly notable is that many industries grew despite the loss of skilled workers to military service. The shortage of workers was overcome by the use of unskilled women and children and the introduction of new technologies. But many industries, such as cotton textiles and shoes, suffered because of the loss of the southern market and the redirection of capital to production of war-related goods that had little long-term civilian use.

The South also experienced rather substantial industrial development, as the Confederate ordnance chief, General Josiah Gorgas, established dozens of factories across the South to produce arms and ammunition. But war-induced industrialization was temporary. As the Union armies advanced, they destroyed most of the new factories. By the war's end the South was worse off industrially than it had been before secession.

From a purely statistical perspective, economic growth during the war years was roughly even with the decades before and after the war, but such comparisons must take into account both the North's considerable economic growth and the balancing effect of the destruction of southern resources, productive capability, and purchasing power. It also must be remembered that growth measures for the immediate postwar years reflect the cost of rebuilding the South's productive capability as well as new investment. The Civil War's most important economic consequence, however, was the reordering of the nation's political economy. Just as the North won the war on the battlefield, its industrial might became the driving force in the national economy, and its political power provided the social force behind economic modernization.

The restructuring of the nation's political and economic landscape became apparent well before the war ended. Not only did the Emancipation Proclamation represent the triumph of the free-soil doctrine, but also congressional Republicans enacted a host of bills to advance the development of a modern capitalist economy. In 1862 Congress enacted three pieces of legislation that embodied various forms of capital development. The Homestead Act, which granted 160 acres of public land to settlers who would live on it for five years, provided farmers with land as capital. The Morrill Land-Grant College Act gave every state 30,000 acres for each of its U.S. representatives and senators, with proceeds from the sale of the land to go toward financing colleges to teach "agricultural and mechanical arts." It represented a critical investment in human capital. Similarly, the Pacific Railroad Act authorized a grant of 6,400 acres of public land and $16,000 in federal loans for each mile of a transcontinental railroad between Omaha and San Francisco. This legislation, along with larger grants and loans two years later, was an investment in development capital to expand markets and tap the West's vast natural resources.

Wartime financial needs created an opportunity to build a sound national banking and currency system. The Legal Tender Act, also passed in 1862, authorized the Treasury Department to issue $150 million in treasury notes. Intended for payment of nearly all public and private debts, "greenbacks" served as a ready medium of circulating currency, both facilitating commercial transactions and making it easier for citizens to pay the many taxes levied to finance the Union war effort. The treasury also sold over $2 billion in war bonds, many through Jay Cooke, a Philadelphia banker. Although the bonds were aimed originally at large investors, Cooke's agents blanketed the country, selling securities to average citizens, including the families of soldiers. By making the purchase of war bonds a patriotic act, Cooke helped democratize the marketing of government bonds and forge a stronger link between the general public and the nation's financial community.

The objectives of the National Banking Acts of 1863 and 1864 were to establish a new central banking system, create a market for war bonds, and create a more stable bank note currency. These acts provided for the organization of federally chartered banks, which would issue national bank notes backed by government bonds. The goal was to use the national bank notes to drive less stable state bank notes out of circulation. The system caught on slowly, but in March 1865 Congress enacted a 10 percent tax on state bank notes. By year's end, most state bank notes had been withdrawn, and most state banks had obtained federal charters. The banking system created by the National Banking Acts operated until establishment of the federal reserve system in 1913.

Beyond their individual consequences, the political, economic, and social changes wrought by the Civil War were part of a larger organizational revolution whose effects are still felt more than a century later. When the war began, the United States was still a highly fragmented, unorganized nation. But the demands of total warfare required a high degree of central coordination and affected nearly every aspect of society. Over the four years, millions of soldiers were transformed from raw, undisciplined recruits into highly disciplined fighting units. For more than a century to follow, the same hierarchical army model would serve as the organizing principle for American industry. Likewise, every facet of war support services, from manufacture of ordnance and uniforms to collection of taxes and care of freed slaves, required creation of a specialized government bureau staffed with personnel assigned to plan, organize, and carry out the agency's work.

This organizational revolution also affected the nongovernmental sphere, where it took on a highly voluntaristic character. Primary responsibility for tending sick and wounded Union soldiers was given to the U.S. Sanitary Commission. Organized and governed by civilian directors, the Sanitary Commission recruited thousands of doctors and nurses, established hospitals, stockpiled food and medicine, inspected military camps, and performed many other functions for the care and relief of soldiers. Stressing both efficiency and humanitarianism, it was the forerunner of the American National Red Cross and a model for scores of other charitable organizations founded in the decades ahead.

The war contributed to a resurgence in the labor movement. Workers in numerous industries, pushed to the limit to meet wartime production requirements, organized unions and went on strike for higher wages. In some cases, such as in the anthracite coal fields of Pennsylvania, where the unions were dominated by Irish Catholics, workers combined demands for better wages and working conditions with opposition to emancipation and the draft in strikes against firms owned by Protestant Republicans. This pattern would be repeated again and again in the labor-management strife that accompanied postwar industrialization.

Accompanying the organizational revolution was a self-confident nationalism that emerged from the Union victory. This feeling had many expressions. For the congressional Republicans who drove Reconstruction, it was a single-minded conviction that the nation and its interests were superior to those of the individual states. Tens of thousands of Union veterans expressed similar sentiments by joining the Grand Army of the Republic, a powerful voice of national unity and expansion within the Republican party for the remainder of the century. In the diplomatic

arena, Secretary of State William Seward sketched a blueprint for international economic expansion that undergirded American diplomacy until the Spanish-American War.

The ultimate expression of this new sense of nationhood was Lincoln's
Gettysburg Address, wherein he proclaimed "that this nation, under
God, shall have a new birth of freedom—and that government of the
people, by the people, for the people, shall not perish from the earth."
In these words, Lincoln redefined the United States from a voluntary
union of sovereign states to a unified, democratic nation whose government was superior to the states and responsible directly to the people.
While the Civil War and Reconstruction set the nation on the path toward the "new birth of freedom," Lincoln's vision has yet to be fully
realized. The Emancipation Proclamation and the Thirteenth Amendment ended chattel slavery; the Civil Rights Act of 1866 gave blacks the
same rights as whites; the Fourteenth Amendment gave those civil rights
constitutional protection; and the Fifteenth Amendment ensured adult
black men the right to vote.

But even constitutional rights and protections were not immune to the
resurgent tide of white supremacy that brought down Reconstruction
and ushered in a new era of racial segregation and discrimination.
Throughout the South, blacks were denied civil and voting rights, and
blacks in the North and West were subjected to social and institutional
racism that blocked equal opportunity to education, employment, housing, and public accommodations. The civil rights movement of the 1950s
and 1960s swept away many legal and institutional forms of discrimination, but the aftereffects of centuries of slavery, segregation, and discrimination are still apparent in the disproportionately high levels of
poverty, unemployment, crime, and other social and economic problems
that affect black Americans. Until these disparities are eliminated and
racial equality becomes a reality, Lincoln's new birth of freedom will
remain an unrealized dream, and the Civil War will continue to a play
a central role in defining the American social agenda.

SELECTED BIBLIOGRAPHY

Beringer, Richard E., Herman Hattaway, Archer Jones, and William N. Still, Jr.
    Why the South Lost the Civil War. Athens: University of Georgia Press, 1986.
    Argues that the Confederate defeat resulted not so much from military
    and economic weakness as from the weakness of Southern nationalism
    and a loss of will rooted in evangelical Protestantism.
Bernstein, Iver. *The New York City Draft Riots: Their Significance for American So-*

ciety and Politics in the Age of the Civil War. New York: Oxford University Press, 1990. A vivid account not only of the riots themselves but of their long-term impact on New York City's political culture.

Bestor, Arthur. "The American Civil War as a Constitutional Crisis." *American Historical Review* 69 (January 1964). The classic statement of the argument that the Civil War was a conflict among the free-soil, popular sovereignty, and state sovereignty positions on the issue of expansion of slavery into the territories.

Catton, Bruce. *This Hallowed Ground: The Story of the Union Side of the Civil War.* Garden City, NY: Doubleday, 1956. A vivid narrative treatment of the Union war effort.

Cornish, Dudley Taylor. *The Sable Arm: Negro Troops in the Union Army, 1861–1865.* New York: W. W. Norton, 1966. A pioneering study of the northern struggle to allow African Americans to fight for their own freedom.

Davis, William C. *"A Government of Our Own": The Making of the Confederacy.* New York: Free Press, 1994. The definitive examination of the creation of the Confederacy and its government.

———. *Jefferson Davis: The Man and His Hour.* New York: HarperCollins, 1991. A balanced, well-written biography that depicts the Confederate president as a complex and misunderstood figure whose strengths fully equaled his weaknesses.

Donald, David H. *Lincoln.* New York: Simon & Schuster, 1995. A distinguished study of President Lincoln as political leader, statesman, husband, and father.

Foner, Eric. *Free Soil, Free Labor, Free Men: The Ideology of the Republican Party before the Civil War.* New York: Oxford University Press, 1970. An excellent analysis of the Republicans' attitudes and beliefs about labor and human rights that undergirded the party's opposition to the extension of slavery.

Fredrickson, George M. *The Inner Civil War: Northern Intellectuals and the Crisis of the Union.* New York: Harper & Row, 1965. A pathbreaking analysis of the reaction of northern thinkers to the Civil War and the impact thereof on postwar science, humanitarianism, and social thought.

Genovese, Eugene D. *The Political Economy of Slavery: Studies in the Economy and Society of the Slave South.* New York: Random House, 1961. A collection of pioneering essays by a leading student of slavery and the southern way of life.

Hattaway, Herman, and Archer Jones. *How the North Won: A Military History of the Civil War.* Urbana: University of Illinois Press, 1983. Examines the North's military triumph from the perspective of strategy and tactics, logistics, diplomacy, resources, and command and organizational competence.

McFeely, William S. *Grant: A Biography.* New York: W. W. Norton, 1981. The definitive biography of the Union's commanding general and eighteenth president of the United States.

McPherson, James M. *Battle Cry of Freedom: The Civil War Era.* New York: Oxford University Press, 1988. The best single-volume narrative of the Civil War and its causes.

Marszalek, John F. *Sherman: A Soldier's Passion for Order.* New York: Free Press, 1993. An outstanding biography of the Union's leading exponent of total war.

Nichols, Roy F. *The Disruption of American Democracy.* New York: Macmillan, 1948. The best analysis of the division of the Democratic party before the Civil War.

Potter, David M. *The Impending Crisis, 1848–1861.* Completed and edited by Don E. Fehrenbacher. New York: Harper & Row, 1976. A masterful analysis of the events between the Mexican War and the attack on Fort Sumter.

Pressly, Thomas J. *Americans Interpret Their Civil War.* New York: Free Press, 1952. An excellent discussion of historical viewpoints on the Civil War and its meaning from the beginning of the conflict through the early 1950s.

Rable, George C. *The Confederate Republic: A Revolution against Politics.* Chapel Hill: University of North Carolina Press, 1994. An insightful treatment of Confederate political culture and the conflicts between political ideals and political behavior in the absence of political parties.

Rawley, James A. *The Politics of Union.* Hinsdale, IL: Dryden Press, 1974. A concise summary of northern politics during the Civil War.

Thomas, Emory M. *Robert E. Lee: A Biography.* New York: W. W. Norton, 1995. An outstanding profile of the Confederate commander by a distinguished historian of the Confederacy.

Wert, Jeffery D. *General James Longstreet: The Confederacy's Most Controversial Soldier—A Biography.* New York: Simon & Schuster, 1993. A probing yet sympathetic assessment of one of Lee's top lieutenants, including Longstreet's opposition to Lee's frontal assault at Gettysburg on July 3, 1863.

Wiley, Bell I. *The Life of Johnny Reb.* Indianapolis: Bobbs-Merrill, 1940. The definitive work on soldier life in the Confederate army.

———. *The Life of Billy Yank.* Indianapolis: Bobbs-Merrill, 1952. The definitive account of soldier life in the Union army.

Williams, T. Harry. *Lincoln and His Generals.* New York: Alfred A. Knopf, 1952. A pioneering study of Lincoln as a strategist and commander-in-chief by a distinguished Civil War historian.

Wills, Garry. *Lincoln at Gettysburg: The Words That Remade America.* New York: Simon & Schuster, 1992. A brilliant analysis of Lincoln's Gettysburg Address and its role in redefining the meaning of the United States in the light of the Civil War.

Woodward, C. Vann, ed. *Mary Chesnut's Civil War.* New Haven, CT: Yale University Press, 1981. A fascinating day-by-day account of life in the Civil War South through the eyes of the wife of a powerful South Carolina politician.

Woodworth, Stephen. *Jefferson Davis and His Generals.* Lawrence: University Press of Kansas, 1990. Argues that the Confederate defeat stemmed in part from contentious relations between Davis and his generals in the western theater of operations.

8

The Industrial Revolution, c. 1860s–1890s

INTRODUCTION

The industrial revolution in the United States, usually thought of as a phenomenon of the Gilded Age (1877–1901), had its origins in the early years of the nineteenth century with the development of textile mills in New England. By the 1830s, farm machinery was being manufactured in considerable quantity, and railroads were beginning to replace canals as the country's principal means of transportation.

The census of 1850 showed for the first time that the value of all industrial products was greater than that of agricultural products, although the figures were close and agricultural products regained their lead in the 1860 census. By the 1860s, the beginnings of the North's industrial revolution were quite clear. Abundant natural resources, growing numbers of immigrants, an inventive people, and a flow of investment capital contributed to this transformation of the northern economy, a transformation accelerated by the demands of the Civil War. Still, in 1860, most of the richest men in America were merchants, not industrialists, and the relative weakness of U.S. industry was shown at the beginning of the war by the urgent missions abroad to buy arms and woolen cloth for uniforms, paid for with the proceeds from agricultural exports.

The railroad was the backbone of the industrial revolution in the United States. This scene of a railroad station in Pennsylvania, probably in the 1890s, was typical of hundreds of American towns. (Reproduced from the Collections of the Library of Congress)

The factory system had become firmly established after the War of 1812 with New England's textile manufacturing. This, along with shoe-making, iron, and lumber, were the major industries, and by 1860, factory employment had risen to over 1.3 million, not including construction workers, who, when added, drove the total industrial force to around 2 million workers.

The first few miles of American railroad service began in 1830; by 1840, there were 2,808 miles of track, by 1850, 9,029 miles, and by 1860, 30,626 miles. Chicago and St. Louis were connected by rail with the Atlantic coast by the 1850s, and Chicago was the nation's rail center by 1856. The great majority of track mileage was in the North, although by 1860, rail lines connected Memphis, New Orleans, Atlanta, and Charleston with the major cities of the North and, except for New Orleans, with each other.

After the Civil War, the pace of industrialization rapidly picked up, fueled by the convergence of a number of important factors. Further discoveries of natural resources, particularly iron ore, coal, and oil, provided the raw materials needed in the factories. Technological advances, from Thomas Edison's brilliant inventions to subtle changes in machine tools, greatly increased production. More and more immigrants arrived every year and provided a cheap labor supply, and more and more money, earned during the Civil War or drawn from real estate holdings, provided investment capital. Finally, aid from a friendly federal government in the form of protective tariffs, railroad subsidies, and an unwillingness to regulate industrial abuses did its part in helping pave the way for unparalleled industrial growth.

The period was also marked by the emergence of several important new industries that had never existed before on a national scale. Among these was the petroleum industry, which developed quickly after the first producing oil well was drilled in Pennsylvania in 1859. Oil was valuable first as an illuminant and lubricant; gasoline for automobiles was not a factor until the end of the century. John D. Rockefeller founded the Standard Oil Company in 1867 and led the way in the formation of large monopolistic businesses. Another important new industry was meat packing, which came about with the rise of beef cattle raising on the Great Plains and the growth of railroads in that region. In the 1870s, Kansas City, St. Louis, and Chicago became centers of the meat-packing industry, from where meat products could be safely shipped east in newly invented refrigerator cars. In some ways, the steel industry may have been the most important new industry of the age because of the many applications of steel, from railroad tracks to machine tools. This industry developed because of the development of both the open-hearth and Bessemer processes during the 1860s, both of which greatly increased the supply and decreased the price of steel.

The steel industry had an important impact on the railroad industry, perhaps its largest customer. Track mileage increased by a factor of six during the last third of the nineteenth century, from 30,000 miles to 180,000 miles, and the nation's coasts were linked by the completion of several transcontinental routes. Other technological improvements played a large role in railroad expansion. The safety coupler allowed trains to be much longer and thus carry more goods. The air brake enabled trains to stop more quickly, and the Pullman sleeping car made passenger travel over long distances bearable by creating a hotel-like atmosphere for travelers. The federal government helped railroads through land grants, loans, and subsidies, and state and local governments, aware of the importance of rail routes for economic survival, plied railroad officials with stock purchases and various kinds of financial inducements, including outright bribes, to persuade them to route their lines through a particular state or locality.

Accompanying the expansion of America's industrial production was the growth of big business, the administrative arm of industry. Fundamental to all ambitious businessmen was the belief that combination and consolidation (and the consequent elimination of competition) were essential to success and the prosperity that came with success. Thus most American industrialists engaged in a ruthless struggle for existence, battling their competitors for dominance of their industry. Although this period has been called the era of trusts, a trust was only one of several different methods by which business combination and the reduction or elimination of competition could take place. These methods ranged from very simple, informal gentlemen's agreements, wherein two businessmen would agree to share a market or divide a territory, to more formal arrangements called pools, in which a written, specific set of rules were made among a number of people in the same line of business to govern their production or market share. A trust was a still more sophisticated arrangement, whereby a number of corporations would agree to place control of their stock into the hands of a board of trustees (hence the name), which would make decisions for all the corporations as if they were one. Trusts often controlled a large proportion of trade in their field and could easily force smaller companies out of business (or into the trust) by undercutting their prices or harassing them in other ways. Toward the end of the century, some business managers moved in the direction of outright amalgamation or merger, wherein the total structures of two (or more) companies were combined into a single new company.

Although business combinations brought many advantages to the successful business manager, they often brought higher prices and limited choices to the consumer. Yet the general public accepted business combinations, at least early in the Gilded Age, because of a preference for laissez-faire economics, which mandated no governmental interference into what were thought to be the natural laws of economics and because of a sense that the rich and powerful were so because God had intended for them to be so, and that the reward of the poorer classes would come in heaven.

Public acceptance of big business organization did not extend to labor organization. When labor activists, often with experience in the radical politics of their European homelands, tried to create labor unions in the years following the Civil War, they ran into great resistance from the public and politicians alike. As a consequence, most of the earliest labor unions tried to be secret organizations, a tactic that never worked very well. The most prominent of the early labor unions was the Knights of Labor, organized in 1869 to combat the poor pay and working conditions that were the hallmarks of America's industrial revolution. At the end of the 1880s, for example, only 45 percent of industrial workers earned more than $500 per year, then considered the poverty line, and the average day worker earned $1.50 for up to 12 hours of work. Working conditions too were often atrocious. On the railroads, 72,000 workers were killed on the tracks and another 158,000 were killed in shops and roundhouses between 1890 and 1917. Similar casualty rates existed in the steel and coal industries, and few factories of any description paid much heed to worker safety issues.

Workers tried to attract the attention of their employers about these issues through strikes, often accompanied by violence, and through unions such as the Knights of Labor. Although strikes seldom accomplished anything constructive, the union showed some promise, as when the Knights blossomed in the 1880s under the leadership of Terence V. Powderly. With 700,000 members in 1886, the Knights were potentially a significant political force, but the organization dissipated its energy on marginal political issues such as an income tax and then bore the brunt of the blame for the Haymarket Square "massacre," in which a number of policemen were killed or injured by a bomb thrown while they attempted to break up a labor rally in 1886. Seven anarchists, four of them members of the Knights, were convicted and given death penalties, and the incident was a virtual death penalty for the Knights, whose membership declined sharply after the affair.

Far more successful was the American Federation of Labor (AFL), created in 1886, which limited its membership to skilled workers (the Knights took in anybody) and focused its efforts on the much narrower goals of better pay and working conditions for its members. Strong leadership and disciplined members enabled the AFL to survive the depression years of the 1890s with a steady core of 550,000 members and move into the twentieth century as the most important labor union in the United States.

By the 1870s, farmers in the Plains states and the rest of the Midwest began to express their discontent with what they perceived as unfair and discriminatory treatment at the hands of the railroads. For example, railroad companies usually controlled warehouses where farmers stored their crops and charged extremely high prices for the service, knowing that the farmers had no alternative. This unrest led to the formation of the Grange, a widespread political movement in the 1870s that had some success in persuading state legislatures to adopt state regulatory laws against the railroads. Although the Supreme Court initially upheld the constitutionality of these laws, it reversed itself in the early 1880s, leading to calls for a federal effort at railroad regulation. In the mid-1880s, the Cullom Committee, named for Senator Shelby Cullom, a Republican from Illinois, investigated the railroads and uncovered many malpractices. The Cullom Committee report resulted in the passage by Congress of the Interstate Commerce Act (1887), a landmark act that established the first great regulatory agency, the Interstate Commerce Commission (ICC). Under the law, the ICC could require that railroad rates be "reasonable and just," with no pooling, no rebates, and no discriminatory practices. But enforcement of the law was left up to the courts, and the understaffed commission found it difficult to prove its allegations. Farmers' dissatisfaction with their treatment at the hands of the railroads continued, however, and helped lead to the creation in the early 1890s of the Populist movement, a rural-based political movement that brought a number of reforms to national attention for the first time.

Businesses apart from railroads began to come under criticism in the 1880s, led by some well-known literary figures. Henry George wrote *Progress and Poverty* (1879), a best-seller that pointed out the great contrast between the rich and the poor, and advocated a "single tax" on land values, which George felt increased because of social evolution and not the efforts of the landowner. Although the single tax never came into being, the book raised the consciousness of many Americans about the way in which the industrial revolution was shaping society. Other books, such as Edward Bellamy's *Looking Backward, 2000–1887* (1887), which painted a utopian picture of a future America, and Henry D. Lloyd's *Wealth against Commonwealth* (1884), which attacked monopolies, added to public concern.

In 1890, Congress responded by passing the Sherman Anti-Trust Act, which declared any business combination "in restraint of trade" to be a misdemeanor. Theoretically designed to outlaw trusts and other nefarious kinds of business combinations, the Sherman Anti-Trust Act was ineffective during the 1890s. Unlike the Interstate Commerce Act, no agency was created to investigate business malpractices, and the government was reluctant to bring cases to court. Indeed, the only times the act was enforced during the 1890s was against labor unions, which on a number of occasions were declared to be combinations "in restraint of trade."

Despite the ineffectiveness of early reform measures such as the Interstate Commerce Act and the Sherman Anti-Trust Act, the attention surrounding them kept the important issues in the public arena, and when the progressive movement matured after 1900, during the presidency of Theodore Roosevelt, a suitable climate for constructive reform was at hand.

INTERPRETIVE ESSAY
Julia A. Woods

Industrialization was more than building factories and railroads, although factories and railroads were the most visible signs of the changes that were occurring. Industrialization transformed the American economy, the landscape of both cities and countryside, and the lives of people everywhere.

Industrialization transformed the functioning of the American economy. Building factories and railroads was expensive and risky. Entrepreneurs created enormous companies that dominated the industries. Andrew Carnegie consolidated the steel industry, John D. Rockefeller created a monopoly in oil production and distribution, and Cornelius Vanderbilt and Jay Gould built railroads. Many of these entrepreneurs were not born to wealth. Andrew Carnegie, for example, rose from modest beginnings in Scotland and emigrated to the United States at the age of 12 in 1848. He rose through the ranks of the Pennsylvania Railroad, invested shrewdly, and with his investment fortune built Carnegie Steel. He paid his workers low wages, prevented them from joining unions, and crushed the violent Homestead strike in 1892. In 1888, Carnegie Steel produced more steel than all the steel companies in Great Britain. In 1901, he sold Carnegie Steel to J. P. Morgan and devoted himself to philanthropy.

Rapid industrial growth created problems. In the railroad industry, for example, competition led to disaster. Speculators like Jay Gould built tracks parallel to established lines to force competitors to buy the tracks or to drive them out of business. The railroad companies fought bitterly to control important routes, offering reduced rates to large shippers, while smaller companies paid inflated prices. Gould and others bought and sold railroads, stripped their assets and watered, or inflated, railroad stock. People who had invested their savings in railroad stocks suffered enormous losses. After the panic of 1893, many railroads, which had undertaken tremendous debts to expand their lines, were bankrupt. The banking industry, which stood to lose large sums of money in bad loans, stepped in. J. P. Morgan, in particular, showed how banks could control businesses by controlling money. He and other bankers refinanced many of the financially troubled railroads' loans and, as a condition for not foreclosing, required that the railroads undertake sound financial and business practices. Soon the railroads were controlled by a handful of financially sound and efficient companies, and Morgan and other bankers became rich and powerful.

The pattern for American industrialization began with competition among a large number of small companies, followed by the emergence of a few dominant companies, causing a concentration of money and industrial power in the hands of a few wealthy industrialists. For example, Rockefeller's Standard Oil company controlled 90 percent of the oil industry, having ruthlessly bought out or driven out competitors. This emergence of big business created efficiently run industries and a powerful banking and investment industry, but at the expense of small businesses and investors.

The emergence of huge industrial enterprises had a profound effect on the lives of ordinary people. Many small entrepreneurs lost their businesses in the rush to consolidate, and they and their employees were often forced to go to work for the big companies. Fewer people worked in small factories and shops where everyone knew the owner on personal terms. Instead, they worked in huge buildings and factories, where they might never even glimpse the owner. Greater efficiency meant that industrial workers were often required to work at their utmost physical limits, making jobs in factories and on railroads exhausting and dangerous work. Skilled craftsmen were not needed as much in highly mechanized factories, so much of the work was unskilled and low paying. Industrialists had little motivation to reduce workplace hazards as long as there were more unskilled laborers, often immigrants, so desperate for work that they would risk their lives in dangerous jobs. Many workers were killed and maimed, with minimal if any compensation. One in every 26 railroad workers was injured on the job every year and one in every 399 was killed. More workers found their bodies and spirits steadily broken down by the strenuous, dangerous physical labor: 6 days a week for at least 10 hours a day. Managers fired workers who complained about conditions or joined unions, and gave their names to managers at other factories and railroads, preventing troublemakers from finding work anywhere. Few industrial workers earned enough money to support their families decently. Women and children in these families typically had to work to make ends meet, earning substantially lower wages for difficult and often hazardous work. The loss of a family member to illness, injury, or death caused not only anguish but also a catastrophic loss of income. The life of an industrial worker was an exhausting round of work and sleep, with the constant risk of injury, job loss, illness, and death.

One of the most striking aspects of the lives of industrial workers was the treatment of children and women. Children, small and quick, and thus able to dart among moving machinery in spaces that an adult would find too confining, were very useful for factory work. They were also cheap, earning significantly less than adult men. Child labor laws at first provided minimal restrictions on the number of hours that a child could work daily and limited the jobs that the youngest children could work. The idea of childhood at that time was different from the modern view of it as a time to be set aside for education and emotional growth. Nineteenth-century children, especially the children of poor immigrants, were regarded essentially as smaller adults, with as much right to sell their labor and take risks as any adult. Parents were largely unrestricted in their power to treat their children as they pleased. Also, the nineteenth-century idea of women as delicate creatures who needed to be spared the rigors of the commercial world simply did not apply to poor women. Young women, like children, were small and quick and were paid less than men, and thus were very useful for factory work. Women with small children often earned meager pay doing piecework at home, sewing or other small manufacturing tasks, and were paid a few cents at most per item. This work required long hours to make any significant amount of money. The wages these women and children earned were often the only way the family avoided complete destitution.

Many of the workers in these dangerous jobs were immigrants. Shifting industrial and agricultural patterns, war, ethnic strife and other pressures in many European countries encouraged poor farmers and workers to come to America in search of work. Many industries distributed flyers throughout Europe, claiming that workers in America earned higher wages than anyone could expect to find in Europe. Immigrants often brought their families, enduring an unsanitary and uncomfortable crossing of the Atlantic. These workers often found life difficult in America. Their appearance and unfamiliarity with English made them easily identifiable, and many people regarded them with suspicion and hostility.

Railroads were responsible for bringing in another group of immigrants—Chinese workers, who arrived on the West Coast in large numbers, imported by the railroads to work on building the western railroads. Railroad companies had found that few American workers were willing to endure the miserable and dangerous working conditions at the low wages the railroads offered; hence, they brought in Chinese workers to do the hardest work, including building the tracks that ran over the Rocky Mountains. Large numbers of these men died, and the survivors' endurance in the face of horrible conditions seemed only to reinforce prejudices against them. Only subhuman beings could survive sleeping at night in winter in the tunnels under the Rockies, or so the foremen thought. After the worst of the railroad-building work was done, many people became alarmed at the large number of such foreign-seeming people living in the United States, and Congress passed laws excluding further Chinese immigration.

The industrial revolution caused one of the most important changes in the nineteenth century: the transformation of the cities. City planning, which had never been entirely systematic, could not keep up with the rapid growth in population as European immigrants and rural Americans flooded the cities in search of industrial jobs. Agricultural depressions, in which the prices for farm products plummeted even as the costs of growing them remained the same, drove large numbers of farm workers to the cities in search of work.

A major change in American demographics resulted from an internal migration: the movement of African Americans from the rural South to northern and midwestern industrial cities. Struggling small landowners and sharecroppers found it hard to farm profitably in the face of low prices, stable costs, and the increased mechanization of farming. Mechanical harvesters, pulled by horses, enabled wealthier farmers to produce crops more cheaply and with lower labor costs. African American workers found the cities less ruthlessly segregated than those in the South. Chicago, for example, was residentially segregated, with African Americans living mostly on the South Side and different immigrant groups living in separate neighborhoods. Though they faced discrimination in all aspects of life, African Americans were not treated significantly worse than any other ethnic group and were not required to ride in separate streetcars or to show the same level of deference to whites as in the South. Many African Americans who migrated north found the industrial work very hard and were often relegated to the lowest-paying and most dangerous jobs. However, they also found that their opportunities were not as restricted as in the South, and the luckiest and most industrious of the migrants' children and grandchildren were able to buy their own homes and small businesses.

The neighborhoods built to house industrial workers were not comfortable places to live. Many European immigrants, drawn to industrial jobs by advertisements promising high wages, were shocked at the high cost of living in industrial cities. Tenements were often divided into tiny, windowless rooms, housing large families or even multiple families in small spaces. Factory workers often both worked and slept in shifts, with sleeping people occupying the entire apartment both day and night. Sanitation was typically inadequate, and residents were often required to haul water, which was often contaminated, over long distances. Some cities passed laws requiring multifamily dwellings to have windows for ventilation and plumbing for water taps and toilets, but the laws often applied only to new buildings, and many landlords evaded these requirements by bribing inspectors.

Street life in the industrial cities was also not pretty. In the nineteenth century, most urban transportation was by horse, streetcar, or train. Horses made life difficult for pedestrians, who needed to be nimble to dodge the horses pulling wagons and carriages and the manure on the streets. Streetcars, pulled at first by horses, then electrically powered, were also a terrible hazard for pedestrians. Chicago streetcar conductors were admonished in their rule books not to throw unruly male passengers from the cars without stopping first, but contemporary accounts indicate that this rule was often ignored. Streetcar conductors only slowed to let men and boys disembark, and anyone leaping from a moving streetcar was risking a fall under its wheels. Traffic regulation was often minimal, with few or no lane designations or pedestrian crossings. Women in particular found the streets hazardous since the fashions of the day required them to wear long, heavy skirts and corsets that restricted their breathing. For women, moving quickly enough to evade an oncoming streetcar or wagon was especially difficult. Many people lost limbs or were killed on the streets by streetcars and horse-drawn vehicles.

Pollution was a terrible problem in industrial cities. A city full of horses created two sources for pollution: manure and horse carcasses. Both were often deposited in dumps, which produced foul odors and contaminated the water, hardships that fell hardest on poor people who lived near the dumps and polluted waterways. Coal was an important fuel for residential and industrial use, as many factories were powered by coal-fired steam boilers. Much of the heating in cities was in coal-burning furnaces, stoves, and fireplaces. In some cities, winter weather conditions caused nearly unbreathable air. The term "pea soup," used to describe fog, refers not only to the fog's density but also to the floating coal particles that resembled tiny peas. At times, air pollution in some cities was so severe that the sky was darkened, making day resemble night. For a typical industrial worker, who worked long hours in windowless factories and lived in filthy, dark tenements, the sight of a clear sunny sky and a breath of fresh air were rare treats.

Industrialization and immigration also affected city politics. The nineteenth century saw the rise of machine politics, in which a few powerful individuals dominated political life by controlling the vote in various immigrant neighborhoods. Reformers were horrified at corrupt voting practices, in which voters, often poor immigrants, were paid to vote several times for candidates they knew nothing about. For the immigrants, machine politics had some important advantages. A poor worker who allied himself with a local politician could get help applying for his naturalization papers, and then trade his support for a job, help with problems at work, or other assistance when times were bad. For many workers, the local political boss was their only source of help if a family member was sick, and thus out of work, or if a family member died and had to be buried. A significant risk was getting on the wrong side of a political boss, which meant that these benefits were cut off and that finding employment or a decent place to live might suddenly become impossible.

The industrial revolution caused broader changes in Americans' lives. Most people's standard of living improved as a wider variety of manufactured goods became available at lower prices. Factories and railroads meant that mass produced, cheaply transported goods were available to people who before had been able to purchase only handmade, locally produced goods. For example, a typical family who before may have owned only a few locally made chairs, a table, and a bed would be able to afford such novelties as mass-produced upholstered sofas and chairs. Many of the carpenters who once made furniture by hand for local sale may have been forced to go to work in factories by the competition from cheaper manufactured goods. Other people benefited not only from cheaper manufactured goods but also from the increase in white-collar jobs for large enterprises, where they worked as managers, accountants, and clerks. Young, unmarried women worked as clerks, earning less than men but more than they could earn in occupations traditionally held by women. Although the industrial revolution made life harder for many working people, others benefited by finding jobs in the offices of large industrial enterprises.

Another result of the industrial revolution was the industrialization of transportation. Railroads did more than make the cheap transportation of goods possible. The advent of the cheap and speedy transport of people meant that the United States was not only a nation of immigrants but a nation of migrants as well. Railroads transformed journeys that once took weeks or even months into trips of just a few days. People moved from rural areas to the city and from east to west in large numbers, and far fewer people lived all their lives in the place where they were born.

Improved transportation also meant that information traveled faster. For the first time, national publications could be transported quickly by railroad, and the telegraph, which was vital to railroads, also made it possible for news to travel quickly. Reporters could telegraph their stories to their newspaper offices instead of sending dispatches that took days or weeks to reach print. For the first time, people all over the United

States were reading the same magazines, making purchases based on the same advertisements, and getting news within a day or two of the events.

Many Americans saw these changes as beneficial, not only for individuals but also for the nation as a whole. *Progress* was a term that encompassed technological advancement, industrial development, and economic enrichment. American exceptionalism—the idea that America has a unique destiny that will serve as an example to the rest of the world—has been around since the first settlements in the New England colonies. Many people believed that the fact that industrial production in the United States surpassed Old World industrial nations such as Germany and England was further proof of a unique American destiny. Progress was seen not only as a positive good but as inevitable, and that opposition to the building of factories or railroads was not only misguided but doomed to failure. America would demonstrate to the rest of the world how progress improved everyone's lives and made the world a better place.

Many of these people also believed in social Darwinism, an idea described by Herbert Spencer, an English social scientist. Spencer applied Charles Darwin's theory of natural selection to society and concluded that the "survival of the fittest," in his phrase, meant that people who prospered were naturally stronger than those who did not. Interference with poverty and wealth was a bad idea, in Spencer's view, because it interfered with the natural process that ensured that society as a whole was strong. If poor people died young, according to Spencer, then it was simply nature's way of eliminating the insufficiently fit, making room for those better suited to survival. Social Darwinism applied to nations suggested that America's economic success marked it as one of the nations best adapted to survive and dominate the world.

One of the important institutions changed by the idea of progress was the law. In the preindustrial era, people regarded the law as a moral force. The idea that progress, in the form of industrial development, was both inevitable and good influenced the operation of the law. Judges and lawyers began to regard the law as a neutral set of rules instead of a moral force. This transformation of the basic concept of law meant, for example, that industrial workers who sued their employers were unable to recover the costs of job-related injuries. In their opinions, judges often expressed sympathy toward an injured worker, acknowledging that the employer had a moral obligation to help the worker but that there was no legally enforceable requirement to compensate for injuries. Such rulings functioned as a subsidy to industry that spared industrial enterprises the cost of compensating workers and placing the burden on the injured employee.

At the same time that judges and lawmakers were recommending that industry be permitted to develop without interference, they did not apply this laissez-faire policy to workers who sought to organize. Laissez-faire is often defined as noninterference in the marketplace, but during the nineteenth century it really meant noninterference with industrial development. Workers who attempted to join unions in order to demand higher wages or better working conditions were attempting to consolidate in much the same way that businesses consolidated in order to exert greater influence in the marketplace. Judges, however, did not see unionizing as simply another enterprising activity in a free market. They declared unions to be "unlawful combinations," issued injunctions against strikes, and jailed strike leaders, all the while insisting that they were obliged to do so by the neutral rules that make up the law. Similarly, when state legislatures attempted to regulate working conditions, as in a New York law that regulated the working hours for bakery workers, judges used these same neutral rules to invalidate these regulations. Behind all these neutral rules was the unspoken belief that attempts to interfere with progress were not only futile but terribly wrong.

Not everyone regarded industrialization as positive. Many looked back nostalgically to a time when most men could be independent yeoman farmers, living on the fruits of their labor and manufacturing most of the goods required to satisfy their families' modest needs. Artisans in cities believed in an urban version of these ideas and saw the honest craftsman working in his own shop with a few apprentices as independent and virtuous as the yeoman farmer. Both the pastoral idealists and urban artisans feared that industrial development was creating a nation of employees—men who would always be dependent on their bosses. These employees could never be truly independent voters, since they depended on their employers for their livelihood, and their employers would influence their votes. They believed that dependence is also degrading and crushes the human spirit. As early as 1785, Thomas Jefferson expressed these ideas in his book *Notes on Virginia* and in letters to friends, yet he also hoped that industrial development in the United States would help Americans become independent from buying manufactured goods from England. He, like many others, never completely solved the problem of how a nation could enjoy the benefits of industrialization without also paying a cost in human misery. This problem continued to trouble people through the nineteenth century and beyond.

Another worrisome problem was the demographic effects of industrialization. Some people regarded the large numbers of immigrants with alarm, fearing that they would bring terrible social problems with them from the Old World: poverty, disease, drunkenness, political corruption, undesirable religions, and dangerous political ideas. The last two items particularly reveal something about the biases of the period. Immigrants who brought the "undesirable religions" were Catholics, mostly from Ireland and Italy, and Jews, from Eastern Europe. Anti-Catholic and antisemitic sentiments had been present in the United States throughout its history, and immigration revived these ideas. The "dangerous political ideas" were socialism and Marxism and did in fact originate in Europe. People who feared these ideas preferred to think of them as alien European imports rather than ideas that Americans, both immigrant and native born, might find appealing. The first four items noted above—poverty, disease, drunkenness, and political corruption—were features of immigrant life in industrial cities, but not everyone who was concerned about these problems blamed them on the immigrants.

Reformers saw the problems in the cities and sought to remedy them. Radical socialist and Marxist reformers sought to improve the lives of working people by transforming both political and economic structures. Progressive reformers, many of whom were deeply religious, sought similar goals but preferred to work within existing structures. Some Progressives, in fact, saw their work as important for preventing the spread of radical ideas. Unions were interested in improving the lives of working people, especially by increasing wages and improving working conditions, and their supporters held various political ideas, from Progressive to radical.

Socialism and Marxism were important political and economic theories during the nineteenth century. Briefly, socialism is the advocacy of a political and economic system in which workers both own the means of production and distribution and exert political power. Karl Marx, with his collaborator Friedrich Engels, developed socialist ideas into a system of thought based on class struggle. According to Marx and Engels, this struggle will inevitably move society from a capitalist economy governed by a bourgeois democracy to a socialist society and then to communism. The most radical aspect of Marxist ideas is the prediction that workers will rise in violent revolt to bring about these changes. These ideas were very appealing to people who were appalled at the human costs of industrial development and saw little chance for economic fairness within the economic and social world of the time. These ideas were simultaneously alarming to people who thought industrial development was both inevitable and good. The bourgeoisie—the owners of factories and railroads—were horrified to imagine their employees in violent revolt. Socialists and Marxists sought to bring about social change by a variety of means—some of them peaceful, such as organizing unions, writing pamphlets, and speaking to gatherings about socialist reform, but some of them violent, such as actively seeking revolution. The fact that most middle- and upper-class people, along with law enforcement authorities, regarded all socialists and Marxists as bomb-throwing revolutionaries meant that radical reformers faced great difficulties, including threats to their personal safety.

Unions were faced with and presented tremendous challenges. They presented a challenge to employers, who took the threat of radical ideology and its violent implications very seriously, and who found the idea of overturning American social structures quite shocking. Employers also thought they would be driven out of business if their employees demanded higher wages. Economic instability during the nineteenth century had caused recurring downturns, which made industrialists try to keep profits high during periods of economic stability in order to weather the occasional downturn. Other costs were typically fairly stable, and hiring workers cheaply when needed and firing them when necessary was the most flexible means of controlling costs. Unions threatened this flexibility, and the employers sought to resist unions with every means available to them.

Unions were faced with the challenge as well of persuading workers that it was in their best interests to join, although many workers who joined unions ran the risk of being fired or beaten up by thugs hired by the bosses. If the union did manage to persuade workers to join and pay dues from their meager earnings, it was then faced with the challenge of gaining recognition from the bosses to speak for its members. Employers typically refused to bargain with union leaders and scoffed at threats of a strike. When unions did go on strike, employers hired scabs to replace striking workers and brought in men from the Pinkerton Agency, who intimidated, beat up, or even murdered strikers. Unions responded by intimidating scabs and staging sit-down strikes, where workers occupied the factory in order to keep replacements out. In some strikes, policemen and soldiers from the National Guard or the army protected replacement workers and sought to prevent violence and property damage. Not until the twentieth century, when Congress passed legislation against unfair labor practices, were employers and unions consistently able to negotiate without resorting to violence.

Another reaction to the problems of industrialization was the reform movement known as progressivism. Progressive reformers began their work in the last decade of the nineteenth century, but their work continued through the early years of the twentieth. Progressive reformers employed a variety of means to ease the social problems caused by industrial development. Some used the newly emerging social sciences to study social problems and recommend solutions. Women such as Jane Addams saw problems and took active measures to correct them. Addams founded Hull House, a Chicago institution staffed by college-trained social scientists that offered recreational facilities, vocational training, and child care to immigrants. Temperance reformers such as Frances Willard of the Women's Christian Temperance Union (WCTU) sought not only to reduce drunkenness but also to correct social problems that caused excessive drinking. The WCTU was made up only of women and campaigned for public improvements such as public water fountains and toilets so that men would not have to buy a drink in a bar to relieve their thirst or gain access to restrooms. WCTU members and other Progressive reformers learned how to organize and lobby, and many called on these skills later in the campaign to win votes for women. Some Progressive reformers turned their attention to other reform issues, seeking to break up large business conglomerates, and reform urban machine politics.

Industrial development in the United States created an important international role for the nation. The United States' industrial production of such commodities as steel soon outpaced other industrial nations. The United States became an exporter of manufactured goods and enormous amounts of grain. Before 1800, America had imported most of its manufactured goods and exported raw materials for use in manufacturing in British factories. As the United States became an industrial nation, many American manufacturers looked abroad for potential sources for raw materials. For many, it seemed obvious that the time had come for America to become an imperial power, with colonies of its own. The Monroe Doctrine sought to limit European imperial expansion or recolonization in the Western Hemisphere, and many Europeans regarded this doctrine as an excuse for the United States to dominate the hemisphere. By the century's end, the United States had completed its continental expansion, purchased Alaska, annexed Hawaii, and acquired as colonies the Philippines, Puerto Rico, and Guam. Cuba was a U.S. protectorate, and several other Latin American nations would soon experience U.S. intervention. The urge to expand into new territory in search of new markets for American manufactured goods and new sources for raw materials would strongly influence American international relations for a long time.

The industrial revolution in America caused enormous changes in international relations, American economic development, and especially the lives of ordinary people. In 1800, America was a small nation on the eastern edge of the North American continent. The vast majority of people lived on farms, and American cities such as New York and Philadelphia were quite small in comparison to European cities. By 1900, America had been transformed. The nation spanned a continent and looked far beyond for wider spheres of influence. It had surpassed European nations in the size of its manufacturing and transportation industries. New cities like Chicago joined New York and Philadelphia as important international trade and cultural centers, though most Americans still lived on farms and in small towns. Life was indeed very different for many people. The debate about the effects of the industrial revolution and how to cope with the resulting human costs continues.

SELECTED BIBLIOGRAPHY

Alger, Horatio. *Ragged Dick, and Mark, the Match Boy.* 1870. Reprint, New York: Collier Books, 1962. Alger's novels influenced the way many people thought about upward mobility. These two depict the experiences of plucky young men in an urban, industrial setting.

Banner, Lois W. *Women in Modern America: A Brief History.* New York: Harcourt Brace Jovanovich, 1974. A good general source for information about women's experiences; covers industrialization well.

Bodnar, John. *The Transplanted: A History of Immigrants in Urban America.* Bloomington: Indiana University Press, 1985. Addresses the important subject of urban immigrants.

Bordin, Ruth. *Woman and Temperance: The Quest for Power and Liberty, 1873–1900.* New Brunswick, NJ: Rutgers University Press, 1981. An interesting history of the Women's Christian Temperance Union, an important social movement in the late nineteenth century.

Campbell, Charles S., Jr. *Transformation of American Foreign Relations, 1865–1900.* New York: Harper & Row, 1976. A useful overview, including American imperial aspirations.

Clemens, Samuel Langhorne [Mark Twain], and Charles Dudley Warner. *The Gilded Age: A Tale of Today.* 1874. Reprint, New York: New American Library, 1969. The title of this book became the name for the entire era, and the book is still worth reading.

Cronen, William. *Nature's Metropolis: Chicago and the Great West.* New York: W. W. Norton, 1991. An original and fascinating study of Chicago and its regional influence.

Cruden, Robert M. *Ministers of Reform: The Progressives' Achievement in American Civilization, 1889–1920.* Urbana: University of Illinois Press, 1989. Presents an unsentimental and informative account of Progressive reform.

Eller, Ronald D. *Miners, Millhands and Mountaineers.* Knoxville: University of Tennessee Press, 1982. Addresses the neglected subject of industrialization in the Appalachian South.

George, Henry. *Progress and Poverty.* 1879. Reprint, New York: Robert Schalkenbach Foundation, 1970. In this influential book, George depicted the depths of American poverty amid wealth and shocked many of his readers.

Gould, Lewis L., ed., *The Progressive Era.* Syracuse, NY: Syracuse University Press, 1974. An informative book covering the period from varying perspectives.

Gutman, Herbert G. *Work, Culture and Society in Industrializing America.* New York: Vintage Books, 1977. An especially perceptive treatment of industrial society and workers.

Handlin, Oscar. *The Uprooted.* 2d ed. Boston: Little, Brown, 1973. A study of immigrants in America that influenced many historians and remains a useful survey.

Hindle, Brooke, and Steven Lubar. *Engines of Change: The American Industrial Revolution, 1790–1860.* Washington, D.C.: Smithsonian Institution Press, 1986. Presents a good survey of early industrial development.

Horwitz, Morton J. *The Transformation of American Law: 1780–1860.* Cambridge, MA: Harvard University Press, 1977. Presents the argument that law served the interests of industry; indispensable to anyone interested in the subject.

Kennedy, Susan Estabrook. *If All We Did Was to Weep at Home: A History of White Working Class Women in America.* Bloomington: Indiana University Press, 1979. Presents a useful approach to an interesting, and neglected, subject.

Kirkland, Edward C. *Industry Comes of Age: Business, Labor and Public Policy, 1860–1897.* New York: Holt, Rinehart and Winston, 1961. Presents a detailed survey of this subject.

Marx, Leo. *The Machine in the Garden: Technology and the Pastoral Ideal in America.* New York: Oxford University Press, 1964. The most lucid analysis of American thought and industrialization.

McCraw, Thomas K. *Prophets of Regulation.* Cambridge, MA: Harvard University Press, 1984. An especially interesting profile of Charles Francis Adams and his efforts to regulate railroads.

Pursell, Carroll. *The Machine in America: A Social History of Technology.* Baltimore, MD: Johns Hopkins University Press, 1995. An especially good source on the effects of the industrial revolution on ordinary people.

Salvatore, Nick. *Eugene V. Debs: Citizen and Socialist.* Urbana: University of Illinois Press, 1982. A biography of the socialist labor leader and presidential candidate, as well as a good examination of socialism in unions and politics at the turn of the century.

Sinclair, Upton. *The Jungle.* 1906. Reprint, Cutchogue, NY: Buccaneer Books, 1984. Sinclair once said that he aimed at the nation's heart and hit it in the stomach; his vivid descriptions of working conditions in Chicago slaughterhouses are both unforgettable and nauseating, but he also tells a gripping story of immigrant life in an industrial city.

Spear, Allen H. *Black Chicago: The Making of a Negro Ghetto, 1890–1920.* Chicago: University of Chicago Press, 1969. An excellent study of the African American community in turn-of-the-century Chicago.

Steffens, Lincoln. *The Shame of the Cities.* 1904. Reprint, New York: Hill and Wang, 1957. A collection of articles that Steffens wrote for *McClure's Magazine* exposing corruption in city governments across the nation.

Stilgoe, John R. *Metropolitan Corridor: Railroads and the American Scene.* New Haven, CT: Yale University Press, 1983. An excellent source for information on the railroad industry.

Wall, Joseph F. *Andrew Carnegie.* New York: Oxford University Press, 1970. A sound biography of one of the Gilded Ages' "captains of industry."

Warner, Sam B. *The Urban Wilderness: A History of the American City.* New York: Harper & Row, 1972. An interesting look at the role of technology in city development.

———. *Streetcar Suburbs: The Process of Growth in Boston, 1870–1900.* New York: Oxford University Press, 1962. An intensive look at the growth of one American city.

Wertheimer, Barbara Mayer. *We Were There: The Story of Working Women in America.* New York: Pantheon Books, 1977. A good general work on women's experiences in the industrial revolution.

Woodward, C. Vann. *Origins of the New South, 1877–1913.* Baton Rouge: Louisiana State University Press, 1971. A classic work describing the southern experience during this period.

Mining was the first stage in the settlement of the American West, and gold and silver discoveries in Montana and other territories lured many people across the plains. (Reproduced from the Collections of the Library of Congress)

9

The Closing of the Frontier, c. 1890s

INTRODUCTION

Following the Louisiana Purchase in 1803, settlement of the West proceeded rather slowly until midcentury, when the Oregon Treaty (1846) and the Treaty of Guadalupe Hidalgo (1848) completed the territorial expansion of the United States, with the minor exception of the Gadsden Purchase (1853). The additional territory opened up new frontiers that stretched to the Pacific Ocean, and the discovery of gold, silver, and copper, especially in the lands acquired from Mexico, caused a rush across the Plains to the West that changed that region and the lives of its indigenous people permanently.

The settlement of the West that led to the closing of the frontier occurred in three stages. Between 1849 and the 1860s, mining was predominant, with the dream of striking it rich drawing thousands of people to the areas that are now California, Nevada, Colorado, and Montana. From the 1860s to the 1880s, conflicts with Indians were the major concerns of those interested in western settlement. And as the Indians were subdued, an influx of farmers and ranchers into the Plains region between 1870 and 1890 completed the process of western settlement.

The mining phase of western settlement began with the discovery of gold in California in the late 1840s that brought enough people to the newly acquired territory in 1849 to produce a folklore and a nickname—the Forty-Niners—and to make California a state by 1850. The gold in California played out quickly, however, and prospectors next looked to Colorado, where significant gold discoveries in the late 1850s gave rise to the nickname Fifty-Niners and the slogan "Pike's Peak or Bust!" Enough of the Colorado prospectors stayed on and went into farming or ranching so that Colorado became a territory in 1861 and a state in 1876. In Nevada, gold was discovered at Virginia City in 1858, and the legendary Comstock lode, located in the middle of the desert, yielded $15 million in gold and silver in 1859, bringing enough people to the area for Nevada to achieve territorial status in 1861 and statehood in 1864. Similar mining booms led to the creation of the Idaho, Montana, and Arizona territories in the early 1860s. Mining towns declined fairly rapidly, however, as accessible sources of gold and silver disappeared, and by the 1880s, most places were little more than ghost towns. Montana was an exception; there, gold and silver mining was replaced by copper, which allowed towns like Butte to flourish well into the twentieth century.

The rush of settlers across the Plains in search of gold and silver inevitably brought them into conflict with the Indians. In an effort to head off trouble, the federal government negotiated the Treaty of Fort Laramie (1851) with Indian leaders, in which Indian territory was defined and the Indians agreed to refrain from hostile acts against whites in return for annual government payments. But it was not long before the treaty was violated by the government, which reneged on the annuity payment provisions; by settlers, who refused to recognize Indian territory; and by Indians who did not always agree with what their chiefs had signed.

During the 1860s, Indian-white conflicts continued, and indeed, were marked by a heightening of brutality. In 1862, for example, Sioux warriors killed about 500 settlers on the Minnesota frontier and forced the state to use about half its Civil War recruits to protect remaining settlers. In retaliation, the federal government publicly hanged 38 Sioux leaders and stopped payment of annuities for four years. Two years later, the Sand Creek massacre in Colorado was a particularly shocking incident in which U.S. military forces, commanded by Colonel J. M. Chivington, killed about 450 Indians, including many women and children, and mutilated their bodies. Although Chivington was a local hero in Colorado, where he liked to display his collection of 100 Indian scalps, a storm of protest from easterners finally forced his resignation from the army.

As a result of this kind of hostility, a peace commission toured the

Plains in 1867 and recommended that Indians end their nomadic ways and be placed permanently on reservations. Subsequent treaties tried to implement these recommendations, but renegade Indians, upset by poor conditions on the reservations, continued to hunt buffalo and raid settlers' herds. This brought the army out again, and a new series of Indian-white clashes ensued. The Indians initially gained the upper hand with their devastating victory at the Battle of Little Big Horn in eastern Montana, where a large Indian force annihilated a smaller cavalry force led by General George A. Custer in June 1876. But it was the last great Indian victory. Gradually weakening from the effects of disease, alcohol, and the disappearance of the buffalo, the Indians eventually had no choice but to accept government terms.

After the Civil War, reports of high casualties in Indian battles and poor conditions on Indian reservations began to stir the American conscience. By 1880, this growing concern over Indian welfare had resulted in the creation of several Indian aid organizations such as the Indian Rights Association, which investigated Indian conditions and lobbied Congress for better treatment of Indians, and the National Indian Association, composed principally of women, which sponsored missions among Indians. Helen Hunt Jackson, a writer and Indian reformer, published *A Century of Dishonor* (1881), an exposé of broken Indian treaties that attracted much attention to the cause.

In 1887, Congress responded with the Dawes Severalty Act, which attempted to bring about a new policy toward Indians by assimilating them into mainstream America. *Severalty* refers to the partitioning of land among the Indians, and the main feature of the Dawes Act was the survey of Indian reservation land and the allotment of parcels of that land to the resident Indians. The land was to be held in trust for the Indians for 25 years to ensure that they would not sell or be cheated out of their allotment. Each family was given 160 acres, and each head of a family was granted U.S. citizenship. Any surplus land was made available for sale on the open market. The idea was to make Indians into small independent farmers, but this was an idea the Indians, who had no concept of private land ownership, could not comprehend.

As a consequence, the Dawes Act was generally a complete failure. Reformers who had pushed for the act lost interest as soon as it was passed, assuming the problem was solved. The land allocated to the Indians was often the least productive on the reservation; the surplus land sold to speculators was much more desirable. Clever speculators found loopholes through which they could obtain control over an Indian's allotment, sometimes through the device of persuading the Indian to appoint him as his guardian. Less clever speculators talked Indians into writing wills naming the speculators as beneficiaries and then killed the Indians in order to inherit their land.

Incompetent or corrupt federal agents added to the problem. The Board of Indian Commissioners made the first appointees and often chose naive or uninformed (if well-meaning) agents in the West; these were later replaced by standard political appointees, who were often people of very low character. One Republican said of an appointee: "His character is such that he ought not to hold office even if he is a Republican." Missionaries were not much better. Most Indians were not receptive to the standard versions of Christianity; only when a missionary was perceptive enough to mix Christianity with the indigenous religion by giving sermons utilizing Indian legends and the like could he hope to win souls.

Other laws and regulations attempted to augment the policy of assimilation (or acculturation, as it is sometimes called). Off-reservation boarding schools took Indian children at a young age and forced a complete separation from their native culture, teaching them skills that would be useless in traditional Indian life and making them outcasts when they returned to their communities. Indian police and Courts of Indian Offenses were used in Indian areas as acculturation agents. Indian police worked as truant officers, ran down bootleggers and rustlers, and gathered census data. They were urged to set an example for other Indians by cutting their hair, wearing white man's clothes, having just one wife, and taking an allotment. Other Indians generally scorned them as turncoats and as part of the common enemy.

At the end of the 1880s, Indians were living in miserable conditions. In South Dakota, government allotments of food were insufficient, and a drought had severely curtailed farm production. A Paiute Indian named Wovoka, who claimed to have had a mystical religious experience, became a prophet to the Indians, predicting the coming of a new Messiah. Wovoka's movement was marked by the Ghost Dance (which lent its name to the movement), in which Indians danced until they passed out. When they awoke, they would tell tales of visits with the dead. In late 1890, the army concluded that this kind of uncontrolled behavior was dangerous and decided to put a stop to it by arresting the Sioux chief, Sitting Bull. The ensuing fracas escalated into the Battle of Wounded Knee, in which some 200 Indian men, women, and children were killed. This event effectively ended Indian resistance to white rule.

By 1890, the former domain of the Plains Indians was largely settled by farmers and ranchers. These activities developed in proportion to the decline of the Indian and the disappearance of the buffalo. Before 1870, enormous herds of buffalo roamed the Plains. They had no natural enemies, but the Indians killed them in limited numbers for their meat, hides, and other useful parts. In 1870, however, there were an estimated 5 to 7 million buffalo in a range that extended from North Dakota to Texas. During the 1870s, the organized killing of buffalo almost made the species extinct. Trains, which first crossed the Plains in 1869, brought parties of hunters from the East who shot thousands of buffalo for the sport of it or to feed the current fashion trend of buffalo robes. In addition, a tick-borne disease killed many more buffalo at this time, so that by 1883 only 1,000 survived. Buffalo bones were collected for years afterward and sent east to be ground into fertilizer.

With the removal of the buffalo, federal policies encouraging farmers to go west could be more fully implemented. The Homestead Act (1862) provided a family with 160 acres of public land if it stayed five years. The Timber Culture Act (1873) stipulated that a settler would receive 160 acres of public land if he agreed to plant 40 acres in trees. These acts were well intentioned, but much of the land ended up in the hands of speculators. Others discovered that 160 acres was not enough farmland to support a family in the arid West. Still others did not have the money to get out West to claim their land. All in all, it was a difficult life, with a lack of timber for houses and fuel, unpredictable weather, and invasions of grasshoppers or locusts at periodic intervals.

As the popular musical *Oklahoma* pointed out, there were frequent conflicts between farmers and ranchers. Cattle raising on the Plains became popular with the growing popularity of beef in the East and the ability of railroads to get it to hungry easterners. Cowboys could herd cattle in great numbers and drive them from Texas or the Dakotas to rail points in Kansas or Nebraska, where they would be shipped to meat-packing centers in Kansas City, St. Louis, or Chicago. The range cattle industry was relatively cheap and thus a good investment that attracted a good deal of U.S. and European capital. By the mid-1880s, however, conflicts with growing numbers of farmers and their enclosed lands, overstocked ranges, and a succession of severe winters had greatly reduced the number of cattle and the attractiveness of the range cattle industry, which was replaced on a smaller scale by ranching. An important cultural legacy, though, was the legend and lore of the American cowboy, immortalized in literature, film, and music during the twentieth century.

Farmers enjoyed some success on the Plains in the early 1880s, despite the hard living conditions. Railroads brought many settlers out to the region, and windmills, iron plows, and barbed wire helped increase productivity. In the northern Plains, the population increased sixfold between 1870 and 1890, and cities like Omaha, Topeka, and Kansas City developed. What boom there was, however, collapsed in 1887, when a very dry summer was followed by a harsh winter. Farmers returned to the Midwest and East, with the jingle, "Fifty miles to water, a hundred miles to wood; To hell with this damned country, I'm going home for good," fresh in their minds.

In 1890, the census declared that there were no more unsettled parts of the United States. The basic frontier problems of Indians, water, and fencing were largely solved, and by 1900, all the western territories except Oklahoma, New Mexico, and Arizona had achieved statehood. Clearly the time was appropriate in 1893 for Frederick Jackson Turner to speak of the significance of the frontier and to warn about the dangers to American democracy of its closing.

INTERPRETIVE ESSAY
Michael J. Devine

Near the end of the nineteenth century, when America's sparsely inhabited frontier regions began to vanish, the idea of the closing of the frontier created anxiety about the very survival of the nation. The settlement of successive frontiers had occupied the attention and absorbed the energies of the American people for nearly three centuries. From the establishment of the earliest colonies in the first decades of the seventeenth century through the creation of new states in the Rocky Mountains at the end of the nineteenth, millions of pioneers, speculators, prospectors, developers, and adventurers had sought new opportunities on America's western frontier. Americans had come to view the conquest and settlement of vast territories as their special mission, and they accepted the claim of John L. O'Sullivan, a journalist and politician, that "our manifest destiny [is] to overspread the continent allotted by Providence for the free development of our multiplying millions." As the dawn of the twentieth century approached, national leaders grew concerned about stability without the social safety valve that had allowed room for those unhappy with their condition to start anew on the frontier. Fears arose that the nation might soon become overpopulated, face food shortages, and rapidly exhaust vital natural resources. Policymakers began to consider the need to abandon the country's traditional posture of nonalignment and isolation in favor of a more assertive foreign policy, which sought new foreign markets and overseas sources for raw materials. Meanwhile, historians came to view the passing of the frontier as a significant turning point; they began to pay greater attention to America's frontier experience, and during the first decades of the twentieth century, a new and contentious western American historiography established itself.

The frontier can be defined in various ways and, in the study of American history, the term is almost synonymous with "the West." Generally a frontier region is one that is in transition from an unsettled wilderness to a more modern, complex society, and the line of the frontier is that part of the developed area which fronts an unsettled wilderness region. The North American frontier usually was occupied by nomadic native peoples, traders, hunters, miners, and various sorts of adventurers. In most instances, there was an evolutionary pattern to the frontier's development, from basic trading, hunting, and trapping to a more complex social and economic system featuring farms or ranches, permanent urban communities, and a cultural life of some sophistication. In America, the frontier experience consisted of three general phases. In the first, following the establishment of colonies along the eastern seaboard, pioneers moved inland to the Appalachian Mountains. The second phase, following the American Revolution, saw the settlement of the Old Northwest (the Ohio River Valley and Great Lakes Region); and the third and final phase, which occupied most of the nineteenth century, consisted of trans-Mississippi migration across the Great Plains to California, and then back inland to fill in the Rocky Mountain regions and the Southwest. In recent decades historians have paid increasing attention to the settlement of the southwestern frontier by Spanish-speaking people and noted the permanent communities established in California and New Mexico prior to the American Revolution. Throughout the nineteenth century, the U.S. census officially defined a frontier as having fewer than two inhabitants per square mile.

The cost of frontier settlement was high in both capital and human suffering. The advancement of the frontier produced demands on the federal government for policies favorable to and supportive of the settlement of frontier or western lands. The westerners wanted cheap land or—better yet—free land. Their constant demands ultimately led to the passage of the Homestead Act in 1862. Upon arrival in the frontier region, settlers called for government protection, removal of the Indians, and the construction of internal improvements, principally roads, canals, and railroads. Meanwhile, people of the frontier regions usually insisted on high protective tariffs to create a market for their products. Near the close of the nineteenth century, settlers in the remaining frontier regions, including land speculators and developers, successfully secured federal assistance in the construction of huge dams and irrigation projects to open the less desirable, arid lands to homesteading. Throughout the era of frontier settlement, the constant conflict between the Native Americans and the pioneers resulted in hundreds of thousands of deaths, the devastation of Indian culture, and the eventual displacement of the Indian tribes from their traditional homelands. The advancing frontier also caused, in large part, the rupture of the federal union and the Civil War in 1861, as political leaders were unable to resolve questions related to the extension of slavery into the frontier regions.

The frontier's unstructured society and individual freedom influenced the character of the American people, and this phenomenon was noted by Europeans who visited the new nation. In 1782, J. Hector de St. John de Crèvecoeur observed that as people from many nations arrived in America to settle new regions, they quickly "melted into a new race of men, whose labors and property will one day cause great changes in the world." A naturalized citizen of New York, the French-born Crèvecoeur went on to write in his *Letters from an American Farmer*, "He is an American, who leaving behind him all ancient prejudices and manners, receives new ones from the new mode of life he has embraced, the new government he obeys and the new rank he holds. . . . The American is a man who acts upon new principles." In the 1830s, Alexis de Tocqueville, a French sociologist, saw Americans as an energetic and restless people, practicing greater equality than the Europeans and enjoying a wider distribution of land. He observed American women enjoying greater freedom and individual liberties than in the more authoritarian and socially stratified European nations. However, he expressed deep concern over the institution of slavery and questioned whether American individual liberties and democratic institutions could survive as the nation became more industrialized and urbanized. Other European observers, such as British writer Charles Dickens, found Americans, particularly on the frontier, materialistic, vulgar, and crude.

By the 1880s, careful observers of American life began to notice that the frontier was rapidly disappearing, and they expressed concern.

Americans had been conditioned to think of their nation as an agrarian utopia, an "American Eden," with unlimited resources. Some recalled that in the previous century Thomas Jefferson had warned James Madison that Americans would "remain virtuous . . . as long as they are chiefly agricultural; and this will be as long as there shall be vacant lands in any part of America. When they get piled up upon one another in large cities, as in Europe, they will become corrupt as in Europe, and go to eating one another." Suddenly in the late nineteenth century, some American policymakers noted with dismay that much of the land in the United States was controlled by foreign syndicates, railroads, or giant monopolies. They worried that American stability would be threatened by further immigration, and they endeavored to curtail it. A few of the most anxious worriers considered annexing Canada as a means of providing the growing population of the United States with additional lands to settle. The popular theologian and philosopher Josiah Strong noted "pressure of population on the means of sustenance" would inevitably lead to a drive for overseas expansion. Government actions during the decade reflected the growing public anxiety. The administration of President Grover Cleveland sought to restore to the public domain lands acquired through fraud, and an executive order in 1885 called for the removal of fences placed on the public domain by private individuals and corporations. Two years later, the Dawes Severalty Act opened millions of acres of Indian land for white settlement. Even with these actions, Americans remained fearful that the loss of the agrarian ideal envisioned by Jefferson would cause disaster.

Events in the 1890s tended to confirm the nation's worst fears about the closing of the frontier. Prior to 1890, the U.S. Census Bureau report had always featured a map with a frontier line, but the new figures from the 1890 census indicated that now such a line would be meaningless. In effect, the bureau declared the frontier officially closed. This news arrived just as the nation entered into a devastating and prolonged economic depression. Meanwhile, the rise of the radical Populist party, growing out of agrarian discontent, threatened the nation's ruling class, and increasingly militant labor unions demonstrated through strikes their dissatisfaction with low wages and abysmal working conditions. Suddenly America seemed too crowded. Hoping to stem the tide of European immigrants, worried Americans formed the Immigration Reduction League in 1894. In 1893 economist Richard Ely predicted overpopulation and disaster in the near future. "We have practically reached the limit of our free land supply," social reformer Ignatius Donnelly wrote in 1893. "That free land has been the safety valve of Europe and America. When the valve is closed, swarming mankind every day will increase the danger of explosion. Nothing can save the world but greater wisdom, justice, and fair play."

Donnelly, a Minnesotan, may have written his warning after learning of a scholarly paper recently presented by a young historian from the neighboring state of Wisconsin. At the 1893 annual meeting of the American Historical Association in Chicago, Frederick Jackson Turner of the University of Wisconsin delivered what would become one of the most influential essays in American history. Historian Walter LaFeber has written that Turner's name will be associated with the importance of the frontier "as long as historians are able to indent footnotes." In "The Significance of the Frontier in American History," Turner contended that the development of the frontier was the principal factor in the emergence of a uniquely American character and civilization. Among the first generation of American historians trained in the new analytical methods of German historical writing, Turner, like his contemporaries, believed historical evidence, particularly economic data, could be scientifically studied to provide useful knowledge. In his study of the successive American frontiers Turner observed that "American History has been in a large degree the history of the colonization of the Great West. The existence of an area of free land, its continuous recession, and the advance of settlement westward, explain American development." Turner found that Europeans were "Americanized . . . in the crucible of the frontier" and developed the "stalwart and rugged qualities of the frontiersman." Furthermore, "each frontier" had, in Turner's view, provided the liberated and increasingly democratic and individualistic settlers with "a new field of opportunity, a gate of escape from the bondage of the past." Turner concluded by stating: "And now, four centuries from the discovery of America, at the end of one hundred years of life under the constitution, the frontier has gone, and with its going has closed the first period of American history."

Following his presentation in Chicago, Turner lectured widely and published in the nation's most influential magazines, elaborating on his frontier thesis. He raised questions about the impact the loss of the frontier would have on the nation's democratic institutions and American society. In 1896, he wrote in the *Atlantic Monthly* that the loss of the frontier "demands a vigorous foreign policy . . . and the extension of American influence to outlying islands and adjoining countries." Similar articles and speeches followed. Throughout his long and productive career, Turner refined and modified his frontier thesis and attained wide recognition among the nation's leading intellectuals. Theodore Roosevelt expressed his admiration for Turner in 1894, writing, "I think you . . . have put into shape a good deal of thought which has been floating around rather loosely." Woodrow Wilson, another future American president who had known Turner at Johns Hopkins University, agreed that with the closing of the frontier, the United States needed to seek new frontiers overseas, in Asia and the Pacific. In the halls of Congress, politicians cited the frontier thesis in debating naval appropriations. In 1910, Turner assumed a chair at Harvard University. He won election by his peers to the presidency of the American Historical Association, and he was posthumously twice awarded the Pulitzer Prize. But he was not without his critics.

Historians have noted that the frontier did not abruptly close in 1890, and many challenged Turner's glowing description of the American character, which he believed featured "coarseness and strength combined with acuteness and inquisitiveness, that practical, innovative turn of mind . . . that restless nervous energy, that dominant individualism . . . that buoyancy and exuberance that comes with freedom." Critics of Turner's frontier thesis questioned the extent to which the frontier experience actually led to increased democracy, noting that the frontier's democratic institutions were usually copied from and modeled after those in the more settled states. Also, scholars pointed out the contradiction between individualism and community effort in the taming of the frontier, where all settlers relied heavily on government assistance, neighbors, and voluntary associations. Turner's critics maintained that few urban workers actually left the crowded cities for a farm or ranch on the frontier and that solutions other than a return to the agrarian ideal of Jefferson had to be found to stem depression, social unrest, and political radicalism. Finally, since the 1970s, revisionist or new western historians, among them Donald Worster, Richard White, and Patricia Nelson Limerick, have disagreed with Turner's heroic interpretation of the settlement of the frontier and have dismissed his sharp division of American history into pre- and postfrontier epochs. Historians of the new western history have attacked Turner for neglecting the issue of slavery and the critical roles blacks, Hispanics, and women played in the development of the West. Their studies have tended to emphasize exploitation of natural resources, racial conflict, and the excessive lawlessness of the frontier. However, the attacks on Turner have not lessened his influence, and Patricia Limerick has observed that "the New Western

History's campaign to declare Turner irrelevant revitalized Turner's reputation."

After the turn of the century, as the anxiety over the closing of the frontier subsided, the debate over the frontier's significance was just beginning. With the twentieth century came economic stability, a new overseas empire, and a more assertive national foreign policy. However, the frontier stubbornly refused to vanish for another generation. More homesteads were established in the first two decades of the twentieth century than in the final four decades of the nineteenth, and the center of the nation's population continued to move steadily westward. American leaders came to understand that solutions to social and economic problems required more than just free and open land. Turner himself modified his reviews on the frontier and in the 1920s urged his countrymen to abandon the "squatter ideal," which allowed "individual freedom to compete unrestrictedly for the resources of a continent." Convinced that some of his followers had misinterpreted his thesis, Turner confided to a colleague, "Some of my students have approached only certain aspects of my work and have not always seen them in relation."

Some Americans recognized that the myth of rugged, pioneer individualism had warped the American consciousness, but the myth had a seductive appeal. In a radio address to the nation in 1935, President Franklin D. Roosevelt told Americans, "We can no longer escape to virgin territory: we must master our environment." He added that Americans needed to "unlearn the too comfortable superstition" that all the nation's economic and social problems could be resolved simply with the mere application of the "American spirit of individualism—all alone and unhelped by the cooperative efforts of government." But many Americans, perhaps most of them, ignored Roosevelt's eloquent appeal and remained convinced that the American pioneer spirit and rugged individualism provided all that was required to conquer any frontier. Whether intentionally or not, Turner's writings on the frontier clearly helped advance the myth of America as an agrarian garden populated by virtuous and heroic white people. However, the myth was being vigorously perpetuated long before Turner entered the history profession. The myth has origins at least as far back as the era of Jefferson. From the very beginning, Americans seem to have viewed their nation as a new beginning, a fresh start on a unspoiled wilderness, an escape from injustice, tyranny, and corrupt social systems. Some have even viewed the nation as anointed by God for a special mission, a concept called "exceptionalism." Throughout the nineteenth century, a frontier mythology grew with the widely read novels of romantic writers like James Fenimore Cooper and the popular fiction surrounding the lives of Daniel Boone, Davy Crockett, William F. "Buffalo Bill" Cody, and other heroes who achieved mythic status.

While the physical frontier eventually vanished in the twentieth century, the frontier myth emerged stronger than ever as a popular theme for innumerable books and stories known as the western, which came to constitute an entire literary genre. During the twentieth century, thousands of movies, radio shows, and television programs have employed the western frontier as a setting for a heroic tale. Furthermore, government officials and political leaders have frequently turned to the history of the frontier, as they envision it, to explain their policies to the American public. For example, in 1945 the director of the Office of Scientific Research and Development entitled his report to the president, *Science: The Endless Frontier*. The highly technical study received a favorable review in the White House, and natural science research received generous funding in Congress the following year. In 1960, John F. Kennedy's use of the slogan "New Frontier" in his acceptance speech for the Democratic presidential nomination "tapped a vein of latent ideological power," according to historian Richard Slotkin, as the candidate attempted to portray himself as a new type of frontiersman. Governor Michael Dukakis, the Democratic candidate for president in 1988, spoke of science as the "next American frontier," and many Americans have turned to outer space as the frontier of the future. President Ronald Reagan, perhaps the nation's most effective politician in the use of symbol and myth and a fervent believer in American exceptionalism, proclaimed in his Thanksgiving Day speech in 1982, "I have always believed that this anointed land was set apart in an uncommon way, that a divine plan placed this great continent here between the oceans to be found by people from every corner of the earth who have a special love of faith and freedom."

America prepares to enter the twenty-first century with scholars continuing their debate over the nature of frontier history, the public demanding more western movies and western literature, and political leaders still looking to the symbol of the frontier to help rally public opinion. As the nation moves ever further from the time when the frontier was a physical reality, Americans hold to the belief that there are still frontiers yet to be conquered. It appears that the influence of the frontier on American civilization is a permanent and indelible characteristic.

SELECTED BIBLIOGRAPHY

The American Heritage Book of the Frontier Spirit. New York: American Heritage Publishing, 1959. An extensive summary of the traditional, heroic version of the frontier experience, with essays by a number of notable historians of the West.

Athearn, Robert. *The Mythic West in Twentieth Century America.* Lawrence: University Press of Kansas, 1986. Studies the impact of western mythology from a scholarly but highly personal perspective.

Billington, Ray Allen. *Frederick Jackson Turner: Historian, Scholar, Teacher.* New York: Oxford University Press, 1973. A sound biography by one of the most highly regarded historians of the American West.

————, ed. *Frontier and Section: Selected Essays of Frederick Jackson Turner.* Contains a good selection of Turner's writings.

Cronon, William, et al., eds. *Under an Open Sky: Rethinking America's Western Past.* New York: W. W. Norton, 1992. Contains essays tracing the changing debate over the validity of the Turner thesis.

Etulain, Richard W. *A Bibliographical Guide to the Study of Western American Literature.* Lincoln: University of Nebraska Press, 1982. A good introduction to the sources for study of the frontier.

LaFeber, Walter. *The New Empire: An Interpretation of American Expansion, 1860–1898.* Ithaca, NY: Cornell University Press, 1965. Discusses the impact that the closing of the frontier had on overseas expansion.

Slotkin, Richard. *Gunfighter Nation: The Myth of the Frontier in Twentieth Century America.* New York: HarperCollins, 1993. A careful examination of the impact of the frontier on modern American culture.

Smith, Henry Nash. *Virgin Land: The American West as Symbol and Myth.* Cambridge, MA: Harvard University Press, 1950. A seminal work discussing how the idea of the West stirred the consciousness of Americans and influenced public affairs.

Turner, Frederick Jackson. *The Frontier in American History.* New York: Henry Holt, 1920. Contains many of Turner's most important writings, including "The Significance of the Frontier in American History."

Webb, Walter Prescott. *Divided We Stand: The Crisis of a Frontierless Democracy.* Rev. ed. Austin, TX: Acorn Press, 1944. A classic study of the concern raised by the closing of the frontier.

Weber, David J. *The Spanish Frontier in North America.* New Haven, CT: Yale University Press, 1992. The most thoughtful and comprehensive study of the long-neglected Spanish frontier.

Williams, William A. *The Roots of the Modern American Empire: A Study in the Growth and Shaping of a Social Consciousness in a Marketplace Society.* New York: Random House, 1969. Places the West and the closing of the frontier in the historical context of America's development as an international economic giant in the twentieth century.

Wrobel, David. *The End of American Exceptionalism: Frontier Anxiety from Old West to New Deal.* Lawrence: University of Kansas Press, 1993. An excellent analysis of the crisis in American life generated by anxiety over the closing of the frontier.

10

The Spanish-American War, 1898–1901

INTRODUCTION

The Spanish-American War was the culmination of a generation of U.S. diplomacy that, while often low key and unnoticed by the public, prepared the nation for the world leadership role that it came to assume after the turn of the century. For many years, historians neglected the diplomacy of this period, emphasizing instead domestic matters, such as Reconstruction, industrialism, and the settlement of the West.

To some degree, the lack of emphasis on diplomacy is appropriate. There was a great deal of concern with internal matters, and the press, for instance, had little to say about foreign affairs. Henry Cabot Lodge, a senator from Massachusetts, said in 1889, "Our relations with foreign nations today fill but a slight place in American politics and excite generally a languid interest."

More recently, diplomatic historians have discovered that the 1865–1900 period may not have been so dormant as was thought. Evidence on various fronts indicates that this period contained personalities and events that hinted strongly at a new manifest destiny and the imperialist surge of the 1890s. Although the diplomatic history of the late 1800s may at first glance seem somewhat chaotic, many of the events can be linked in the ways that they contributed to the success of America's first entrance onto the global stage.

Although naval engagements in the Spanish-American War are more celebrated, there was also a significant land war in Cuba. Here U.S. troops survey the scene near Santiago in eastern Cuba in 1898. (Reproduced from the Collections of the Library of Congress)

One concern of quite a number of people during the years after the Civil War was the sorry state of the diplomatic service. Many, concerned with other matters, denounced the foreign service as too costly or nothing more than a medieval relic and tried to reduce its funding. There were, however, strong currents in the business community to strengthen, not curtail, the consular service—that part of the diplomatic corps that promoted American business abroad. The reason was made evident in 1889 when America's manufacturing potential reached a point where domestic consumption could no longer buy all that was produced. Thus foreign markets became essential to assume the surplus of industrial goods.

By 1889, the consular service had been revitalized in a process begun ten years earlier under Secretary of State William M. Evarts, who appointed consuls with business experience and began a system of monthly consular reports. The well-qualified consuls themselves used their reports to advise American businessmen in an overseas venture and give them local assistance when they came on site to develop their business.

Interest in a strengthened U.S. Navy was also a forerunner of the imperial days of the late 1890s. In the 1870s and 1880s, there were frequent comments about the rusting and obsolete navy, and boosters pressed Congress to appropriate money to build a new, modern fleet. Congress responded in 1881 with the first in a series of steel ship construction authorizations, which by the time of the Spanish-American War gave the United States a navy that easily destroyed the Spanish fleet. Much of the interest in a new navy, as it was called, came from the founding of the Naval War College in 1883 and from the publication of Captain Alfred Thayer Mahan's seminal work, *The Influence of Sea Power upon History* (1890), which demonstrated convincingly how a strong navy was essential for the continuance of national greatness.

Public interest in foreign matters was heightened by hardy bands of missionaries who traveled to remote places in search of souls to win over to Christ and who frequently wrote or spoke about their activities, and by a number of literary figures who wrote of the foreign scene or used it as a setting in their novels. William Dean Howells, Henry James, Mark Twain, and other well-known writers brought a more cosmopolitan spirit to the American reading public. Other less well-known individuals traveled to Asia, Africa, or the Middle East and wrote descriptive accounts or gave public lectures, often accompanied by pictures, of their adventures. The popularity of stereoscopic viewers and the colorful pictures that could be seen through them brought the world into the average American home.

As political and popular interest in foreign affairs increased, so too did a philosophical rationale to justify American expansion overseas. The old manifest destiny of the 1840s had used geographical determinism and a romantic sense that America was God's chosen nation to explain continental expansion; the new manifest destiny relied on the newer and more controversial ideas of Charles Darwin, altered into social Darwinism by sociologists like Herbert Spencer.

Darwin's ideas, spelled out in his 1859 book, *Origin of Species,* included the notions of "survival of the fittest," "natural selection," and "struggle for existence." In social Darwinism, human life (like plants and animals) was also viewed as a struggle for existence, and success in life was seen as evidence that an individual was among the fittest. This observation was easily converted into terms of nationhood, with those nations that had the attributes of a great power—industrial and military strength, population, wealth—obviously being the fittest nations, chosen to be world leaders and to instruct and guide less fortunate nations up the path of civilization.

Inevitably the ideas inherent in the new manifest destiny were wrapped up in a belief in Anglo-Saxon racial superiority. While belief in the white man's superiority was common before Darwin, the concept of social Darwinism left no doubt. All one had to do was note which nations had the attributes of a great power—the United States, Great Britain, Germany—and then note what race governed these nations. It logically seemed to follow that if the Anglo-Saxons were the leaders of the greatest nations on earth, then the Anglo-Saxons must be the most superior race on earth. Scientists scurried to find proofs of this. Some used the so-called race-climate hypothesis, which asserted that darker races, living in warm climates near the equator, never had to work very hard in order to survive, while whites, living in temperate climate, had to work harder to provide shelter, food, and clothing sufficient to get through the long, cold winters. Consequently they evolved into a more intelligent, harder-working race.

Believers in the new manifest destiny had an important ally in organized religion, with many leaders promoting their denominations along social Darwinist lines, emphasizing the obligation of Anglo-Saxons to spread the Gospel to the darker races and help them along the path of civilization. The British writer Rudyard Kipling popularized this with the phrase "White Man's Burden." Josiah Strong, one of the most widely known religious leaders in the Untied States in the 1880s, published *Our Country: Its Possible Future and Its Present Crisis* (1885). This book declared that because of the rapid expansion of the Anglo-Saxon race, it would soon come to dominate the world, and because the United States was so much larger than Great Britain, the United States would become the center of Anglo-Saxon civilization. According to Strong, this was the desire of God, whose commandment, "Prepare ye the way of the Lord," was directed at Anglo-Saxons.

In 1893, the United States suffered a severe economic downturn that developed into a four-year depression. Many people were thrown out of work, labor discontent simmered, and, given the laissez-faire economic beliefs of the time, virtually no government action was taken to relieve the crisis. One remedy that was frequently the topic of discussion was the need to develop foreign markets more aggressively, since one of the causes of the depression was thought to be overproduction. The depression of the 1890s went far in convincing many in the business community to embrace a more activist and expansionist foreign policy, a need made more pressing by the fact that Great Britain, France, and Germany were all engaged in a race to colonize Africa, Asia, and the Pacific islands.

By the mid-1890s, America had exerted some clout in Latin America, under the aegis of the Monroe Doctrine, but had been very quiet with regard to diplomacy in other parts of the world. And although the Spanish-American War would originate in Latin America, it would take the United States halfway around the world with a colonial outpost in the Philippines.

Cuba had long been an object of American expansionists. Thomas Jefferson had coveted it, filibusters in the 1850s had tried to conquer it, and American business interests had plowed about $50 million into the burgeoning sugar industry by the 1890s. Despite that investment, Americans were not much concerned when a civil war broke out between Cubans and their Spanish colonial masters in 1895. By the 1896 election, however, Cuban rebels had adopted a policy of trying to force U.S. intervention by wantonly destroying American property. The Spanish, meanwhile, sent a new military commander, General Valeriano Weyler, to suppress the rebellion. Weyler's tactic of herding Cuban civilians into "reconcentrado" camps, where many died under terrible conditions, was widely noted in the U.S. press and helped turn American public opinion against the Spanish. By late 1897, due largely to a much heralded press war between William Randolph Hearst and Joseph Pulitzer, publishers of rival New York newspapers, American opinion was solidly on the side of the Cubans, although President William McKinley and a majority of Congress opposed any kind of active intervention.

Two events in early 1898 were responsible for pushing the United States into war with Spain. In January, the Spanish minister to the United States, Enríque Dupuy de Lôme, wrote a letter to Madrid characterizing McKinley in decidedly unflattering terms. The letter was intercepted in New York and its contents released to the press. Dupuy de Lôme's undiplomatic language symbolized to many the perfidy of the Spanish and served to drive the two countries even further apart. The second event was the sinking of the battleship *Maine* in Havana harbor on February 15, 1898, killing 266 Americans. No one knows who or what caused the explosion that sent the ship to the bottom of the harbor, but the press and many American politicians blamed the Spanish. The crisis escalated to new emotional heights, and many demanded war with Spain. McKinley, the last Civil War veteran to serve as president, had seen war and was reluctant to commit the United States to another one. But the pace of events overtook the president, who finally passed the issue to Congress in early April. Congress passed a joint resolution making impossible demands on the Spanish, who responded by declaring war on the United States.

Militarily, the war was an easy win for the United States. The navy destroyed Spanish fleets in Manila Bay and off the Cuban coast, and a brief land war secured victory over Spanish forces in Cuba. The war was concluded with the Treaty of Paris (1898) in which the United States received title to the Philippines, Puerto Rico, Guam and a protectorate over Cuba in return for $20 million. Opponents in Congress criticized the responsibility the United States was taking on by acquiring overseas possessions and nearly kept the treaty from being ratified when the vote was taken in February 1899.

Just at the time the treaty vote was taking place, native Filipinos, expecting independence and realizing that they had traded one colonial master for another, launched an insurrection against U.S. occupation troops. At first the war was fought between well-equipped U.S. forces and native armies led by Emilio Aguinaldo. After a series of defeats in late 1899, the Filipinos abandoned conventional warfare and adopted guerrilla tactics: ambushing small patrols, sniping, committing acts of sabotage, and committing assorted atrocities.

In early 1900, the situation began deteriorating for the Americans, and the U.S. commander, General Arthur MacArthur, invoked General Order 100, which dated from the Civil War and attempted to set up codes of conduct between the warring parties. It did not change the situation markedly, and MacArthur proceeded to build U.S. troop strength up to

70,000, including over 5,000 Filipino scouts. In another part of the islands, General J. Franklin Bell rounded up 300,000 civilians and placed them into concentration "zones," like Weyler's "reconcentrado" camps, where there was much suffering.

By early 1901, the insurgency had weakened badly, and Aguinaldo was captured. He issued a proclamation urging his followers to surrender, and many did, but in September 1901, a guerrilla massacre of a U.S. infantry company in a rural area prompted brutal retaliation under General Jacob H. "Hell-Roarin'" Smith. By April 1902, all resistance had ended.

The result of the insurrection was a widespread anti-imperialist sentiment in the United States. Congress demanded an investigation, which friends of the administration managed to whitewash, but it was hard to ignore the fact that the insurrection had cost nearly 5,000 American lives and $160 million. In addition, 20,000 Filipino soldiers and 200,000 civilians died in the conflict, many from famine and disease. While the Philippines remained an American colony until 1946, the insurrection convinced the Theodore Roosevelt administration and those that followed it that there must be other, better ways to be an imperial power than by acquiring overseas colonies.

INTERPRETIVE ESSAY
Henry E. Mattox

"It has been a splendid little war," wrote John Hay to Colonel Theodore Roosevelt in July 1898. At that time, before the end of hostilities between the United States and Spain, Hay served as U.S. ambassador in London, and a few months later President William McKinley named him U.S. secretary of state. Students of the era often include Hay's striking phrase in their accounts of the Spanish-American War of 1898.

The senior American diplomat made appropriate use of the word *little* in one sense to describe the conflict. While military and naval action took place in both the Caribbean and the distant western Pacific Ocean, the conflict was short. It began when Spain and the United States declared war on each other in April 1898, and was followed that spring and summer by major naval battles in the Philippines and off the coast of Cuba and by clashes on land in Cuba. The fighting ended in August, less than four months after the opening of hostilities. Representatives of the two powers signed a formal peace treaty in December. Further, an American might be excused for calling the war "little" in the sense that "only" 5,462 U.S. servicemen perished from all causes, including diseases (fewer than 400 died in action, with 1,700 wounded). These casualty figures contrasted starkly with the total of more than 625,000 dead in the nation's most recent experience of combat a generation earlier, the Civil War.

Hay's choice in this letter of the adjective *splendid* might seem to indict him as a warmonger. But John Hay had been private secretary to President Abraham Lincoln during the Civil War and had witnessed the effects of that dreadful bloodletting. He explained himself in this regard in another letter written from London, this one in May 1898. After expressing happiness to a friend, Theodore Stanton, over the United States's victory earlier that month over the Spanish fleet at Manila Bay, he continued: "I detest war, and had hoped I might never see another, but this [war] was as necessary as it was righteous." He termed "splendid" the resounding success of American arms and what he saw as the "necessary" and morally "righteous" effort to overthrow oppressive Spanish rule in Cuba, the last of that nation's major colonies in the Western Hemisphere.

The war had its immediate causes in a mix of factors that included Spain's less-than-enlightened rule of Cuba, the eruption once again in early 1895 of long-standing Cuban desires to gain independence, the political dangers to the Spanish government of appearing to be overly accommodating in the face of demands, the American public's sympathy for the rebels, and an American press campaign featuring the plight of the Cuban peasantry. Spain did not help its own cause with its policy, devised by General Valeriano Weyler, of "reconcentrating" the populace in camps to control rebel activities. The Hearst and Pulitzer newspapers in New York competed for the more sensational coverage of these events. Additionally, the Spanish ambassador in Washington, Enríque Dupuy de Lôme, indiscreetly discussed President McKinley in derogatory terms in a private letter, which found its way into a New York newspaper in early February 1898. This diplomatic gaffe angered segments of the American public, not to mention the president. Further, certain U.S. business interests expressed concern about investment holdings on the island totaling as much as $50 million, mainly in sugar cane, and other leaders saw a need to obtain markets for American exports. Diplomatic negotiations continued, but official relations between the United States and

Spain worsened steadily, and by early 1898 had reached a stage of considerable strain.

It took the tragic destruction of the U.S. battleship *Maine* to provide the spark to set off this volatile mix. Dispatched to Havana in January 1898 to show the flag, the warship blew up in a terrific explosion the evening of February 15 while riding at anchor in the harbor. More than three-fourths of the 354–man crew perished. The exact cause of the disaster has never been determined, but a U.S. Navy board of inquiry at the time concluded in a voluminous report—without fixing responsibility on any particular party—that a submerged mine had destroyed the *Maine.* The report was promptly leaked to the newspapers. Much of the American public, urged on by sensationalist press reports, and nearly all of the Congress immediately blamed Spain, as contrary to Spanish interests as such drastic action would have seemed to be. Reflecting the opinion of many Americans, Theodore Roosevelt, then assistant secretary of the navy, privately attributed the sinking to "the dirty treachery" of the Spaniards.

The die was cast. The following month, President McKinley obtained a $50 million appropriation from Congress for arms. By April, despite the last-minute efforts of U.S. ambassador Stewart L. Woodford in Madrid, who hoped that a peaceful resolution could be reached, President McKinley found the gathering impetus toward war irresistible. In Madrid, the government of Prime Minister Praxedes Mateo Sagasta made conciliatory moves, measures that were short of granting independence yet largely met Washington's demands. McKinley by many accounts was reluctant to opt for war; he placed the matter in the hands of Congress, with his own intentions still a matter of historical debate. On April 19, the Congress adopted a bellicose joint resolution making war virtually unavoidable, while at the same time, by adopting without dissent an amendment to the resolution introduced by Senator Henry M. Teller (R.–Colorado), the Congress disclaimed any intention to exercise U.S. sovereignty over Cuba. Two days later, Spain and the United States went to war.

The course of the conflict can be recounted briefly. The U.S. Navy, well prepared to take on the obsolete Spanish fleet, carried the fight to the enemy almost immediately. The first decisive action took place, unexpectedly, in the distant Philippine Islands. After sailing from Hong Kong promptly at the end of April, the nine-ship U.S. Asiatic Squadron, commanded by Commodore George Dewey aboard the *U.S.S. Olympia*, attacked at dawn on May 1 and destroyed ten Spanish warships in Manila Bay under the command of Admiral Patricio Montojo y Paseron. It was a complete victory, achieved at little cost to the American side but with comparatively heavy Spanish losses.

Closer to home in the Caribbean Sea, the U.S. North Atlantic Squadron under Rear Admiral William T. Sampson blockaded Cuba and bombarded the port city of Matanzas early in the war. At the end of May, Sampson's powerful flotilla, which included four new battleships and two modern cruisers, bottled up at Santiago a naval force sent out from Spain commanded by Admiral Pascual Cervera. The Spanish admiral's hand eventually was forced by defeats administered to the Santiago army garrison. On Sunday morning, July 3, Cervera's six ill-equipped warships took to sea to challenge the Americans, temporarily led by Commodore Winfield Scott Schley. "Poor Spain!" exclaimed one of the Spanish captains when ordered to break the blockade. Barely five hours later, the American fleet had destroyed all of the Spanish warships, killing well over 300 Spaniards. Only one American lost his life in the action. The 200,000 Spanish troops scattered throughout Cuba now found themselves cut off from their homeland with no naval support.

The American army, by nearly all reports as ill prepared for war as the navy was ready, underwent a brief phase of training for the volunteer units that were added to the small number of regulars available for duty. The forces then experienced organizational and logistical confusion at the invasion embarkation point at Tampa, Florida. With the focus of the military campaign on Santiago because of the presence in that harbor of Cervera's warships, the inexperienced troops encountered sporadic but frequently fierce opposition once they came into contact with the Spanish in Cuba. On June 10, marines landed, to establish a base at Guantanamo Bay to the east of Santiago on the southeastern coast; they soon drove off the defenders. Some 17,000 army troops under General William Rufus Shafter began landing closer to Santiago on June 22. Two days later they clashed with Spanish soldiers at Las Guasimas, only eight miles from the city. On July 1, the American force fought ill-coordinated battles at El Caney, Kettle Hill, and the adjacent San Juan Heights overlooking Santiago (it was here that Roosevelt led the disorganized but successful charge of his famed Rough Riders). The soldiers of Spain resisted stoutly in each instance, but eventually gave way and retreated into the Santiago defensive perimeter. General Shafter considered withdrawing to regroup, but at Washington's insistence he forged ahead and enveloped the city. On July 17, two weeks after the decisive defeat of Admiral Cervera's fleet, the near-starving, disease-ridden Spanish defenders of Santiago surrendered.

The brief war had nearly run its course. American troops invaded Puerto Rico against light opposition at the end of July. On August 12, the French ambassador in Washington, acting at the request of Spain, signed an armistice agreement that provided for the transfer to the United States of Puerto Rico and Guam, and for the U.S. occupation of Manila until a decision was made on the final disposition of the Philippines. There, on August 13, Commodore Dewey's forces and General Wesley Merritt's army troops, unaware of the peace move, attacked Manila. The Spanish in the Philippines promptly surrendered, and the war was over.

With peace negotiations underway in the fall, the consequences of victory in the brief war became evident. Most significant, President McKinley decided that the United States should keep all of the Philippine archipelago, not just a base at Manila; he so instructed the U.S. delegates to the peace talks in Paris. The Spanish objected but could do nothing under the circumstances. After two months of discussions, the two nations signed the Treaty of Paris in December. The United States agreed to pay $20 million to obtain Spain's agreement to relinquish title to the Philippines, Guam, and Puerto Rico, along with its express grant of independence to Cuba. Defeated Spain's overseas empire virtually disappeared.

In July 1898 during the course of the war Congress had resolved a long-simmering issue, the annexation of the Hawaiian Islands, by joint resolution. Washington's expansion-minded leaders viewed Hawaii as vital to U.S. interests as a stepping-stone to the Orient. In addition, the navy claimed Wake Island in the mid-Pacific. Finally, late in 1898 during an outbreak of fighting between rival factions, U.S. sailors landed in the Samoan Islands in the South Pacific, where for the past nine years the United States had participated in a protectorate arrangement with Great Britain and Germany.

At the beginning of 1898, that fateful year in American history, the United States consisted almost entirely of contiguous states and territories on the North American continent. The only geographically separate area of note was the territory of Alaska, with just 35,000 inhabitants. By year's end, the American flag flew, or was very shortly to be raised, over a number of places beyond the continental limits of the United States, many of which lay outside the Western Hemisphere. Newly acquired colonies and areas occupied by U.S. troops stretched from the Caribbean far across the Pacific to East Asia. Approximately 9 million people overseas, most of them Filipinos, had come under American rule for the indefinite future. In addition, U.S. troops occupied Cuba, now a protectorate of the United States, on a temporary basis.

More changes from the United States's long-standing practice of avoiding involvement beyond its shores were to come, and soon. By April 1899, the American takeover of the Philippines had led to the beginning of a particularly vicious guerrilla war against the "insurrectos" of General Emilio Aguinaldo, who sought independence (it took three years for American forces to repress the movement and establish firm U.S. control). In September, Secretary of State Hay sent to four European powers the first of two Open Door notes concerning far-off China: the United States endeavored to ensure equal commercial opportunities in that ancient nation ruled by the enfeebled Manchu dynasty. Late in 1899, a portion of Samoa formally came under American rule following negotiations with Britain and Germany. The second Open Door note, issued by Hay in July 1900, restated the U.S. trade position and in addition avowed America's interest in China's maintaining its territorial and administrative integrity. That summer 2,500 American soldiers formed part of an international force sent to China to put down the Boxers, an anti-foreign, anti-Christian armed sect that had besieged the Western diplomatic community in Peking. America found itself engaged in military actions in both the Philippines and China. Soon after, old Rough Rider Teddy Roosevelt, as president, engineered and abetted Panama's independence from Colombia in 1903, thereby clearing the way for the United States to build and control the Panama Canal. As evidence of its dominance in the Caribbean, the United States assumed a protectorate over the Dominican Republic in 1905 and sent marines to that Caribbean nation. U.S. forces occupied Vera Cruz, Mexico, for six months in 1914 in response to what was deemed to be an affront to the American flag. Haiti came under protectorate status and military occupation in 1915. In 1916, the United States bought from Denmark its part of the Virgin Islands in the Caribbean. That year also brought U.S. intervention in Mexico against the depredations of Pancho Villa in an invasion that lasted until early 1917. In April, the nation entered World War I, the first time the United States had become involved in a conflict in Europe.

Thus, the Spanish-American War marked a clear turning point in American history. During the nineteenth century, the nation had significantly expanded its territorial holdings on the North American continent, but America had not taken over noncontiguous lands. Not until almost the turn of the twentieth century did the United States acquire overseas colonies. Establishing dominance in the Caribbean and Central America, the United States laid the groundwork for construction of the strategically crucial Panama Canal. America also instituted a significant, if exposed, presence in East Asia through the acquisition of the Philippines. The Pacific suddenly became the equivalent on the west of the Atlantic on the east, a focus of strategic interest. The nation, long potentially an important world power, had now become a major player on the international scene. As a result directly or indirectly of the "splendid little war," in Hay's phrase, the United States had come into possession of a far-flung empire that promised to rival that of the major imperial European powers of the day and soon threatened competition with the rising sun of Japan.

Not all Americans supported these policy initiatives, as evidenced by a close vote in the Senate on ratification of the peace treaty with Spain, and the Congress's resort to a majority vote and joint resolution to annex Hawaii because a treaty would have occasioned another Senate fight. Anti-imperialist forces, including important congressional and intellectual leaders, objected strenuously, if in a disunited fashion and for different reasons. Individuals as varied in their interests and backgrounds as Senator George F. Hoar, steel tycoon Andrew Carnegie, Democratic party leader William Jennings Bryan, reformer Jane Addams, and author Mark Twain all protested. In particular, opponents objected to the annexation of the Philippines. Those who saw problems, moral or practical, with the U.S. moves overseas organized the Anti-Imperialist League in Boston in late 1898, but no effective, cohesive action ever was taken to reverse the course of empire.

Those favoring America's expansion abroad—those who pushed for a "large policy" in the power struggle following victory in the 1898 war—included President McKinley (at least when it came to negotiating a peace) and his successor, Theodore Roosevelt; leading senators such as Henry Cabot Lodge and Nelson Aldrich; naval strategist Captain Alfred Thayer Mahan; influential newspaper editors and publishers, including the Hearst chain; many of the less conservative business leaders; and a large percentage of a younger generation of intellectuals. In consequence, while the issue was disputed, the United States propelled itself promptly onto the world scene following the defeat of Spain, notwithstanding a long-held belief in the benefits of isolation from overseas complications. The nation for a time abandoned its traditional policy, attributed to President George Washington in his Farewell Address of 1796, of avoiding entanglements abroad.

Historians have been no more united on the reasons for this sudden policy change than were the contemporary policymakers and opinion leaders on its adoption. The scholarly issue has centered on whether the acquisition of empire was more or less accidental or the result of deliberate policy. A related question has focused on the role of McKinley in U.S. expansion: did he effectively plan and implement the move abroad, or was he a reluctant participant?

Traditional interpretations of American expansionism at the turn of the twentieth century tend to deny planning and deliberate intent as central factors. These scholars see political considerations and the element of chance as playing large roles. The government had no prior plans to expand American hegemony and territorial holdings from the Caribbean to the Philippine seas. The president sought peace until almost the last hour, and leading businessmen did not want the interruption and uncertainties of war. The nation fell heir to an empire largely as a result of a short-lived swell of public opinion and American outrage at the sinking of the *Maine*, followed by reluctance to give up to international rivals the gains from the successful pursuit of the war. America took the Philippines because "they were attractive and available." In the 1930s, Julius W. Pratt's arguments along these general lines influenced a generation of researchers.

Beginning in the 1960s with increased U.S. involvement in the Vietnam War and the rising level of public controversy over that ill-fated venture, a revisionist school of scholars began a reinterpretation of the Spanish-American War, among other important episodes in American history. Influenced by the earlier writings of historian Charles A. Beard, these diplomatic historians founded their explanations of causality on trade and investment interests—on economic determinism. They saw McKinley as virtually Machiavellian in the subtlety of his machinations for war in response to the "large policy" views of (mainly) Republican political figures and the promptings of big business. Proponents of expansionism advanced the need for overseas markets in an economy that had begun to overproduce for the home market. Many such leaders, especially in the business community, looked to China as the principal potential outlet. For the United States to tap the supposedly vast China market, it was necessary to establish a forward base in the Philippines and to protect the sea lanes across the Pacific, eventually along with those that led through the Panama Canal. Economic considerations were paramount in the deliberate buildup of American territorial and trade interests abroad.

Whatever the factor or combination of factors advanced later to explain the Spanish-American War, by the beginning of the 1900s, the American people had adopted and implemented, even if without unanimity, policies that set the tone for their active engagement in the world during a large part of the twentieth century. That participation ranged from various interventions in the politics of Latin American neighbors to participation in two world wars and a decades-long global confrontation with the Soviet Union, a series of events that affected virtually every American living during the century. By the pivotal year of 1898, which saw the nation fighting and winning a war against Spain, the events of a decade or more had converged toward the time when the United States would be obliged to depart from its established attitude of relative political, economic, and cultural isolation. The nation reinterpreted its view of the Monroe Doctrine, thereby redefining its stance toward Europe, and adopted a revised view of manifest destiny, thereby opening a new chapter in its relations with the Pacific and East Asia. During the following century, the United States would be unable to avoid the associated obligations, advantages, complications, and dangers.

SELECTED BIBLIOGRAPHY

Beisner, Robert L. *Twelve against Empire: The Anti-Imperialists, 1899–1900.* New York: McGraw-Hill, 1968. Investigates the actions and motivations of leading anti-imperialists.

————. *From the Old Diplomacy to the New, 1865–1900.* New York: Crowell, 1975. Suggests that the nation moved from passive approaches to a new paradigm of diplomatic activism, a change not primarily related, however, to economic factors.

Brands, H. W. *Bound to Empire: The United States and the Philippines.* New York: Oxford University Press, 1992. A study in power relationships; an overview of U.S. relations with the Philippines from the 1890s to the 1990s.

Chadwick, French Ensor. *The Relations of the United States and Spain: The Spanish-American War.* 2 vols. New York: C. Scribner's Sons, 1911. The first general history of the war but one that still rewards attention.

Challener, Richard D. *Admirals, Generals, and American Foreign Policy, 1898–1914.* Princeton, NJ: Princeton University Press, 1973. Study of civil-military relations and the influence of the military during the period covered.

Foner, Philip Sheldon. *The Spanish-Cuban-American War and the Birth of American*

Imperialism. 2 vols. New York: Monthly Review Press, 1973. A denunciation of the American role, stressing economic motivations.

Friedel, Frank. *The Splendid Little War.* Boston: Little, Brown, 1958. A popular, readable account including numerous contemporary letters, reports, and photos.

Grenville, John A. S., and George B. Young. *Politics, Strategy and American Diplomacy: Studies in Foreign Policy, 1873–1917.* New Haven, CT: Yale University Press, 1966. Emphasizes strategic factors as an explanation for war and expansion.

Harbaugh, William H. *Power and Responsibility: The Life and Times of Theodore Roosevelt.* New York: Farrar, Straus & Cudahy, 1961. Good survey of Roosevelt's career by one of the leading scholars in the field.

Healy, David. *U.S. Expansionism: The Imperialist Urge in the 1890s.* Madison: University of Wisconsin Press, 1970. A review of the decade, with attention paid to both expendiency and morality in expansionist ideas.

LaFeber, Walter. *The New Empire: An Interpretation of American Expansion, 1860–1898.* Ithaca, NY: Cornell University Press, 1963. One of several important interpretations highlighting economic motives for the war and U.S. expansion.

Leech, Margaret. *In the Days of McKinley.* New York: Harper and Brothers, 1959. A detailed, sympathetic treatment of McKinley's role in policy determination.

Linderman, Gerald F. *The Mirror of War: American Society and the Spanish-American War.* Ann Arbor: University of Michigan Press, 1974. Considers the effect of the war on both ordinary Americans and their leaders.

Livezey, William E. *Mahan on Sea Power.* Norman: University of Oklahoma Press, 1947. An account of the American naval theorist's contemporary influence.

May, Ernest R. *American Imperialism: A Speculative Essay.* New York: Atheneum Press, 1968. Notes that American leadership was influenced in favor of expansion by political ideas from abroad.

McCormick, Thomas J. *China Market: America's Quest for Informal Empire, 1893–1901.* Chicago: Quandrangle, 1967. Emphasizes economic factors in the McKinley administration's commitment to market expansion as a rationale for East Asia policy.

Morgan, H. Wayne. *America's Road to Empire: The War with Spain and Overseas Expansion.* New York: Wiley, 1965. Cites expansion as part of a conscious program to extend U.S. power in the world.

Offner, John L. *An Unwanted War: The Diplomacy of the United States and Spain over Cuba, 1895–1898.* Chapel Hill: University of North Carolina Press, 1992. A detailed account, based on multiarchival research, with a focus on domestic U.S. political considerations in the decision for war.

Plesur, Milton. *America's Outward Thrust: Approaches to Foreign Affairs, 1865–1900.* DeKalb: Northern Illinois University Press, 1971. Discusses diplomatic activities during the Gilded Age in the context of preparations for America's imperial surge.

Pratt, Julius W. *Expansionists of 1898: The Acquisition of Hawaii and the Spanish Islands.* Baltimore, MD: Johns Hopkins University Press, 1936. Classic presentation of noneconomic reasons for expansion, emphasizing the support of religious groups.

Rickover, Hyman G. *How the Battleship* Maine *Was Destroyed.* Washington, D.C.: Naval Historical Division, 1976. The final verdict: an internal explosion, probably from coal gasses and munitions.

Sprout, Harold, and Margaret Sprout. *The Rise of American Naval Power, 1775– 1918.* Princeton, NJ: Princeton University Press, 1946. A lesson of the war was the need for supply stations abroad.

Trask, David F. *The War with Spain in 1898.* New York: Macmillan, 1981. Comprehensive study with somewhat positive interpretation of army's readiness; views McKinley as imperialist, albeit reluctant.

Varg, Paul A. *The Making of a Myth: The United States and China, 1897–1912.* East Lansing: Michigan State Press, 1968. Includes nonofficial as well as official reports on Sino-American relations; emphasizes factors other than economic.

Williams, William Appleman. *The Tragedy of American Diplomacy.* Cleveland: World Publishing Co., 1962. Highly influential economic explanation for expansion, based on policymakers' belief that foreign markets were essential.

Appendix A

Glossary

American System. The American System was the name given to a plan for U.S. economic development during the Madison administration. It called for the creation of a national bank, improvements in communication and transportation, and high tariffs to protect America's young industries.

Anti-Imperialist League. The Anti-Imperialist League was an organization created in 1898 to campaign against American acquisition of colonies. Andrew Carnegie funded the organization, which included a number of prominent politicians and intellectuals.

Articles of Confederation. The Articles of Confederation, ratified in 1781, established the first national government for the United States. It was replaced by the Constitution in 1788.

Border states. The border states of Delaware, Maryland, Kentucky, and Missouri, were situated between the North and the South in the Civil War. Slavery was legal in these states, but none of them joined the Confederacy.

Boxer Rebellion. This was a terrorist campaign waged against foreigners in the late 1890s by the Boxers, a secret society in China. In 1900, the Boxers besieged the diplomatic community in Peking, which was saved by the arrival of a multinational force that had marched inland.

Burr, Aaron (1756–1836). A New York politician, Burr was elected vice president under Thomas Jefferson in 1800. He killed his political rival, Alexander Hamilton, in a duel in 1804 and led a suspected separatist expedition to the lower Mississippi River Valley, where he was captured and tried for treason but acquitted. In later life, he practiced law in New York.

Clayton-Bulwer Treaty (1850). This treaty between the United States and Great Britain provided that any isthmian canal that might be built across Central America would be under joint Anglo-American control. It was superseded in 1901 by the Hay-Pauncefote Treaty, which allowed for a canal built and operated solely by the United States.

Compromise of 1850. This was a series of political measures devised to calm growing sectional tensions. It included the admission of California as a free state, the adoption of the doctrine of popular sovereignty, or the vote of the people, regarding slavery in other territories, an end to the slave trade (but not slavery) in Washington, D.C., and a new, tough fugitive slave law to help southerners recover slaves who had fled to the north.

Democratic party. This political party was created in 1826 by Martin Van Buren and others dissatisfied with the results of the election of 1824 and the growing centralism of the Republican party, sponsors of the American System. They rallied behind Andrew Jackson, who was elected in 1828. This party is sometimes referred to as the Democratic-Republican party and is the direct ancestor of the modern-day Democratic party.

Douglass, Frederick (1817–1895). A former slave in Baltimore, Frederick Douglass escaped and went to New England, where he became a leading lecturer and publisher in the abolitionist movement. After the Civil War, he held a number of government posts and continued to work for black equality.

Dred Scott decision (1857). This U.S. Supreme Court decision established that a slave was still a slave, even though he or she had lived in a state or territory where slavery was illegal. In the decision, the Court ruled that slaves were property, not people, and were forever barred from U.S. citizenship. The decision fanned the flames of sectionalism shortly before the Civil War.

Evarts, William M. (1818–1901). Secretary of State under President Rutherford B. Hayes (1877–1881), Evarts helped promote the growth of foreign commerce by raising the standards of consular appointments and negotiating commercial treaties with China and Japan.

Falkland (Malvinas) Islands controversy. In the 1830s, Great Britain occupied this group of islands, which Argentina also claimed. The United States chose not to invoke the Monroe Doctrine against Britain, and the islands remained in British hands. In 1982, Britain and Argentina fought a short war over the islands, which Britain won.

Federalist party. The Federalists developed as a faction during the constitutional ratification process, where they supported ratification and a strong central government. During the 1790s, they evolved into a loosely organized party headed by George Washington, Alexander Hamilton, and John Adams. They favored Great Britain over France in the European wars and the centralization of power in the federal government.

Filibuster. A filibuster refers to any of a number of private adventurers who led expeditions to Cuba or various Central American countries during the mid-nineteenth century, with the object of overthrowing their governments and colonizing them under the U.S. flag.

Fugitive Slave Act (1850). Part of the Compromise of 1850, this law obliged northern law enforcement officials to return escaped, or fugitive, slaves to their southern owners.

Gould, Jay (1836–1892). Jay Gould was a speculative investor, principally in railroads during the late 1850s and 1860s. He and his associates waged a titanic battle with Cornelius Vanderbilt for control of the Erie Railroad in 1868, and in 1869, he attempted to manipulate the gold market by persuading President Ulysses S. Grant to withhold federal gold from public sale. Before Grant released the gold to the market, Gould and his partners had made an $11 million profit.

Habeas corpus, writ of. This legal term refers to an accused person's right to appear before a court to determine whether he or she should be charged with a crime or released. During the Civil War, President Abraham Lincoln suspended this right, allowing persons to be held without charges for an indefinite period of time.

Hoar, George F. (1826–1904). A Republican from Massachusetts, George F. Hoar was a member of the U.S. House of Representatives from 1868 to 1877 and the U.S. Senate from 1877 until his death. He is best known for his leading role in the anti-imperialist movement.

Holy Alliance. The Holy Alliance, created in 1815 by Czar Alexander of Russia, joined his country with Prussia and Austria in a "Christian unity of charity, peace, and love."

Homestead strike (1892). This strike occurred at the Homestead steel factory in Pennsylvania, owned by Andrew Carnegie. When workers walked out over a proposed wage cut, a battle broke out between the striking workers and detectives from the Pinkerton Agency, sent in to protect the plant. The workers forced the surrender of the Pinkerton detectives, but the governor sent in the state militia, who restored order and took control away from the strikers. Their union never recovered from its defeat.

Houston, Sam (1793–1863). Sam Houston was the principal leader in the fight for Texas independence and subsequent annexation to the United States. He was the military commander of Texan forces in their civil war against Mexico, the first president of the Republic of Texas, and, after statehood, one of Texas's first two senators.

Lodge, Henry Cabot, Sr. (1850–1924). A long-time Republican senator from Massachusetts (1893–1924), Henry Cabot Lodge was an ardent supporter of U.S. expansion and a close friend of Theodore Roosevelt. Later he became a leading opponent of President Woodrow Wilson in the fight to ratify the Treaty of Versailles (1919), ending World War I and creating the League of Nations.

Louisiana Purchase International Exposition (1904). A great world's fair held in St. Louis (one year late) to celebrate the centennial of the Louisiana Purchase. Almost 20 million visitors attended the fair, which sprawled over 1,270 acres in Forest Park.

Missouri Compromise (1820). The Missouri Compromise was an early attempt to resolve the growing sectional strife between North and South. Under its terms, Missouri was admitted to the Union as a slave state and Maine as a free state, and the latitude of 36° 30′ was to be extended to the west as a demarcation of slave territory (south of the line) and free territory (north of the line).

Nativism. This term refers to the dislike of immigrants and their beliefs and values and the consequent opposition to further immigration. During the 1890s, nativist organizations argued that excessive immigration threatened American traditions and values.

New Frontier. President John F. Kennedy's (1961–1963) term refers to his domestic program of aid to education, urban renewal, and other social legislation.

Oregon Trail. The Oregon Trail was the most famous of the several trails taking people to various parts of the American West. Beginning in 1843, large-scale migration occurred over the Oregon Trail, so named because it went to the Oregon Country in the Northwest.

Panic of 1819. The Panic of 1819 came about after the Second Bank of the United States tightened credit and called in loans in an attempt to put the brakes on land speculation. The policies of the bank went too far and caused a six-year economic depression.

Pinckney's Treaty (1795). This treaty settled a number of problems between the United States and Spain. Most notably, the United States acquired full navigational rights on the Mississippi River and the right to use the port of New Orleans.

Pinkerton Agency. This private detective agency was established by Allan Pinkerton in 1850. During the Civil War, Pinkerton agents worked behind Confederate lines, and after the war, they frequently were used as strikebreakers and factory police.

Republican party. This name was first used for a political faction that emerged in the 1790s in opposition to the Federalist party and its beliefs in a strong central government and friendship with Great Britain. Under the leadership of Thomas Jefferson and James Madison, the Republicans, who believed in a weak federal government and supported France in Europe, became the dominant party in the United States between 1800 and 1824. The party is sometimes referred to as the Jeffersonian-Republican party in order to distinguish it from the Republican party of the 1850s, which developed in the North among those who opposed the extension of slavery into the territories.

Roosevelt Corollary. Named for President Theodore Roosevelt (1901–1909), the Roosevelt Corollary is an addition to the Monroe Doctrine in which the United States reserved the right to intervene in a Latin American nation in order to forestall a European intervention. Roosevelt announced the corollary in 1904. It was implemented on several occasions between 1905 and the 1920s before being renounced in the 1930s.

Santa Anna, Antonio López de (1794–1876). A resilient Mexican general, Santa Anna served several times as president of Mexico between the 1830s and the 1850s. He is best remembered for leading Mexican forces to defeat in the civil war with Texas (1836) and again in Mexico's war with the United States (1846–1848).

Three-fifths compromise. A compromise made at the Constitutional Convention (1787), wherein five slaves were counted as three people in determining the number of U.S. representatives to which a state would be entitled under the new Constitution.

Trafalgar, Battle of (1805). This was a major naval encounter off the Spanish coast near Cadiz between a fleet of thirty British ships, commanded by Admiral Horatio Nelson, and a combined Franco-Spanish fleet of thirty-three ships, commanded by Admiral Pierre Villeneuve. Nelson's victory ensured British control of the seas and the admiral's reputation as a great naval commander.

Turner, Nat (1800–1831). Nat Turner was a Virginia slave who, with seven followers, launched an insurrection in the Virginia countryside in August 1831. Turner's following grew, as did the level of violence, and as a result, 57 whites were killed, and Turner and 20 of his followers were captured and executed. The rebellion heightened sectional tensions and convinced many southerners that blacks and whites could never live peaceably together in a free society.

War Hawks. War Hawks was the name given to a group of U.S. congressmen, principally from the West, who enthusiastically urged war with Great Britain in the year before the outbreak of the War of 1812.

Whig party. This political party formed around 1834 as a coalition of groups and factions opposed to President Andrew Jackson and his policies. The name "Whig" came from the English party of the same name, which was usually associated with antimonarchical policies; American Whigs thought that Jackson, as president, had become too powerful.

Appendix B

Timeline

1800	Federal government moves from Philadelphia to Washington, D.C.
1801	Tripoli declares war on United States
1803	In *Marbury v. Madison* Supreme Court overturns a U.S. law for the first time
	France sells Louisiana to United States
1804	Lewis and Clark expedition leaves from St. Louis
	Aaron Burr kills Alexander Hamilton in a duel
1805	Zebulon Pike explores Colorado and New Mexico
1807	Robert Fulton builds first steamboat
	Embargo Act bans all foreign trade
1808	Slave importation outlawed
1811	William H. Harrison defeats Indians at Battle of Tippecanoe
	Cumberland Trail opens
1812	War of 1812 with Britain begins
	British capture Detroit
1813	Oliver Perry defeats British fleet on Lake Erie
1814	British burn Capitol and White House

	British fleet repulsed at Fort McHenry
	Francis Scott Key writes "Star Spangled Banner"
	Treaty of Ghent ends War of 1812
1815	United States wins Battle of New Orleans
	Congress authorizes peacetime army
1816	Second Bank of the United States chartered
1817	Rush-Bagot treaty signed limiting armaments on the Great Lakes
1819	Spain cedes Florida to United States in Adams-Onís Treaty
	U.S.S. Savannah makes first partial steam crossing of the Atlantic
1820	First immigration of blacks back to Africa begins
	Missouri Compromise passed by Congress
1821	First college for women, Troy Female Seminary, founded by Emma Willard
1823	Monroe Doctrine pronounced
1825	Erie Canal completed
	John Stevens builds first steam locomotive in United States
1828	South Carolina declares that states have the right to nullify federal laws
	American Dictionary of the English Language, published by Noah Webster
	Baltimore & Ohio, first passenger railroad, inaugurated
1830	Joseph Smith founds Mormon church
1831	Abolitionist newspaper, the *Liberator,* started by William Lloyd Garrison
	Nat Turner leads slave insurrection in Virginia
1832	South Carolina threatens withdrawal from the Union
	Congress passes compromise tariff act; South Carolina remains in Union
1833	First coeducational college, Oberlin College, founded
1835	Seminole war begins
	Texas declares right to secede from Mexico
	Oberlin College refuses to bar students because of race

1836	Battle of the Alamo
	Battle of San Jacinto; Texas wins independence
	First white women cross Oregon Trail
1838	Cherokee forcibly removed to Oklahoma in "Trail of Tears"
1841	First wagon train reaches California
1842	Seminole war ends; Indians removed to Oklahoma
	Webster-Ashburton Treaty establishes border between Canada and Minnesota and Maine
	First use of anesthetic
1844	Samuel Morse sends first telegraph message
1845	Texas annexed and admitted to Union
1846	Mexican War begins
	California declares itself a republic
	United States and Great Britain sign Oregon Treaty
	Mormons under Brigham Young settle in Utah
	Elias Howe invents sewing machine
1847	First adhesive postage stamp issued
	Henry Wadsworth Longfellow publishes *Evangeline*
1848	Treaty of Guadalupe Hidalgo, ending Mexican War; cedes California, Arizona, Nevada, Utah, Colorado, and New Mexico to United States
	Women's Rights Convention, led by Elizabeth Cady Stanton and Lucretia Mott, held at Seneca Falls, New York
	Gold discovered in California
1850	Compromise of 1850 allows admission of California to Union
	Slave trade in District of Columbia forbidden
1852	Harriet Beecher Stowe publishes *Uncle Tom's Cabin*
1853	Commodore Matthew Perry negotiates treaty to open Japan to trade
	Gadsden Purchase settles boundary with Mexico
1854	Republican party formed
	Henry David Thoreau publishes *Walden*
1855	Walt Whitman publishes *Leaves of Grass*

	First railroad crosses Mississippi River
1856	Lawrence, Kansas, sacked by proslavery forces
1857	*Dred Scott* decision
1858	Lincoln-Douglas debates
1859	First commercial oil well drilled
	John Brown leads raid on Harpers Ferry
	John Brown hanged for treason
1860	Abraham Lincoln elected president
	Pony express between Sacramento, California, and St. Joseph, Missouri, begins
1861	Seven southern states set up Confederate States of America
	Firing on Fort Sumter starts Civil War
	Lincoln calls for 75,000 volunteers
	First Battle of Bull Run
	First transcontinental telegraph in operation
	Trent Affair strains relations with Britain
1862	Homestead Act passed by Congress
	Morrill Act passed by Congress, leading to establishing state land grant universities
	New Orleans falls to North
	Battle of Shiloh
	Battle of Antietam
1863	Emancipation Proclamation
	Battle of Gettysburg
	Vicksburg falls to North
	Lincoln gives Gettysburg Address
	Draft riots in New York City
1864	Sherman takes Atlanta
	Indian massacre at Sand Creek, Colorado Territory
1865	Robert E. Lee surrenders to Ulysses S. Grant, ending Civil War
	Abraham Lincoln assassinated
	Thirteenth Amendment abolishes slavery
1866	Ku Klux Klan formed

	Fourteenth Amendment gives blacks citizenship and protection of civil rights
1867	Alaska purchased from Russia
	The Grange organized
1868	Andrew Johnson impeached, but Senate fails to convict
1869	Attempt to corner gold market causes "Black Friday" in New York
	First transcontinental railroad completed
	Knights of Labor formed
	Women suffrage law passed in Wyoming Territory
	First college football game played
1871	Great fire destroys much of Chicago
	Civil Service Commission established
1872	Amnesty Act restores civil rights in South
	Congress makes Yellowstone first national park
1873	First postal card issued
	Bank panic and beginning of depression
	William "Boss" Tweed convicted of stealing public funds
1875	First Kentucky Derby held
1876	General George A. Custer killed by Indians at Battle of Little Big Horn
	National [Baseball] League established
	Mark Twain publishes *Tom Sawyer*
	Centennial Exhibition held in Philadelphia
1877	Molly Maguires, a radical labor group, broken up
	Troops used to end railroad strike
1878	First commercial telephone exchange opened
	Thomas Edison founds Edison Electric Light Co.
1879	First five-and-dime opened by F. W. Woolworth
1881	President James A. Garfield assassinated
	Tuskegee Institute founded by Booker T. Washington
1883	Brooklyn Bridge opened
1886	Haymarket riot in Chicago
	Statue of Liberty dedicated

	American Federation of Labor formed
1887	Interstate Commerce Commission established
1888	Great blizzard paralyzes East Coast
1889	Oklahoma opened for white settlement
	Johnstown, Pennsylvania, flood
1890	Indians massacred at Wounded Knee, South Dakota
	Sherman Anti-Trust Act passed
1892	Homestead steel strike
1893	Financial panic leads to depression
	World's Columbian Exposition held in Chicago
1894	First showing of Edison's motion picture machine
	Jacob Coxey leads march of unemployed on Washington
1896	William Jennings Bryan delivers "Cross of Gold" speech
	Plessy v. Ferguson permits "separate but equal" doctrine in race relations
1898	Battleship *Maine* sunk in Havana harbor
	Spain declares war on United States
	United States annexes Hawaii
	Spain cedes Philippines, Puerto Rico, and Guam and permits Cuban independence, ending Spanish-American War
1899	United States declares Open Door Policy in China

Appendix C

Presidents, Vice Presidents, and Secretaries of State in the Nineteenth Century

President	Vice President	Secretary of State
Thomas Jefferson (1801)	Aaron Burr (1801)	James Madison (1801)
	George Clinton (1805)	
James Madison (1809)	George Clinton (1809)	Robert Smith (1809)
	Elbridge Gerry (1813)	James Monroe (1811)
James Monroe (1817)	Daniel D. Tompkins (1817)	John Quincy Adams (1817)
John Quincy Adams (1825)	John C. Calhoun (1825)	Henry Clay (1825)
Andrew Jackson (1829)	John C. Calhoun (1829)	Martin Van Buren (1829)
	Martin Van Buren (1833)	Edward Livingston (1831)
		James McLane (1833)
		John Forsyth (1834)
Martin Van Buren (1837)	Richard M. Johnson (1837)	John Forsyth (1837)
William H. Harrison (1841)	John Tyler (1841)	Daniel Webster (1841)
John Tyler (1841)		Daniel Webster (1841)
		Abel P. Upshur (1843)
		John C. Calhoun (1844)
James K. Polk (1845)	George M. Dallas (1845)	James Buchanan (1845)
Zachary Taylor (1849)	Millard Fillmore (1849)	John M. Clayton (1849)
Millard Fillmore (1850)		Daniel Webster (1850)
		Edward Everett (1852)
Franklin Pierce (1853)	William King (1853)	William L. Marcy (1853)

James Buchanan (1857)	John C. Breckinridge (1857)	Lewis Cass (1857)
		Jeremiah S. Black (1860)
Abraham Lincoln (1861)	Hannibal Hamlin (1861)	William H. Seward (1861)
	Andrew Johnson (1865)	
Andrew Johnson (1865)		William H. Seward (1865)
Ulysses S. Grant (1869)	Schuyler Colfax (1869)	Elihu B. Washburne (1869)
	Henry Wilson (1873)	Hamilton Fish (1869)
Rutherford B. Hayes (1877)	William A. Wheeler (1877)	William M. Evarts (1877)
James A. Garfield (1881)	Chester A. Arthur (1881)	James G. Blaine (1881)
Chester A. Arthur (1881)		F. T. Frelinghuysen (1881)
Grover Cleveland (1885)	Thomas A. Hendricks (1885)	Thomas F. Bayard (1885)
Benjamin Harrison (1889)	Levi P. Morton (1889)	James G. Blaine (1889)
		John W. Foster (1891)
Grover Cleveland (1893)	Adlai E. Stevenson (1893)	Walter Q. Gresham (1893)
		Richard Olney (1895)
William McKinley (1897)	Garret A. Hobart (1897)	John Sherman (1897)
	Theodore Roosevelt (1901)	William R. Day (1897)
		John Hay (1898)

Index

About the Editors and Contributors

THOMAS CLARKIN is a graduate student in American history at the University of Texas at Austin. His research interests include the Civil Rights Act of 1968 and federal Indian policy during the Kennedy and Johnson administrations.

MICHAEL J. DEVINE is director of the American Heritage Center and adjunct professor of history at the University of Wyoming. He received his doctorate from Ohio State University in 1974 and has held administrative posts with the Ohio Historical Society and Historic St. Mary's City, Maryland. From 1985 to 1991 he was Illinois State Historian and Director of the Illinois State Historical Society. He is the author of *John W. Foster: Politics and Diplomacy in the Imperial Era, 1873–1917* (1981) and was twice named a Senior Fulbright Lecturer, to Argentina in 1983 and Korea in 1995.

PETER G. FELTEN received a Ph.D. in United States and Caribbean history from the University of Texas. He teaches history and leadership development at Tulsa Community College.

JOHN E. FINDLING is professor of history at Indiana University Southeast. He earned his Ph.D. at the University of Texas and is the author of

Dictionary of American Diplomatic History (1980; 1989); *Close Neighbors, Distant Friends: United States–Central American Relations* (1987); and *Chicago's Great World's Fairs* (1995). With Kimberly D. Pelle, he co-edited *Historical Dictionary of World's Fairs and Expositions, 1851–1988* (1990), and *Historical Dictionary of the Modern Olympic Movement* (1996), and with Frank W. Thackeray, he co-edited *Statesmen Who Changed the World* (1993) and the other volumes in the Events That Changed the World and Events That Changed America series.

SALLY E. HADDEN is assistant professor of history and law at Florida State University. Her forthcoming book about slave patrollers in Virginia and the Carolinas is slated for publication in 1997. She received her B.A. from the University of North Carolina and her M.A., J.D., and Ph.D. from Harvard.

CARL E. KRAMER is president of Kentuckiana Historical Services, a historical consulting firm, and adjunct lecturer in history at Indiana University Southeast, where he teaches Civil War and reconstruction and American urban history. He received his Ph.D. from the University of Toledo and is the author of *Capital on the Kentucky: A 200-Year History of Frankfort and Franklin County* (1986).

THOMAS C. MACKEY divides his time between Louisville, Kentucky, and Long Island, New York. He completed his undergraduate studies at Beloit College (1978) and his doctoral studies at Rice University (1984). Constitutional and political issues are his specialties.

HENRY E. MATTOX retired from the U.S. Foreign Service in 1980 after 24 years of service, mostly abroad. Since that time he has earned a doctorate in U.S. history at the University of North Carolina at Chapel Hill and has engaged in teaching and writing. Among his publications are *Twilight of Amateur Diplomacy* (1989) and *Army Football in 1945* (1990). Currently he teaches at North Carolina State University in Raleigh.

DONALD A. RAKESTRAW is associate professor of history at Georgia Southern University. Specializing in U.S. diplomatic history, he has authored a number of works, including *For Honor or Destiny: The Anglo-American Crisis over the Oregon Territory* (1995), and is co-author with Howard Jones of a forthcoming volume on the mid-nineteenth-century Anglo-American rapprochement.

STEVEN E. SIRY is associate professor of history at Baldwin-Wallace College. He received his Ph.D. from the University of Cincinnati in 1986. His publications include articles in the *Journal of the Early Republic*, *Locus*, *Political Parties and Elections in the United States* (1991), and *Statesmen Who Changed the World* (1993).

FRANK W. THACKERAY is professor of history at Indiana University Southeast. He received his Ph.D. from Temple University. He is the author of *Antecedents of Revolution: Alexander I and the Polish Congress Kingdom* (1980) as well as articles on Russian-Polish relations in the nineteenth century and Polish-American relations in the twentieth century. With John E. Findling, he co-edited *Statesmen Who Changed the World* (1993) and the other volumes in the Events That Changed the World and Events That Changed America series. He is a former Fulbright scholar in Poland.

JULIA A. WOODS is a Ph.D. candidate in history at the University of Texas at Austin. She has an M.A. in history from the University of Texas and a law degree from the University of North Carolina at Chapel Hill. She is currently researching her dissertation, tentatively titled, "Not Yet Sharks: Antebellum Southern Lawyers."